modern management
and
information systems

modern management
and
information systems

Joel E. Ross
Professor of Management
Florida Atlantic University

RESTON PUBLISHING COMPANY, INC.
A Prentice-Hall Company
Reston, Virginia

Library of Congress Cataloging in Publication Data

Ross, Joel E
    Modern management and information systems.

    Includes index.
    1. Business—Data processing.   2.   Management
information systems.   I.   Title.
HF5548.2.R629   658.4′03   75-38942
ISBN 0-87909-499-0

© 1976 by
Reston Publishing Company, Inc.
A Prentice-Hall Company
Reston, Virginia   22090

10 9 8 7 6 5 4 3 2 1
Printed in the United States of America.

to
Mary Beth
and
Susan

contents

preface

I have a simple purpose in writing this book. It is to assist the reader in improving his productivity by becoming a better manager and decision maker. By reading these easily understood principles and evaluating his own and his organization's compliance with them, he should be able to significantly improve his operations through the use of sound and basic fundamentals.

A secondary purpose of this book is to assist the many people engaged in computer and related operations in realizing better economies in this resource, and in designing better systems for managerial, rather than clerical use.

The book is intended to serve as a practical guide for both the user of computers and the college student. Each chapter concludes with a summary checklist that provides an easy method of self-evaluation and a guide for practical action.

The combined subjects of management and information systems are not easy to treat properly. On the one hand is the highly technical and sometimes extraneous (to the manager) computer jargon, while on the other hand is the esoteric systems theory. One must avoid the popular custom of writing to one extreme or the other. I have attempted in this book to reach a practical middle ground. The book describes the very latest approach to the processes and functions of management and shows how the reader can facilitate this approach through participation in information systems design. Above all, I have tried to make the subject *operational*. This means that the reader should be able to put it to use *immediately*.

I would like to express my appreciation to the many hundreds of university students and business managers who have participated in seminars around the world. They have served as the proving ground for this material and I am grateful for their enthusiasm.

Joel E. Ross

the computer and management: broken promises and future potential

1

So widespread will be the use of computers in the 70's that banks of computers will be commonplace on the streets, and families may own their own computers for home use.

—Irene Hughes
Psychic

Like most predictions about computer use, this one by the psychic Irene Hughes has proven to be somewhat wide of the mark, but it is typical of the many forecasts made in recent years by responsible people both in and outside the industry. Government and technological forecasters, economists, business users, and the general public have all anticipated a much greater penetration by the computer in our personal lives and in business operations.

It hasn't happened. Despite enormous technological advances, the computer has not yet reached anything approaching maturity in business use. Indeed, as far as management is concerned, it has been something of a bust.

THE INDUSTRY

Except for fortress IBM, the computer industry has not enjoyed a profitable success. It has been labeled "Snow White and the Seven Dwarfs (RCA, GE, Univac, Control Data, NCR, Burroughs, Xerox)" and characterized as snatching defeat from victory.

> Harold Geneen, the colorful chairman of IT&T, was one chief executive who realized that computers were a business and not a technological romance. His conclusion: "Do you know we actually had two guys whose job it was to keep us out of the computer business? It probably saved us a half a billion dollars. The worst thing we could have done is gone down that road."

Several firms probably wish that they had taken a position similar to Geneen's. Consider RCA Corporation which lost $500 million and abandoned the manufacture of computers one year after its chairman, Robert Sarnoff, assured everyone that the product would be the company's most important growth area in the seventies. General Electric got out of the business after incurring similar losses. Xerox was so anxious to get into the business that it paid $1 billion (yes, $1 billion in stock) for Scientific Data Systems (SDS), a small company whose revenues and profits amounted to only $100 million and $10 million, respectively. As of this writing, the cumulative losses of Xerox on its computer venture are not known, but the losses amounted to $100 million in the first two years following acquisition of SDS, and in late 1975 the company announced the abandonment of its computer business.

The *software* or *systems* side of the industry is also hurting. Even Texas computer services magnate H. Ross Perot admits this. His Electronic Data Systems (EDS), which specializes in business information systems, was offered to the public in 1968 at $16.50 per share. The stock price subsequently skyrocketed to $160 per share (and a price/earnings ratio over 100), but during the market slide of 1974 the price sank to a low of 10½. It is not known to what extent these market evaluations reflect the failure to achieve anticipated revenues from computer systems.

Equally as disappointing has been the failure of the time sharing industry to take off on its expected boom. This disappointment has not been due to the lack of technology; the hardware and know-how has been available. Has it been the lack of "brainware"—the systems design capability?

THE HARDWARE

Hardware development has been the one bright spot in an otherwise slow process in the evolution of computer application to management problems. This evolution is summarized in Table 1-1.

Hardware technology has outraced our ability to utilize it for management. Processing speed and storage capacity has increased enormously while the cost has been reduced substantially. However, the application of this accelerating technology is another matter. As Booz, Allen, and Hamilton concluded:

> "For the most part, third-generation equipment is being used for first-generation systems design."

FAILURE TO USE THE COMPUTER FOR MANAGING

These are baffling times for most managers. On one hand he is faced with a puzzling array of hardware/software combinations. On the other hand he cannot seem to get the promised results in terms of improved management. A curious dilemma is the result. The manager is aware of the urgency of using the computer to improve his operations, but he knows that the honeymoon with computers is over. There must be an economic payoff, but there is increasing disillusionment about achieving it. Com-

Table 1-1

Evolution of Computer Hardware

Gener-ation	Period	Hardware Characteristics	Software Characteristics	Management Application Potential
First	1953–58	Vacuum tubes, magnetic records	Elementary	Selected clerical. Batch application.
Second	1958–66	Transistors, magnetic cores	Compilers, systems for control of input/output	Wide range of applications with inquiry capability. Mostly clerical.
Third	1966–74	Integrated circuits, interactive terminals	Multifunction systems with communications interaction	Remote processing and inquiry from data network. Remote communications and central data banks.
Fourth	1974–?	Satellite computers with enormous file storage	Virtual machines and general purpose data manipulators	File integration, full transaction processing, management potential limited only by imagination and design capability. Universal system entry for individual problem solving.

puters have transformed clerical and accounting operations but have had surprisingly little impact on the operating problems of management—the area where the real potential lies.

> The consulting firm of McKinsey & Company concludes: "In terms of technical achievement, the computer revolution in the U.S. has been outrunning all expectations. In terms of economic payoff on new applications, it has rapidly lost momentum." *Business Week* reports that "management's romance with computers for their own sake is over. New systems must justify their cost and performance."

Meanwhile, the gap between the potential of the computer and its actual achievement continues to widen as the stakes and costs keep rising. From a profit standpoint, computer efforts in many firms appear to be in trouble. Third- and fourth-generation hardware, more costly staffs, and increasingly complex operations can be found everywhere. However, much less in evidence is the computer application that is profitable. Sometimes the manager is faced with a curious choice: "Damned if I do and damned if I don't."

In short, the bloom is off the rose where unjustified computer applications are concerned. Businessmen are beginning to ask the hard question: "What are our real computer needs and can we justify them in terms of cost/benefit and improved management of the organization?"

The overriding question remains: how do I utilize the computer to provide *management information systems?*

WHAT IS A MANAGEMENT INFORMATION SYSTEM?

Despite the fact that the computer is nothing more than a tool for processing data, many managers view it as *the* central element in an information system. This attitude tends to overrate and distort the role of the computer. Its real role is to provide information for decisions and for planning and controlling operations.

Judging from the business press, the brave new world of *management information systems* is upon us. There is hardly a business magazine today that doesn't contain articles on information systems, data banks, and related subjects. Despite this proliferation of books, articles, seminars, and courses surrounding this area, few efforts have managed to synthesize the separate subjects of *management, information, and systems* and to show how these are related to computers. This synthesis is a major goal of this book. Let's begin by describing how an MIS evolves and then defining the concept.

The Evolution of an Information System

Imagine the operation of a typical small business of not so many years ago—a neighborhood grocery store depicted in Figure 1-1. Mr. Owner is president, proprietor, chief executive, and chairman of the board. Owner, Jr. is vice-president of sales, director of market research, controller, treasurer, and in charge of various other miscellaneous duties. Their entire work force consists of two helpers. The organization chart is indicated by the heavy lines in Figure 1-2.

An examination of Figure 1-1 will reveal Mr. Owner's complete information system. His transaction tickets are skewered on the spindle as they occur. Historical information is contained in ledger books on the top of his desk. With this system, management has what amounts to real-time entry into the basic resource records of the company and on-line access to its entire data bank. Cash budgeting and cash flow information are within sight in the safe in the corner of the office. There is even an advanced system of

Figure 1-1   Owner and Sons Information System

exception reporting on the blackboard on the washroom door. What Mr. Owner has is a *real-time* information system—all information required to run the business is within reaching distance of the manager and is available within the time necessary to affect ongoing decisions. Inventory, payroll, and operating systems are no problem.

As time passes, Mr. Owner's business grows into additional stores and his organization chart looks something like the *after expansion* chart depicted in Figure 1-2. Although the functions are basically the same, the volume and complexity of information needs have increased geometrically. As with all growing companies, new products are developed, sales volume grows, the number of employees increases, factors outside the company become increasingly complex, and the managerial problems surrounding the operation of the organization generally expand even more rapidly than company size. Communications channels are more difficult, authority must be formally delegated, and information needs expand.

This increase in company size results in the need for additional information collection, processing, and distribution. It now becomes necessary to handle many customer accounts, many production records, and many more

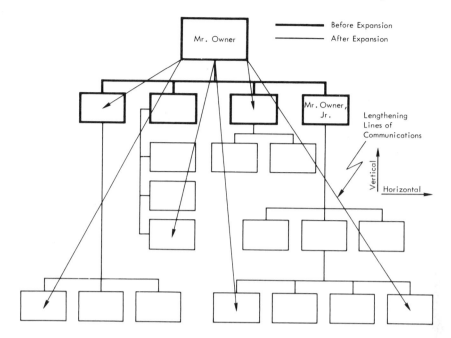

Figure 1-2   Complexities of Growth (Communications, Delegation, Information)

interrelationships among subsystems. In addition to the increased records
with many more interrelationships, it is now necessary to assign people to
supervise other people, and this development expands communications
lines.

As the need for information grows, additional people and equipment
must be added to handle this information. Procedures, rules, position
descriptions, policies, forms, programs, and organization manuals become
necessary to organize the information flow. Typewriters and calculators
are purchased and additional clerks added. The next step is to procure
tabulating and punched-card equipment. Finally, the first-, second-, and
third-generation electronic computers are acquired in order to handle the
need for increased information handling. *An information system is born.*

Meanwhile, what has happened to management? As with the other basic
functions of the company (production, sales, finance, etc.), the functions
of management have not changed and will not change. Management still
plans, organizes, staffs, directs, and controls. However, the communication
network for information has increased enormously. A succession of dele-
gations of duties and authority has lengthened the lines of communications

and increased the complexity of the communication network of Mr. Owner's business a thousandfold.

In spite of these complexities, the management of the larger company would like to be able to operate essentially in the same fashion and with the same information requirements that old Mr. Owner enjoyed. The objective of developing or improving a management information system can be explained largely in terms of the new problems: (a) to provide the type of information environment that will unite the basic operating functions, and (b) to provide management with access to information relative to complex activities in decentralized organizations.

> Most small businessmen ($5–50 million sales) reach a stage of *critical information overload* where their lack of a structured information system prohibits or inhibits the necessary delegation of authority. Many of these managers hesitate to loosen the reins of tight centralized control because they fear the loss of information feedback regarding progress of operations. However, don't conclude that an information system permits total decentralization. Witness the loss of control (despite sophisticated information systems) experienced by Litton Industries and several other conglomerates.

A Management Information System (MIS) Defined

Because this book is largely devoted to the design and utilization of computer based information systems, it is appropriate to clearly define the term MIS.

MIS is not new; only its computerization is new. Before computers, MIS techniques existed to supply managers with the information that would permit them to plan and control operations. The computer has added one or more dimensions, such as speed, accuracy, and increased volumes of data, that permit the consideration of more alternatives in a decision.

The scope and purpose of MIS is better understood if each part of the term is defined. Thus:

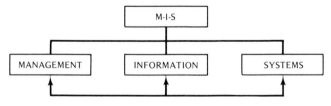

Management

Management has been defined in a variety of ways, but for our purposes it comprises the processes or activities that describe what managers do in the operation of their organization: plan, organize, initiate, and control operations. They *plan* by setting strategies and goals and selecting the best course of action to achieve the plan. They *organize* the tasks necessary for the operational plan, set these tasks up into homogeneous groups, and assign authority delegation. They *control* the performance of the work by setting performance standards and avoiding deviations from standard.

Because *decision making* is such a fundamental prerequisite to each of the foregoing processes, the job of an MIS becomes that of *facilitating decisions* necessary for planning, organizing, and controlling the work and functions of the business.

Information

Data must be distinguished from *information,* and this distinction is clear and important for our purposes. Data are facts and figures that are not currently being used in a decision process, and usually take the form of historical records that are recorded and filed without immediate intent to retrieve for decision making. An example would be any one of the supporting documents, ledgers, etc. that comprise the source material for profit and loss statements. Such material would only be of historical interest to an external auditor.

Information consists of data that have been retrieved, processed, or otherwise used for informative or inference purposes, argument, or as a basis for forecasting or decision making. An example here would also be any one of the supporting documents mentioned above, but in this case the data could be used by an internal auditor, the management services department of an external auditor, or by internal management for profit planning and control, or for other decision-making purposes.

> The analogy is sometimes made between the accountant (and his role as advisor to the manager) and the automobile driver. Can you imagine the difficulty of driving an automobile while blindfolded and depending on the advice of a backseat driver who is looking out the rear window telling you where you've been? This situation is somewhat like the accountant advising the manager regarding future action based solely on historical accounting records.*

Systems

A *system* can be described simply as a set of elements joined together for a common objective. A subsystem is part of a larger system with which

---

*With apology to the accountants. Let it be said that we are now witnessing in the accounting profession a trend away from data and into information. Moreover, the profession is becoming increasingly concerned with measuring the "non-dollar" type of transactions such as labor productivity, lost sales, turnover, and optimum assignment of production crews and maintenance factors.

we are concerned. *All* systems are parts of larger systems. For our purposes the organization is the system and the parts (divisions, departments, functions, units, etc.) are the subsystems.

Whereas we have achieved a very high degree of automation and joining together of subsystems in scientific, mechanical, and factory manufacturing operations, we have barely scratched the surface of applying systems principles to organizational or business systems. The concept of synergism has not generally been applied to the business organization, particularly as it applies to the integration of the subsystems through information interchange. Marketing, operations, and finance are frequently on diverse paths and working at cross purposes. The systems concept of MIS is therefore one of optimizing the output of the organization by *connecting the operating subsystems through the medium of information exchange.*

> The objective of an MIS is to provide information for decision making on planning, initiating, organizing, and controlling the operations of the subsystems of the firm and to provide a synergistic organization in the process.

WHAT IS THE SYSTEMS APPROACH?

The systems approach can be explained by describing *what it is not.* As one chief executive recently commented, "Marketing seems to be selling what can't be designed and what manufacturing can't produce and to customers that finance wouldn't approve anyway!" Imagine also these hypothetical but typical questions in a manufacturing organization that reflects non-integration:

> What has purchasing done with the parts for the rush order?
> Why wasn't production notified of the changed sales forecast?
> What is the impact on my operations of the change in prime rate?
> Why is assembly working half-time while other departments are working overtime?

The systems approach in business was an idea born in the decade of the 1960s. The notion was one of *Synergism*—the sum of the parts is greater than the whole—2 + 2 = 5—the output of the total organization can be enhanced if the component parts can be integrated. This concept was the rationale for the conglomerate form of organization—a concept that subsequently fell into disrepute because of widespread conglomerate near-failure.

For our purposes the systems approach to management is designed to utilize scientific analysis in complex organizations for (a) developing and managing operating systems (e.g., money flows, manpower systems), and (b) designing information systems for decision making. The link between these two is obvious because the reason for *information systems* design is to assist in decision making regarding the management of *operating systems*.

A basic and fundamental notion of the systems approach to organization and management is the interrelationship of the parts or subsystems of the organization. The starting point of the approach is a set of objectives, and the focus is on the design of the whole as distinct from the design of components or subsystems. The *synergistic* characteristic of the systems approach cannot be overemphasized. In organizational and information systems design we want to achieve *synergism,* which is the simultaneous action of separate but interrelated parts that together produce a total effect greater than the sum of the individual parts. The result obtained by a team of eleven well-coached football players is greater than that achieved by eleven individual players "doing their own thing." The analogy for the business organization is clear. The MIS can go a long way toward achieving the integration we seek.

In the past, the effectiveness of business organizations has been somewhat less than optimum because managers failed to relate the parts or functions of the systems to each other and to the whole. The sales function was performed without a great deal of integration with design or production; production control was frequently not coordinated with financial or personnel planning; and the classic management information system was concerned largely with variance reporting on an historical basis and was constructed around the chart of accounts without too much regard for organizational information needs.

A basic tenet of systems theory is that every system is held together by information exchange. This is certainly true of the business system or the organizational system. Yet information systems and computers have not focused in on this essential characteristic or need for integration. The need, and the potential, for such integration through information can be demonstrated conceptually in Figure 1-3. The heavy solid line indicates classical authority relationships and the hierarchical structure of the typical organization. The dotted lines show the same organizational structure but with the parts joined together in a system by means of information flow.

Students of management, and businessmen, frequently express some criticism of an overemphasis on the systems approach. They say that it is nothing new, that managers have intuitively known of synergism and reckoned with it in the past. While I must admit that this is a valid comment, it becomes necessary to point out two shortcomings of "systems thinking" in the past. First, we have been unable to design very many MIS that facilitate organizational integration and second, the absolute need for the systems approach will continue to accelerate in the '70s and '80s. There

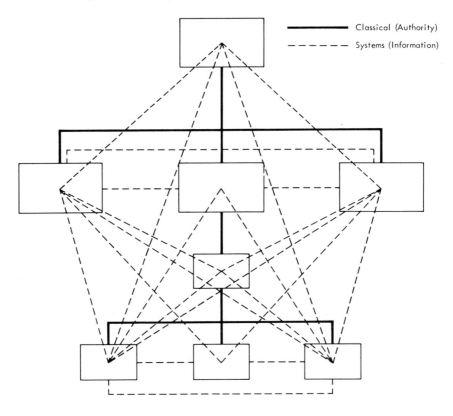

Figure 1-3   The Classical and Systems Approach to Organization and Information Flow

are two main reasons for this acceleration: (1) increased complexity in business, and (2) recent managerial advances.

1. *Increased complexity* requires systems thinking as never before. This complexity can be attributed to four causes:

   a. *The technological revolution* demands that we stay on top of changes that affect our products, techniques, output, and productivity. Few companies are immune from the geometric acceleration of change.

   b. *Research and development,* although slackening somewhat from its breathtaking rate, looms large in its effect on the life cycle of products and related considerations.

   c. *Product changes,* stemming partly from technology and research and development, have an impact on every facet of the organization. Tomorrow's products are not yet invented, designed, financed, sold, or produced. This is lengthening the time required for future commitments and demands a central course of action to integrate the subsystems of the organization.

    d. *The information explosion* has profound impacts upon the complexity of management and organizations, and a modern computer based MIS is becoming more essential for the storage, processing, retrieval, and use of information for the right decision.

2.   *Advances in management* also suggest renewed attention to the systems approach. Indeed, these modern breakthroughs demand and permit a systems approach to management that was not formerly available. These advances are:

    a. *The theory of information feedback systems* has been around a long time in the science of engineering but has only recently been applied to the management of organizations. Although we have had such feedback systems as historical variance reporting, the notion of automatic correction through information feedback has not been exploited. This notion says: the output of the system leads to a decision, which results in some type of action, corrects the output, and in turn leads to another decision. Very few of today's information systems incorporate the features of this theory.

    b. *Decision making* has advanced considerably from the coin-flipping choices of the past that were based solely on hunch or experience at best. The modern systems notion of *programming* decisions by *decision rule* is now a basic consideration of management and of information systems design.

    c. *Management science* has given us the quantitative approach to reduce heretofore complex decisions to a system of known or predictable variables. The potential for problem solving and decision rule design is enormous.

    d. *The electronic computer* is nothing more than a tool for processing data or making computations. Nevertheless it is the *one* breakthrough that makes the other three advances in management possible. Because of its incredible capability, the computer allows us to utilize management science to design the decision rules and process the information needed for modern information feedback systems. It is not *the* central element in a modern information system, but it is an exceedingly important tool in the systems approach to organization and management.

MIS READINESS CHECKLIST

	Yes	No

1. Have I reviewed my computer hardware configuration   ( ) ( )
   to determine whether:
   (a)   it is justified in view of present use?
   (b)   it achieves a balance between cost and benefits?
   (c)   it is appropriate for future MIS plans?

2. Am I utilizing my computer for: ( ) ( )
   (a)   developing and recording operational plans?
   (b)   organizing tasks and organizational elements for
         subsequent control?
   (c)   controlling the achievement of plans?

3. Have my systems kept pace with the increased need   ( ) ( )
   for integration due to growth? Communications?
   Authority delegation?

4. Do I emphasize information systems rather than data   ( ) ( )
   systems?

5. Do I take a systems approach to management of the   ( ) ( )
   organization? Have I adopted a systems philosophy?

6. Have I designed or do I plan to design my manage-   ( ) ( )
   ment information systems to facilitate the systems
   approach?

7. Have I identified those areas of increased complexity   ( ) ( )
   (technology, research and development, product
   changes, information explosion) that affect my business?

8. Have I designed my reporting systems to provide in-   ( ) ( )
   formation feedback for improved decisions rather
   than for historical reporting?

9. Have I identified those operations and decisions that   ( ) ( )
   lend themselves to improvement through a pro-
   grammed decision rule?

10. Have I utilized the techniques of management science   ( ) ( )
    to improve operations?

*Three or more NO answers indicate that you have a
lot of work to do.*

the use and misuse of computers: ten ills that cause MIS failure

2

"I wish I could put my arms around every customer our computers screw up and say, 'There, there, we'll figure a way between us to make the computer cry, just for once.' "

—William Fine, president,
Bonwit Teller

Most businessmen know through personal experience some inconvenience or expense that can be traced to the failure of some computer systems design. Every manager can tell a classic story of a particular goof caused by a computer.

> Penn Central Railroad literally lost entire trains and hundreds of boxcars due to a computer error. The joke around Wall Street was that the trains were not lost, they were stolen! Later, the case of the missing freight cars came before a federal grand jury in Philadelphia. It was noted that the possibility of the cars having been scrapped was unlikely, because this required a lot of work for a small return, and freight cars are almost impossible to fence.

> Another railroad incident occurred in Akron. There is a grain elevator where railroad cars are emptied by being lifted and tipped over, pouring the grain into bins. One day a bunch of cars came in from Penn Central, and they were lifted and dumped—they were filled with bathtubs.

> Macy's loses $60 million in accounts receivable.

> A little old lady in Iowa receives a $1 million tax refund.

And the stories go on and on. But they reflect a curious dichotomy in American business. On one hand, the manager has the growing need to use the computer to manage increasing complexity and maintain his competitive edge. On the other hand, he cannot seem to break through the barrier of "computerese," "computercrats," and the technical jargon that gets in the way of good systems design for *management*. Moreover, he is convinced that there is significant underutilization of the computer, but he is not clear on how to improve these conditions.

In Chapter 1 we noted the spectacular advance of computer technology and made the point that similar advances in systems design and utilization have been extremely small by comparison. The result is the *MIS gap*. This gap, and indeed almost all cases of individual company failure, can be traced to one or more or a combination of ten basic MIS "ILLS."
These are summarized:

1. Overemphasis on the *clerical system*. This may be called the one-for-one changeover syndrome.

16

2. Failure to close the *communications gap* between technician and manager-user.

3. Overreliance on a *consultant* or *computer manufacturer*.

4. Failure to design to a *master plan*.

5. *Organization* of the MIS function.

6. No *management system* to build upon.

7. No *managerial participation* in MIS design.

8. Failure to identify *information needs*.

9. *Poor system* prior to changeover.

10. Overlooking *human acceptance* of the system.

Each of these are discussed and at the end of the chapter suggestions are made for curing the "ILLS" of MIS sickness.

CLERICAL SYSTEMS

The overwhelming majority (estimates range up to 98%) of computer applications are for clerical data processing and paperwork automation, not for managerial decision making. In this type of system (e.g., payroll, inventory accounting, accounts receivable) the computer is used for the most part as a piece of high-speed tabulating equipment. Despite the fact that this "clerical" automation approach yields minimum benefit in terms of information usage for managerial purposes, it remains the most frequent type of application.

The clerical approach may have been justifiable in the past when cost savings through clerical automation was a major objective. However, this approach has been carried about as far as it can go, and the time has come to adopt improved management as an objective.

The worst possible approach to systems design is what I call the *one-for-one changeover syndrome,* which occurs when a technician takes an existing manual or computer system and converts or modifies it without upgrading or changing it. In other words, ledger accounting remains ledger accounting (instead of being upgraded to *financial planning*), order entry remains order entry (instead of being upgraded into *sales analysis*), and production reporting remains production reporting (instead of being upgraded to *production planning and control*). The conversion process provides an excellent opportunity to upgrade an existing clerical system into a *management information system.* So why not take advantage of the opportunity?

One government agency with over a million employees spent millions of dollars in design cost alone to convert personnel records from one computer hardware configuration to another. No changes were desired or made in records, files, or system outputs. Yet this one-for-one changeover provided an excellent opportunity to redesign for *manpower planning:* requirements determination, recruitment, training, placement, etc.

The art of management has sometimes been defined as the making of irrevocable decisions based on incomplete, inaccurate, and obsolete information. Perhaps this view is the result of past attention to clerical systems that have played a relatively limited role as a management tool. Because decision making has not been the central theme of these systems, they have generally been oriented in one of three directions:

1.   *Problem oriented*—emergency and random retrieval of information to meet a crisis situation of limited duration and scope.

2.   *Project oriented*—used to manage a specific program of limited time and scope.

3.   *Specialty oriented*—ongoing clerical needs in personnel, bookkeeping, accounting, technical data, or other specific functional areas.

Robert Anderson, chief executive of Rockwell International, is one manager who deplores the use of the computer for clerical automation. He believes that MIS should provide four additional managerial functions: (a) serve manufacturing, marketing, and the other real-line operations, (b) instead of providing historical reports of past irretrievable actions, point the way to improvement and alternative solutions to problems, (c) not only point up deviation from plans but show the necessary corrective action, and (d) monitor outside conditions affecting company plans. These functions are a long way from the clerical systems to which we are accustomed, but they can be achieved through proper MIS design.

COMMUNICATIONS GAP

One of the reasons for the overemphasis on clerical systems is the communications gap between the computer technician (EDP* manager, systems analyst, programmer, management scientist) and the manager-user of the system.

It is unlikely that for the foreseeable future the technician will be able to speak the language of management, and managers for the most part

---

*Electronic data processing.

are not prepared to speak the language of the computer. The result—a communications gap that sometimes results in a design standoff.

The technician has little appreciation of the process of management or of the problems of managers. Operation of the machine is their "thing." He measures his performance by how many shifts the computer is running and how much printout or output he can generate. Given the choice, the technician will give the user all the data contained in the system pertaining to the users problem. Thus the sales manager who asks for the sales performance report is likely to get computer printout in a stack two feet high. What he really wants is an exception report that highlights significant variances from plan.

Robert Townsend, of *Up the Organization* fame, summarized the problem with the technicians: "They are trying to make it look tough. Not easy. They're building a mystique, a priesthood, their own mumbo-jumbo ritual to keep you from knowing what they—and you—are doing."

On the other hand, the manager is not without guilt. Unless he's been to a business school or a good seminar recently, he is not likely to be very knowledgeable about the computer and how it can be used to help him improve his operations. The result is frequently abdication to the computer technician. A phrase that is too often heard by the systems analyst or EDP manager is, "You're the expert. You figure it out!"

But the expert can't "figure it out." Because of his training, interests, desires, and peer pressure, his compulsive tendency is to generate massive data bases, install display devices and data-communications techniques, and install newer and grander designs—all for the purpose of empire building but not for improved management—and it is probably too much to expect that the computer technician will change.

Characteristically, there are three stages in the development of an MIS, each stage depending on a fragile process of communications. These stages and the typical communication breakdown are shown:

Development Stage	*Typical Communication Breakdown*
Designer asks user what information he needs	User not accustomed to rigorous self-analysis and cannot adequately express information needs.
Designer works out a plan and gives it to programmer	Designer converts what he *thinks he heard* from the user into flow charts and trappings of systems design, altering information needs in the process.
Programmer implements system	Programmer incorporates his *own ideas and interpretations,* further altering users needs. Final results frustrate user and he becomes hostile or worse, sabotages the system.

RELIANCE ON CONSULTANT OR MANUFACTURER

Some computer manufacturers and some consultants will try to sell the *turnkey* system, one that is designed and debugged and ready for its buyer to push the button or turn the key.

Be careful! These guys are foxes who like to eat chickens! Their natural inclination is to promise everything without too much regard for that eventual day when they depart and leave you holding the key—or bag. In most cases, the consultant or manufacturer is concerned more with the machine than he is with management solutions.

On the average, it is probably true that most companies are over-computerized by about 20%. In many cases this computer "fat" is the result of strong marketing programs offered by manufacturers and to a lesser extent the "overcomputerization" recommended by consultants. This situation is particularly regrettable when more powerful machines are installed in anticipation of *management* systems that never seem to materialize.

There are other good reasons for going slow in allowing consultants or manufacturers to make your computer and MIS decisions. First, there is a good chance that you will have to spend a great deal of time educating them in the operations of your company before they are in a position to make recommendations. Second, installing the system without substantial preparation is likely to result in some chaos. And third—and this is a general rule—if the buyer doesn't have the personnel who are capable of designing the organization's MIS, it is unlikely that they will have the expertise to operate those that were designed and installed by the outsider.

> Borden, Inc. is an example of one company that did some costly floundering around with new hardware and new design before setting down to some good computer systems designed and installed by their own people. The advice of the vice-president in charge is: "If you don't have an in-house staff doing the job of design and also available to maintain it, you are asking for trouble."

If, despite this advice, you want to use the consultant or manufacturer in a major way, remember these do's and don'ts:

> *Don't* let a technological romance with the computer obscure management's objective of improved operations.
>
> *Do* take a return-on-investment approach to expenditures.
>
> *Do* avoid operating in a reactive mode rather than against a master plan.
>
> *Don't* buy the argument of reduced unit processing costs unless it means lower absolute or total costs.

LACK OF A MASTER PLAN

A fourth cause of computer failure is the lack of a master plan to which hardware development and individual MIS design can be related. Without such a plan, the result is likely to be a patchwork approach that will result in *islands of mechanization* with little integration between separate systems. In other words, we need a systems approach to MIS development.

> The National Association of Accountants recently completed a study to determine the state-of-the-art in MIS. Their conclusion: "For the most part, what companies 'have done' shade into 'what we are now doing' which leads to 'what we plan to do' next year."

This patchwork or piecemeal approach to systems development, which lacks a unifying framework and is without a master plan, has several disadvantages. One of these stems from the unrelated nature of the subsystems developed. Frequently autonomous departments and divisions have developed individualistic systems without regard to the interface of such systems elsewhere in the organization. The result has been an inability to communicate between systems and the incompatibility of subsystems of a like nature throughout the company. A second disadvantage is the cost involved—cost in time, resources, and money.

> A fairly common example of failure to relate subsystems lies in the manner in which personnel information is structured. Frequently several departments (sales, production, accounting, personnel) will maintain employee files that overlap with each other and with similar files elsewhere but do not provide for interface between them. I have witnessed the development of critical engineering and labor skills shortages in one or more geographically separated divisions of a multidivision company. But despite the fact that these skills are available elsewhere in the company, no identification can be made owing to the lack of a common personnel skills information system.

The reasons for MIS planning are the same as for planning in general: it offsets uncertainty, improves economy of operations, focuses on the objectives, and provides a device for subsequent control of operations. If the patchwork approach is allowed to progress too far, it may be too expensive to start once again from scratch and redesign to an integrated master plan. You may have passed the point of no return.

> Lack of systems integration and master planning is dramatically illustrated in the case of the merger of two railroads (Pennsylvania and New York Central) into the Penn Central. Alfred Perlman,

former chief executive of the New York Central said that the heart of the merger problem and the ultimate collapse of the Penn Central was due to the incompatibility of the two railroads' computer systems. Penn Central could no longer locate cars in use on its lines and costs went through the roof; shipments that normally required six days to deliver took 18 to 22; and as shippers began routing their business to competing lines, the railroad's traffic volume ebbed to tragic proportions. Even Perlman (of the Penn Central) admitted: "All of a sudden they were in the dark and we were in the dark."

ORGANIZATION OF THE MIS FUNCTION

Another significant cause of computer failure is the lack of proper organization of the EDP and MIS function. When computers first burst upon the business scene in the late fifties and early sixties, the only practical applications were concerned with the automation of clerical work: accounting, payroll, inventory reporting, and similar *financial* jobs. Following the classical organizational principle of assignment of a service activity by *familiarity,* the overwhelming trend at that time was to assign the computer to the controller or the chief accountant. Unfortunately, this is where it has remained in many companies. The result has been a disproportionate emphasis on accounting and related clerical work. This development was a natural one because the computer gave the accountant an added dimension of importance. However, the result has been a reluctance on the part of the financial managers to share the machine with others. Many have forgotten the first rule of the staff man; they exist to serve the line operations.

Fortunately, the trend has reversed itself. More and more academicians and practitioners of business realize that the *information* resource of the company ranks alongside the classical 4-M's (money, manpower, materials, machines and facilities) and deserves vice-presidential attention just as the other resources.

> A 1974 survey by *Infosystems,* a computer trade publication, shows that the data-processing department is no longer a stepchild of the finance function. It has become an independent and increasingly ⋅important support operation in its own right. More than 82% of EDP managers interviewed report directly to top management and in many cases to the president himself, compared with only 27% in 1967.

The exact location in the organization and the authority granted to the MIS manager is, of course, a function of the type of business you are in and how important the information resource is to you. In banking, trans-

portation, many service industries, and perhaps to a lesser extent in manufacturing, data processing and MIS pervade all areas of the business.

> At Chase Manhattan Bank the data processing manager is a senior
> vice-president. His operation, with 1100 employees, pervades all
> areas of the bank from balancing hundreds of thousands of ac-
> counts daily to investment analysis and portfolio management. The
> president says that "Data processing is the glue that holds the op-
> eration together."

Alternative assignments of the MIS function are shown in Figure 2-1.

NO MANAGEMENT SYSTEM TO BUILD UPON

For some reason many managers think they can patch up a company's
shortcomings in basic *management systems* by applying a computerized
management information system as a *Band-aid*. It won't work. If good
planning and control does not exist within the framework of a good organizational structure, no degree of sophistication with a computer is going
to cure the basic ill. MIS must be built on top of a management system
that includes the organizational arrangements, the structure and procedures
for adequate planning and control, the clear establishment of objectives,
and all the other manifestations of good organization and management.

The lack of managerial and operational applications (as opposed to
accounting and clerical) is serious, because it implies that the process of
management is not being performed well. If we can say (as we must) that
information is the raw material of decision making, and if information is
not being generated, disseminated, and used for management, then no
system—manual or computer—is going to solve the problem.

> Litton Industries was known far and wide for the sophistication of
> their computer-based MIS. Roy Ashe, the chairman, was asked by
> then President Nixon to chair the committee for structuring an
> information system for the United States government, a position
> that ultimately led to his powerful job as budget director for both
> President Nixon and later President Ford. However, for a number
> of reasons attributed to the company's *management systems,* the ex-
> pensive MIS didn't do the planning and control job.

It is worth repeating that only the manager-user can establish, repair,
or modify the management system prior to overlaying the MIS on top of it.
The computer technician cannot do it for reasons explained in our previous
discussion of the *communications gap*.

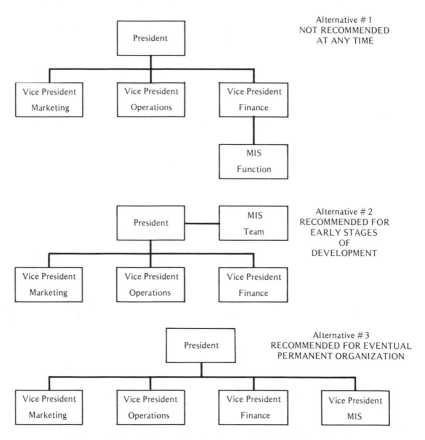

Figure 2-1   Alternative Assignment of MIS Function

There is a widespread complaint among personnel directors associated with computer-related recruitment that while good data-processing people come well schooled in the technological complexities of their craft, most are simply not programmed for managerial jobs. Only a very few business schools have a reputation for turning out computer people with the broad-based skills necessary to function both in the computer room and in meetings with users of their information systems.

A related problem with computer personnel is their apparent loyalty to the machine, or the profession, and not to the company. This fact was pointed out very recently by the president of the American Federation of Information Processing Societies when he concluded that most data processors are notorious for being "machine-mesmerized" and more loyal to their profession than to their corporation.

MANAGERIAL PARTICIPATION

Of all the reasons for MIS failure, this one probably heads the list. Dozens of studies on hundreds of companies have concluded that the most striking characteristic of the successful company is that MIS development has been viewed as a responsibility of management. This includes both top management and operating line management. Even the federal government concluded: "Without question, the single most critical problem in effective computer utilization is the need for understanding and support of top management." The reasonable conclusion that managers must reach is that MIS is too important to be left to the computer technician.

This position is substantiated if one examines the companies that have been successful with computer-based MIS—Weyerhaeuser, IBM, Xerox, Pillsbury, and Ford, to name a few. Their success is attributed directly to the fact that manager-users are required to become involved in the design of their own systems. Moreover, the presidents take a personal interest and participate directly in defining what work the computer should do for the company. Nothing less is acceptable when computers are becoming the largest single item of capital budgets and have such a widespread impact on all operating systems of the firm.

> In a major aerospace firm, a very sophisticated and expensive MIS was recently installed to plan and control the cost, time, and technical specifications of design projects. After significant dissatisfaction with the system, the users were asked their opinion of system malfunction. Their reply was that "the input to the system is no good." Further discussion revealed that the input was provided by the very users who complained. The conclusion emerged that user participation in the design phase would have avoided subsequent expensive and time-consuming rework.

A manufacturing company installed a bigger computer to handle a number of cathode-ray devices in what they called a "communications environment" that was justified by *EDP personnel* in order to strengthen the sales/services functions by providing real-time response to field inquiries. However, inventory and shop-order paper couldn't keep pace. Later, *management* determined objectively that real-time response was not really necessary and the system was scaled down to reality. Three hundred thousand dollars (equivalent to a sales increase of $5 million) were saved.

There are three good arguments for managerial participation. First, the time has come when the up-to-date manager must bring to the job at least a minimal familiarity with the topic of MIS. Second, from the point of view of the organization, the time is rapidly approaching when a company's information system will become a vital part of its operation just as marketing, operations, and finance are today. Third, it simply makes good sense for managers to become involved, because much better and more effective information systems will be the result of that involvement.

FAILURE TO IDENTIFY INFORMATION NEEDS

The failure to identify management's information needs probably accounts for the downfall of more design efforts than any other factor except managerial participation. Indeed, *management participation and identification of information needs* go hand-in-hand.

> Ask any systems analyst or data processing manager what his number one problem is. Almost invariably he will reply: "I can't get the user to be specific about what information he needs in the system output."

A clear statement of information needs is fundamental and necessary to good systems design. Too many companies spend lavish sums on hardware and software to perpetuate existing systems or build sophisticated data banks without first determining the real information needs of management, information that can increase the perception of managers in critical areas such as problems, alternatives, opportunities, and plans.

Unless the manager-user can provide the specifications for what he wants out of an information system, the design effort will produce something less than optimum results. If, on the other hand, the manager-user can define his MIS objectives and spell out those items of information that are needed to reach the objective, he is then at least halfway home in systems design.

Too often design begins without a clear-cut statement of objectives and information needs. If this happens and the manager fails to provide them, the systems analyst or technician will, by default, provide *his* objectives and *his* information needs. These would very rarely meet the needs of the user.

Is is not easy for a manager to spell out his specific information requirements. If you are not convinced of this, try it for your own job. You will probably find yourself stating them in generalities and platitudes that can't be incorporated into systems design.

The real reason for having an information system is to provide the information to meet system objectives, to aid in decision making regarding planning and controlling operations. The information needs must therefore be stated in specifics, not generalities. The computer won't accept generalities. If the manager is to use the system, he must describe (and draw a picture if necessary) what he wants from it.

POOR SYSTEMS PRIOR TO COMPUTERIZATION OR MODIFICATION

Many people apparently attribute some magic power to the computer; they think that by the computerization of a poor manual system (the one-for-one changeover), the results will be improved. Nothing could be further from the truth. Indeed, computerization of a poor system will merely "increase inefficiency at an accelerating rate." You will be getting irrelevant or bad information faster, and the bad decisions can be made sooner.

If left to his own devices, the technician or specialist will dump the manual system into the computer with no changes or improvements. If he does that, nothing will have been improved. On the other hand, the conversion process provides an excellent opportunity to *upgrade* and *improve* the former system. Dozens of opportunities exist to do this. For example:

Clerical System		*Management System*
Ledger Accounting	*upgraded to*	Financial Planning
Order Entry and Billing	*upgraded to*	Sales Analysis
Inventory Accounting	*upgraded to*	Inventory Management
Production Reports	*upgraded to*	Production Planning and Control

OVERLOOKING HUMAN ACCEPTANCE

Most systems designers admit to the unpleasant reality that the toughest part of designing and implementing an MIS is gaining acceptance of the users for whom the system is designed. How many analysts or EDP managers have asked themselves this frustrating question: "Since my system is technically optimum and is obviously going to result in improved performance and more efficient operations, why can't I get the user to accept it and welcome it?"

The fact is that many people will not only resist a new system but what's worse, they will work around it, continue to use the old system, and in many cases *sabotage* the new system. Yet, resistance to MIS is not inherent or automatic. People only resist things that they fear or do not understand.

The first and major step in learning how to overcome resistance to a new MIS is to try and gain some understanding of the *reasons* for resistance. This understanding will give the designer and the manager a new attitude toward resistance and go a long way toward helping him overcome it. Indeed, this understanding and this attitude, if achieved, constitutes about the best answer that behavioral science has to offer. After all, resistance to MIS is nothing more than a special case of the general problem of resistance to change.

The wrong approach, of course, is to try to sell an MIS based on its technical superiority. People are just not interested. They are interested only in how the system will affect them and their jobs. Typical reasons for resistance might be illustrated:

Reason	*Illustration*
Threat to status	Salesmen downgraded below production planners upon installation of production control system.
Threat to ego	Manager's job skills become less important due to computer takeover.
Economic threat	Clerical personnel fear job loss.
Insecurity	Managers may be deprived of personal power or political base due to quantitative measures provided by MIS.
Loss of autonomy and control	Production planning and control function now largely being performed by new MIS.
Interpersonal relations changed	Former relationships built up on personal information exchange are changed.

These illustrations lead to the conclusion that human acceptance of the computer can only be obtained on the basis of how it affects people personally in their job and the way in which they view it as an instrument of social change in their relationship with others. In other words, consider the social and behavioral aspects rather than the technical ones. Here are some do's and don'ts:

> *Don't* design the system first and then try to force acceptance.
>
> *Don't* pay lip service to participation in design.
>
> *Don't* emphasize technical and physical constraints of the system to the exclusion of the social and behavioral.
>
> *Do* begin in the initial stages to take account of the emergent social system and other behavioral variables affecting acceptance.
>
> *Do* remember that the MIS you propose to modify is resident in various individual personnel. Involve them in the early stages.

CHECKLIST
FOR DIAGNOSING YOUR MIS ILLS AND
PRESCRIBING A CURE

	Diagnosis	Yes	No	Cure
1.	Is your computer effort devoted to *clerical data* systems rather than management information systems?	( )	( )	Convert your clerical systems to management systems by *upgrading* them for decision making. Avoid the one-for-one changeover syndrome.
2.	Are you suffering from a *communications gap* between computer technician and manager?	( )	( )	*Management development.* Make the computer man learn the basics of management and how the computer facilitates it. Make the manager learn computer basics—at least enough to communicate with the technician.
3.	Are you placing too much reliance on a consultant or the computer manufacturer?	( )	( )	Develop in-house design and operation talent.
4.	Are subsystems being designed without following the blueprint of an *MIS Master Plan?*	( )	( )	Develop a *master plan* for structure and a timetable for implementation.
5.	Does the head of the computer or information function report to a third-tier manager or the controller?	( )	( )	Provide for an MIS team reporting to the president during the development stage and a vice-president in charge after the shakedown. *Organize and assign near the top.*
6.	Are you developing MIS without adequate underlying *management systems?*	( )	( )	Review and upgrade if necessary your *organization* structure and your *management systems* for planning and control.
7.	Do the manager-users avoid *participation* in MIS design and leave it to the technician?	( )	( )	Get *support* from the chief executive and get him to demand *participation* by users in their own decision systems.

	Diagnosis	Yes	No	Cure
8.	Is failure to identify *information needs* holding up design of systems for improved management?	( )	( )	Get managers to write down their major job responsibilities accompanied by *information needs* to fulfill these responsibilities.
9.	Are you changing or modifying *existing manual systems* that are poor for decision making and management?	( )	( )	Take the redesign opportunity to *upgrade* these systems for MIS.
10.	Have you overlooked the *human acceptance* problem in MIS?	( )	( )	Remember that the social and behavioral aspects of systems design and implementation are as important as the technical. Start in the early stages to gain acceptance.

a system of organization and management

3

synḗrgism, n. 2. the simultaneous action of separate agencies which, together, have greater total effect than the sum of their individual effects.

—Webster's Dictionary, Unabridged, 2nd Ed.

There is an old comedy routine that has been successful for generations and still gets a laugh today. The audience roars with delight as the comedian opens his closet door while the contents pour forth and crash around him in utter disarray and confusion.

Many executives view their organizations in this way. As the door to the "problems" closet is opened, out tumbles a disorganized array of functional crises brought on by subordinates who can't, or won't, work together. He wonders how to make a "system" of the mess.

Somewhat less in disarray, but nevertheless confusing, is the state-of-the-art in the "science" of organization and management. It is the intent of this chapter to bring these pieces together into a system. This integration is necessary because it is a fundamental premise of this book that the process of management must be clearly understood before computer-based information systems can be designed to facilitate that process. Indeed, *the sole reason for MIS is to improve the management process.*

In this "age of synthesis" we should look at a business as a pattern of flows rather than as a collection of parts. This view will avoid suboptimization of the parts at the expense of the whole. Engineers will not overdesign products that are noncompetitive from a cost standpoint; sales managers will not demand product variety and unreasonable deliveries without regard to other considerations; short-range planning will not be emphasized to the exclusion of strategic planning. The systems approach will emphasize the notion that a business is a system composed of parts that interact with other subsystems within and without organizational boundaries.

And so it is with a system of organization and management. The parts should be integrated into a useful whole.

PARTS OF THE MANAGEMENT SYSTEM

Because of the expanding frontiers of management thought and because of the extraordinary interest in the study of management and its related disciplines in recent years, there have developed a number of approaches to its study. What was formerly the province of the practitioner, later to be shared with management scholars, has now become fair game for a variety of persons interested in quite a number of related disciplines. Psy-

chologists, sociologists, anthropologists, statisticians, mathematicians, economists, and political scientists are just a few of those who espouse particular
and specific approaches to the study of management. Consequently, there
has been some confusion about what management theory is and how we
should go about studying it. This confusion has been widely labeled "the
management theory jungle."

In this chapter I will argue that a logical approach to an understanding
of a system of management is to break it down and discuss it under three
parts (subsystems). These parts are: the tools of management, the processes or functions of management, and management information systems
(MIS). The model for this structure is shown in Figure 3-1. The resource
flows of the company are also included in this model because these are the
classical resources that are managed.

TOOLS OF MANAGEMENT

In the brief sketch to follow, it is impossible to deal with the nuances
of each of our "tools" because all lie along a continuum and shade into

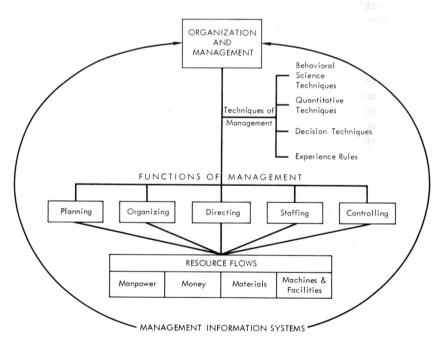

Figure 3-1   Organization and Management—A System

each other. The reader should therefore forgive an approach that is over-simplified for the sake of ease in understanding. Moreover, do not assume that each of these tools is mutually exclusive; indeed, most of them are compatible, at least to the extent that they become subsystems of a system of management.

Experience

If you were to ask the manager-on-the-street his recipe for good management, he would likely reply "get a lot of experience." Until recent years this has been the commonly accepted route to becoming a manager. It has been assumed that good sales managers were experienced salesmen, good product managers were experienced product managers, and so on.

This method of managing, sometimes called the "experience" or "custom" approach, attempts to analyze management by an empirical study of experience. It is probable that a large proportion of practitioners and businessmen belong to this school and hold the view that experience is the single greatest determinant of managerial success. Moreover, in their approach to the problems of management decision making and problem solving, there is a tendency to study the successes and mistakes made by other managers in similar cases. The hope is that by studying these cases, the manager may be able to come up with generalizations concerning similar problems or at least the answer to a specific problem. The subscriber to this school might ask, "How would my predecessor have solved such a problem?" It is more an approach to developing problem-solving skills than an attempt to develop a scientific approach.

The empirical approach, which attempts to transfer knowledge to the learner by a study of experience, is typified by the American Management Association. This group has its roots in the top management people of the nation and views its primary function as providing a forum where practicing managers can gather to trade experiences. The bulk of the association's publications report the experiences of other managers and other companies. In the academic world, this empirical approach is represented by schools of business that teach by the *case method*. The Harvard Graduate School of Business has been the forerunner in this movement.

While few may deny that the knowledge of successful management of yesterday's problems may be helpful in handling similar problems of today's management, there is the danger that yesterday's answer will not be good enough for today's problem nor will it apply to tomorrow's. What fits one organization might not fit another at all, and comparing the past issues with those of present and future is hazardous for the novice. We are all familiar with the type of manager who brags of twenty-years' experience; in reality he only has *one*-year's experience *twenty* times.

In conclusion, we can say that experience is a valuable tool of management but by no means is it the total answer.

> When a manager, in his technical or professional development, falls below that level required for effective performance, he is for all practical purposes obsolete. He will become more obsolete unless he takes corrective action to overcome his shortcomings that are caused by change. Change produces the discrepancy between job needs and managerial capacity. As far as the manager is concerned, he must keep abreast of change in the business environment, in people, in technology, and in the process of management.

Behavioral Science

Those who subscribe to the behavioral school of management can generally be divided as (a) the human behavior group, and (b) the social systems group. In the former case, the approach is based on the notion that management consists of getting things done through people—a notion popularized by Lawrence Apply, former president of the American Management Association. The idea is that the manager, if he is to be successful, should understand human relations, leadership, and the other behavioral science approaches to describing interpersonal relationships among people. People are viewed as the important entity of management, and study is devoted to determining how greater productivity and motivation can be gained by the use of good human relations. Motivation, leadership, training, and communications are among the common topics of those who depend on this tool of management and it has spawned such popular movements as "bottoms-up management" and "management by participation."

The practitioners and scholars in the *human behavior school* are generally oriented toward individual and social psychology. Many of these people equate good management with leadership; others see management as being performed through the study of group dynamics. The approach had its beginnings in the Hawthorne Studies at Western Electric in the 1930s. In more recent years, the approach has been popularized by such writers as the very clever Douglas McGregor, who advanced the notion of the Theory X and Theory Y manager. The classical approach to management is represented by Theory X, which maintains that there is no satisfaction in the work itself, that humans avoid work as much as possible, that positive direction and tight control over workers is necessary, and that workers possess little ambition or enthusiasm for their work. The human relations approach of Theory Y, the antithesis of Theory X, states that workers have much greater potential than is commonly realized and will exercise self-direction and seek responsibility if properly motivated. Theory *Y* is a *participative* approach.

The *social system* group is closely related to the human behavior group but differs in that it looks upon management as a social system, a system of cultural relationships. The sociologists and others who subscribe to this school of organization see the formal organization in terms of cultural relationships of various social groups rather than as a system of authoritative relationships, as has been the custom in the classical approach.

The social system approach to organizational structure and behavior is an outgrowth of the neoclassical or "human relations" approach begun with the Hawthorne studies, but the movement has taken a direction all its own. It has become quite large and influential. Among its pioneers are Abraham Maslow, Chris Argyris, and Frederick Herzberg. Perhaps the greatest impact has been made by Abraham Maslow through his book, *Motivation and Personality,* in which he set out his now famous theory of *hierarchy of needs.* This theory explained that human needs range from those that are physiological to those involving love and esteem. This classification of human needs listed *self-actualization* as the highest human need and hypothesized that workers could be motivated to higher morale and productivity by appealing to their esteem and self-actualization needs, as opposed to the classical idea of workers motivated by monetary rewards and fears of sanctions.

Notwithstanding the overwhelming importance of human behavior and leadership in management, it would be erroneous to equate the entire system of management with behavioral science. The disciplines surrounding the behavioral science approach provide the manager with very valuable tools, but it is one more tool in our system of management.

> Fred Borch, recent chairman of General Electric, commented: "For my money the most difficult decisions that I've made have been organizational and personnel decisions." The recently retired chairman of Montgomery Ward (MarCor) echoed those sentiments with: "In general the most important decisions for the chief executive are about people." And at General Motors, the "organization man's organization," many managers believe that recapturing the interest of their workers—or at least getting them to tolerate life on the assembly line—is one of the crucial problems of the decade.

Decision Techniques

Decision making is the most important task of managers; many scholars believe that decision making and the processes leading up to it account for most of what executives do. Among those who place great importance on the process is Professor Herbert Simon of Carnegie Tech, perhaps the foremost decision theorist of our time. He states, "I shall find it convenient to take mild liberties with the English language by using 'decision making' as though it were synonymous with 'managing.' " Decision making in its broadest context includes among the activities preceding the decision: (1) finding occasions for making a decision, (2) finding possible courses of action, and (3) choosing among courses of action.

Viewed in the foregoing context, decision making becomes the "keyhole" look at management. Moreover, if we accept the thesis of the pure decision theorists, the entire process of management can be explained in terms of decision making. The position taken in this book is that decision making is a fundamental aspect of management. Indeed, the systems approach to management would use the decision as its central focus. However, to say, as some decision theorists do, that the entire body of management theory can rest on the structure of decision making is to oversimplify the matter. While decisions may be the end result of managing, other approaches, schools, disciplines, and techniques provide the manager with the total body he needs for a system of management.

An additional doubt as to whether decision theory has the total answer is raised by the question: does the decision complete the action sought or commence the action? In other words, once the decision is made it must be implemented. This action implies, indeed demands, some form of planning and subsequent control.

As discussed later in Chapter 7, decision making as implemented by the *decision rule,* is a central theme and basic foundation of MIS design. I shall argue that the good computer-based MIS is the one with built-in decision rules that make decisions routine and relieve the manager of this task.

Quantitative Techniques

This approach to the solution of management problems, sometimes called the mathematical school, includes those practitioners and scholars who seek to describe management in terms of mathematical symbols, relationships, and measurable data. They hope that eventually the variables in the problem-solving equation can be quantified and related in an equation so that a quantitative solution will result. In this respect, the school is primarily concerned with decision making and systems analysis. Some applications have been made to organizational behavior.

Included among the proponents of this approach are the operations researchers, the management scientists, and the mathematicians. The methodologies of the school include simulation and modeling. Techniques would include operations research, mathematical programming, Monte Carlo methods, queuing theory, gaming, and heuristics.

Although the quantitative school of management is comparatively new, those who practice it have made some spectacular breakthroughs in specific problem areas that lend themselves to this treatment. The use of its techniques forces the manager to define his problem precisely and encourages careful thinking, logical methodology, and the recognition of definite constraints. Generally speaking, the usefulness of this school is limited by its ability to define and quantify the variables in a management decision-making equation. The complexity of human behavior makes it difficult to describe the problem in quantitative terms in the formulation stage and this appears to be one of the major restrictions of this method at present. However, to the extent that quantitative methods can be used in the design of decision rules and in systems analysis, they are essential to both the theory and to the practical use of management information systems.

The essential point to remember about quantitative techniques is their use in the design of decision rules for inclusion in management information systems.

FUNCTIONS OF MANAGEMENT

The most widespread approach to management is the so-called process or operational school, which defines what managers do in terms of the managerial functions they perform: planning, organizing, and controlling. These three functions also provide the central theme of our management system.

Each of these functions has its body of knowledge and techniques, and each utilizes knowledge from other fields of science. The process school does not deny the existence and validity of the other approaches to management. Indeed, the *functions of management* can absorb or utilize the methodology and techniques of all other disciplines, techniques, and approaches.

The overall job of a manager is to create within the enterprise the environment that will facilitate the accomplishment of its objectives. In doing this, the manager *plans* the work of his subordinates and his own activity, *organizes* the work and task relationships, and *controls* results by measuring performance against plan. These are the traditional functions of the manager.* As distinguished from *operational* functions (manufacturing, engineering, accounting, marketing, etc.), which differ among the various types of organizations, *managerial* functions are common to all.

---

*Two additional functions—*directing* and *staffing*—are also commonly considered to be managerial in nature. However, for our purposes of MIS, these are not considered to be overriding.

This three-part or three-function approach to the job of the manager provides the basic action framework for the systems approach. Its continuing popularity and widespread use are probably due to its approach to the topic—the explanation of the process of management in terms of what managers do. Hence, it reflects the way the manager sees his job and is therefore most useful to him. Moreover, it appears that the functional approach to management will be with us for some time in the future. Although there will continue to be a need for managers with a high degree of *functional* skill, this skill must be accompanied by the essential *managerial* skills of planning, organizing, decision making, and measuring and controlling processes and operations.

The general nature by which management operates is shown in Figure 3-2.

Planning

The most basic and pervasive management function is planning. All managers at all levels plan, and the success of the performance of the other

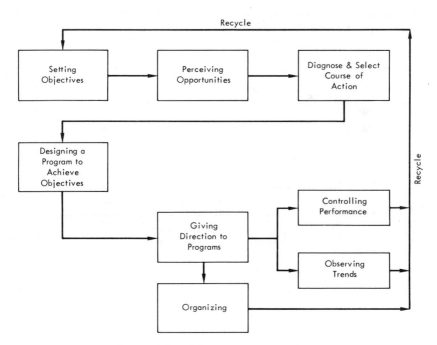

Figure 3-2   A Concept of Management

functions depends upon it. Planning is the deciding in advance of what has to be done, who has to do it, when it has to be done, and how it is to be done. It bridges the gap from where we are to where we want to go. Managers plan for the allocation of resources and the work of other people, in contrast to the nonmanager, who plans only his own activities.

> The North American Society for Corporate Planning (the professional society for full-time planners) identifies a number of reasons for the tremendous upsurge in formal planning. These reasons include: the rapid rate of technological change, growing competition, the increasingly complex business environment, increased complexity of management, and the changing philosophy of management that admits that companies can influence their own future.

The steps in planning are basically the same as in decision making and problem solving: (a) definition of the problem or establishment of the objective, (b) collection and arrangement of facts surrounding the problem, and (c) reaching a decision or solving the problem. These basic concepts can be expanded to provide a logical sequence of steps for operations research and for systems design as well.

Most planning is conducted in an environment that lends itself to a certain basic approach. Expanding on the basic elementary steps of the preceding paragraph, this basic approach can be described in terms of a number of *iterative* steps. The process is shown in Figure 3-3.

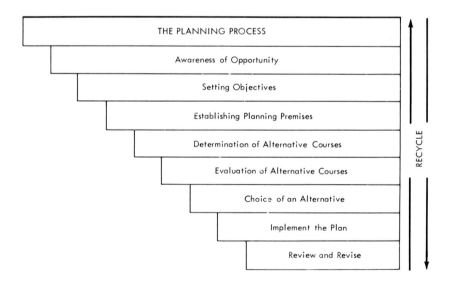

Figure 3-3   The Planning Process

1. *Awareness of Opportunity.* A cardinal purpose of planning is to discover future opportunities and make plans to exploit them. Although, strictly speaking, becoming aware of opportunities is not a step in the planing process, it must precede planning because the most profitable plans are those that identify and exploit opportunities.

2. *Set Objectives.* This step refers to establishing planning objectives as opposed to enterprise objectives, although if the latter have not been set, planning cannot proceed beyond this point.

3. *Establish Planning Premises.* Premises are those data, facts, and information that influence alternative courses of action to reach objectives. It should be evident that a *management information system* is an essential device for gathering, storing, and retrieving planning premises. The nature and organization of this topic is discussed in Chapter 4 and shown conceptually in Figure 4-1.

4. *Determination of Alternative Courses of Action.* This involves the search for and determination of alternative ways to achieve the objective of the plan. In formal planning, this process almost always involves the quantification and documentation of alternatives to permit anaysis.

5. *Evaluation of Alternative Courses.* Evaluation of alternatives involves the weighing of the desirability of each alternative in light of planning premises and goals. Some choices are reduced to mathematical selection because all variables can be quantified. In these cases the new management science techniques are valuable. However, most planning problems are replete with intangibles and uncertainties; it is for this reason that a careful evaluation is so important. A properly designed *management information system* can be of valuable benefit in helping the decision maker perform this evaluation.

> Simulation and forecasting models hold great potential for evaluating alternatives. Fourth-generation MIS is developing to the point at which it is beginning to provide the necessary data to construct effective predictive models. The Pillsbury Corporation is using a model to support a cash flow forecasting system of its chicken-raising business. The model is credited with enabling management to identify and solve problems that have a constraining effect on the profits of the business.

6. *Choice of an Alternative.* This is the point at which a decision is made and a course of action selected. It is taken after a consideration of premises, constraints, enterprise goals, and the factors of expediency, adaptability, and cost.

7. *Implementation of the Plan.* After selection of an alternative, the plan is translated into derivative plans, and its relation to all activities

affected by it are worked out. This includes the details of where the action should be done, by whom, and in what order. Although in a technical sense the planning process stops with the choice of an alternative, there are almost invariably derivative plans to be constructed in order to support and implement the basic plan.

Organizing

Organizing is required of managers because it is the method by which effective group action is obtained. A structure of roles must be designed and maintained in order to make it possible for people to work together to carry out the plans that accomplish objectives. This is the task of organizing. It involves the grouping of tasks necessary to accomplish plans, the assignment of activities to departments, and the provision for coordination through authority delegation.

Organizing, as a process of management, addresses itself to the structural system for achieving coordination and authority delegation, and we can argue convincingly that this structure facilitates the operation of the organization as a system.

Classical, or traditional, organization theory is built upon four basic tenets:

1. *Labor Specialization.* Even before the Industrial Revolution, a major concern with organizational structure was the formation of organizational units around some type of *departmentation,* the manner in which work is divided into homogeneous groups of activities. This is still of major concern today.

Methods of departmentation that experience has proven logical and useful are: by function, by product, by territory, by customer, by process, and by project. An example of each of these methods of departmentation is shown in Figure 3-4. For example, departmentation by *function* is shown at the top level by the common functions of marketing, personnel, operations, research and development, and finance. The breakdown of operations into the furniture division, the metal products division, and the floor-covering division is an example of *product* organization. The sales department is departmented into the eastern district and the western district to establish a *territory* organization, and these territories are further departmented by the *customer* breakdown of retail, government, institutions, and manufacturer's representatives. The manufacturing operation in the metal products division depicts both *process* (assembly, welding, stamping) and *function* (maintenance, power, shipping). Finally, a special *project* team, organized for new product development, reports to the president.

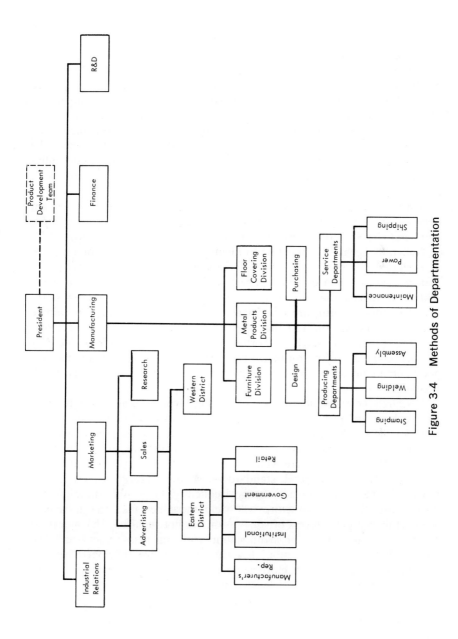

Figure 3-4 Methods of Departmentation

43

2. *Span of Management.* If it were not necessary to coordinate the activities of an organization, departmentation would permit its expansion to an indefinite degree. However, this need for coordination requires a structure composed of levels of supervision. This structure is achieved by establishing these levels of supervision within the confines of the span of management, the number of subordinates that a manager can supervise. The importance of this factor can be appreciated if we consider that were it not for a supervisory limit, there would be no need to organize since everyone in the organization would report to the president. Hence, the reason for organizing is to overcome the limitations of both human ability and time. Additionally, assignment of duties is clarified and control facilitated.

The two basic related questions surrounding the span of management decision are: (a) How many subordinates should be assigned to a superior? and (b) Should the organizational structure be "wide" or "narrow"?

Generally speaking, the effort to identify a specific number or range of subordinates has not been productive. In actual practice the number varies widely. Span of management appears to be a function of the manager's ability to reduce the time and frequency of subordinate relationships. These factors, in turn, are determined by (a) how well the subordinate is trained to do his job, (b) the extent of planning existing in the activity, (c) the degree to which authority is delegated and understood, (d) whether standards of performance have been set, (e) the environment for good communications, and (f) the nature of the job and the rate at which it changes.

Research indicates that the "wide" or "flat" type of organizational structure with a wide span of control is preferable, *provided* that positive values exist for the six determinants of relationships listed in the preceding paragraph. In other words, adopt a wide span of management and organization structure *if* subordinates are well trained, work is well planned, authority is delegated and understood, standards exist, there are good communications, and the work does not change frequently. Given this situation, the "wide" organizational structure will yield these benefits: (a) it is economical in that extra layers of supervision are not required; (b) morale is improved because of better identification with top management and less restriction by close supervision; (c) subordinates are developed because they are required to accept more responsibility; and (d) because of necessity, authority is likely to be delegated more clearly.

3. *Authority Relationships.* Without the delegation of authority, an organization would cease to exist—there would be only one department because the chief executive would be the only manager. It does no good to set up a structure of departmented activities unless authority is delegated to the units within the structure that accomplish particular assignments.

Absolute centralization in one person and absolute decentralization of authority are the two extremes of delegation. Obviously, the tendency is to settle somewhere along the continuum. The major determinant of how well a manager delegates authority is his temperament and personality, but other determinants are beyond his control. Some of these are: (a) cost—the more costly the decision, the more likely it is to be centralized; (b) uniformity of policy—the more uniform and centralized a policy (price, personnel, financial, etc.), the less need there is to delegate authority surrounding it; (c) complexity of the organization—the more complex, the greater the need for coordination and centralization of authority; (d) custom of the business—frequently the delegation philosophy and character of top management determine authority delegation; and (e) environment for good management—the availability of managers and good management practices (including control techniques) in the company that would encourage delegation.

Among the tools and techniques for communicating the delegation of authority and organizational structure are the organization manual, organization charts, position descriptions, activity charts, and procedural flow charts. Others are plans, policies, programs, budgets, and procedures.

4. *Unity of Command.* This last basic tenet of classical organization theory simply means that nobody in the organization reports to more than one boss. Reporting to two or more superiors causes conflict in orders and confusion and frustration on the part of the subordinate. Moreover, violation of the unity of command principle would be in direct conflict to the chain of command principle of authority relationships described in the preceding paragraph.

Classical Organization Theory—Summary

Criticizing the classical or bureaucratic organizational structure is getting to be a profitable vocation; witness the success of such books as *Parkinson's Law, The Peter Principle,* and *Up the Organization.* Robert Townsend, author of the last, a best-selling book, remarks: "It strangles profit and stifles people." I have also had some mild success in this direction.*

Some of the charges leveled at the classical structure are:

It is too mechanistic and ignores major facets of human nature.

It is too structured to adapt to change.

Its formal directives and procedures hinder communications.

---

*See Joel E. Ross and Michael J. Kami, *Corporate Management in Crisis: Why the Mighty Fall* (Englewood Cliffs, N.J.: Prentice-Hall, Inc., 1973).

It inhibits innovation.

It pays the job and not the man.

It relys on coercion to maintain control.

Its job-defensive behavior encourages make-work.

Its goals are incompatible with those of its members.

It is simply out of date for the needs of the seventies and eighties.

The major arguments in favor of the classical approach are:

It has overwhelming acceptance by practicing businessmen.

It works.

It is easily understood and applies.

It isn't set in concrete—it can accommodate modifications.

> There remains much confusion over the application of organization theory. On this subject, *Business Week* magazine reports: "With the behavioralists and humanitarians to the left, orthodox doctrine to the right, and top management just down the hall, it would be natural if organizational planners developed at least a slight case of schizophrenia."

The state-of-the-art in the application of organizational principles does indeed present a paradox. Except for the small organization, the classical structure appears to be the easiest effective way to cope with complexity. Bureaucracy, with all of its "evils," is an organizational requirement when we go beyond the face-to-face stage of communications. On the other hand, there is much in the classical structure that negates what is desirable in the human form. It has a tendency to suboptimize both job satisfaction and productivity.

The task of management is one of modifying the classical structure in order to achieve the potential for increased productivity that exists. It is discussed in Chapter 4 how this might be done with a *systems approach to organizing*.

> Recently the Fellows of the Academy of Management, a group of distinguished senior management professors, were asked to forecast the shape of the organization of the future. The overwhelming conclusion was that the dominant organizational structure in 1985 would be the classical pyramid. Harold Smiddy, a pioneering professor of management, commented, "There will always be experiments, exceptions, etc.—and a continuing deluge of academic claptrap, largely irrelevant, passing as research—but reality will show little widespread change in the periods 1985–2000." Ernest Dale, another respected theorist and consultant agreed: "Despite the

suggestions of the behavioralists, the pyramidal structure is still overwhelmingly used by the majority of business firms and other organizations—and will continue to be."

Controlling

If the manager could depend upon the flawless execution of plans by a perfectly balanced organization, there would be no need for control; results would invariably be as expected. However, plans and operations rarely remain on course, and control is needed to obtain results. The real test of a manager's ability is the result he achieves.

Control is a definite process and is essentially the same regardless of the activity involved or the area of the organization. The fundamental process consists of three steps: (1) setting standards of performance, (2) measuring performance against these standards, and (3) correcting deviations from standards and plans. These three steps are discussed in the following paragraphs.

1. *Standards of Performance.* Setting standards of performance involves defining for personnel in all levels of the organization what is expected of them in terms of job performance. Hence standards are criteria that results can be measured against. These criteria can be quantitative (e.g., 10% increase in sales) or qualitative (e.g., maintain high level of morale). A frequently used definition of standards of performance is a *statement of conditions existing when a job is performed satisfactorily.*

A discussion of standards can be better understood when related to actual examples. Table 3-1 illustrates the basic components of a very important operational plan—the financial plan. Note that a standard of performance is indicated for each of these major items.

The usual criteria for measuring performance against plan for an activity can be stated in terms of cost, time, quantity, or quality. For example, in Table 3-1, the unit *cost* of raw materials for manufacturing a product can be controlled in terms of cost per unit, and this standard would apply in the purchasing operation. *Time* is a standard for sales when performance is measured in terms of meeting sales quotas during established time periods (e.g., weeks, months). In manufacturing, the direct labor hours per unit of output in a process operation is a common *quantity* measure. *Quality* is a common measure in judging the acceptability of such factors as product specification, grades of products sold, and reject rates in quality control.

These are yardsticks and not areas of activity to be measured. Ideally, everyone in the organization should have some standard so that he understands what is expected of him in terms of job performance.

Table 3-1

Standards of Performance for Controlling the Financial Plan

	CRITERIA				
Financial Plan	*Cost*	*Time*	*Quan-tity*	*Qual-ity*	*Illustration of Standard*
Sales	x	x	x		Sales quota during time period at standard cost
Cost of Goods Sold:					
Raw Materials	x		x		Unit usage rate at standard cost
Direct Labor	x	x	x		Hours per unit of output
Manufacturing Expense	x	x	x		Maintenance cost per machine hour
Total					
Gross Margin on Sales	x		x		Percent of sales
Less:					
Distribution Expense	x				Percent of sales
Administrative Expense	x	x	x		Budgeted amount
Total					
Operating Income	x		x		Percent of sales
Federal Income Tax					
Net Income	x		x		Return on investment

Other types of performance standards can be identified:

>*Physical* (e.g., units per man-hour, raw material usage rate)
>*Cost* (e.g., overhead cost per unit of output, distribution costs)
>*Revenue* (e.g., average sales per customer)
>*Program* (e.g., time to complete events, technical specifications)
>*Intangible* (e.g., employee morale, public relations)

In addition to operating standards, there are critical areas of *overall* company performance that are the concern of top management. Is the company achieving its objectives? Are its strategies paying off? By appraising overall company performance in these areas, the company will be evaluating its progress toward its basic purposes and objectives. Some of the areas for checking on overall performance would include: profitability, market standing, productivity, innovation and product leadership, employee and managerial attitudes and development, public and social responsibility, use of resources, and the balance between short-range and long-range objectives.

It is extremely important for both the manager-user and the systems designer to be familar with the control process, because the majority of outputs from the management information system are *control reports.*

2. *Measuring Performance.* Once standards have been established, it is necessary to measure performance against the expectation of the standards. The statement of this measurement, and of any differences, is usually in the form of a personal observation or some form of report—oral or written.

The oldest and most prevalent means of measuring performance is by personal observation. The shop supervisor is on the scene and can personally check the time, cost, and quality of the work under his supervision. Sales managers visit sales offices or make calls with their salesmen to observe performance personally. Advantages include the benefits of immediacy, personal direct contact, and firsthand observation of intangibles such as morale, personnel development, or customer reaction. Disadvantages are those associated with the time-consuming nature of the method and the lack of precision in measurement.

Oral reports of performance may take the form of interviews, informal reports, or group and committee meetings. Measuring performance in this way has many of the advantages and drawbacks of the personal observation method. Additionally, the method of oral reporting does not usually result in any record-keeping of performance.

Control and performance reporting is being increasingly done in written form. This is due in part to the accelerating use of computer-based information systems and related reporting techniques. The written report has the advantage of providing a permanent record, subject to periodic review by the manager and subordinates. This method of measuring performance may take a variety of forms. Among the most common is the statistical report, which presents statistical analysis of performance versus standard, either in tabular or chart form. Special or one-time reports are frequently made in problem areas as they arise. A significant portion of written reports are operational in nature and concern performance rather than standards for the financial plan.

> Hospital rates have risen more than five times as fast as the general consumer price index in the last ten years, but one-third of all hospital costs are related only indirectly to patient care. The potential for cost savings with computer-based control systems is great. Among the functions that can be automated and better controlled are admission and bed control, patient account, reporting, personnel control, cost allocation, scheduling, operations control, and a variety of ancillary applications.

3. *Correcting Deviations.* It does little good to set standards of performance and measure deviations from standard unless corrections are made

in order to get the plan back on course. Methods and techniques for correcting deviations can be described in terms of the functions of management:

Plan—recycle the management process; review the plan, modify the goal, or change the standard.

Organize—examine the organization structure to determine whether it is reflected in standards, make sure that duties are well understood, reassign people if necessary.

Staff—improve selection, improve training, reassign duties.

Direct—better the leadership, improve motivation, explain the job better, and make sure that there is manager-subordinate agreement on the standard.

MIS AND A SYSTEM OF MANAGEMENT

We are now prepared to synthesize the separate parts of the management system with which we have been dealing and construct an integrated, useful approach. The task is to construct a conceptual model with which we can design information systems to help *manage* the transformation of *resource flows* through the *organization* by means of the systems approach. Such an approach should include the *tools of management,* the *functions of management,* and the *management information system* (MIS).

In actual practice the functions of management are interwoven and interrelated; the performance of one does not cease before the next commences, nor are the functions carried out in a sequence. For example, a manager may perform controlling at the same time that he is planning and directing. Although there are times when some function must be performed before others can be put into action (e.g., controlling requires that certain plans be made), there is no sequence, generally speaking, to the operation of these functions. The point to remember is the *interrelationship* between planning, organizing, and controlling.

In carrying out the *functions* of management the *tools* of management are likewise utilized. Rules from experience and behavioral science are constantly used to give meaning and to operationalize plans and controls that are conducted through the organization structure. In the same manner, the quantitative techniques are utilized both in decision making and in carrying on the functions of management. The point to remember is the *interrelationship* between the *tools* and *functions* of management.

Now if we add our last vital component, *a management information system,* the total system of management will have been constructed. This is the component of the system that provides information for planning, activates plans, and provides the essential feedback information necessary to achieve stability through the control process. It is the mortar that holds the bricks of the structure together.

Return to Figure 3-1 for a model of the system. Notice that the envelope called *management information system* encloses the entire model and becomes an integral part of it. This component (MIS) collects, analyzes, stores, and displays data to management decision makers at all levels for the management of the resource flows of materials, manpower, money, and facilities and machines. This component is also vital to the practice of the functions of management.

CHECK YOUR MANAGEMENT SYSTEM

You cannot superimpose an MIS in an organization with a poor management system. Check whether you have the prerequisite management system.

	Yes	No
RELIANCE ON EXPERIENCE*		
Have you been saying lately, "We've always done it this way" or "What's wrong with the way we do it?"	( )	( )
Are you uncomfortable with subordinates when they propose a new managerial solution to problems?	( )	( )
Do you consider yourself a Theory X manager?	( )	( )
BEHAVIORAL SCIENCE		
Can you explain the behavioral science theories of Maslow, Argyris, McGregor and Herzberg?	( )	( )
Have you operationalized Maslow's concept of self-actualization?	( )	( )
Do you apply the synergistic effect of behavioral science on the other functions of management?	( )	( )
DECISION MAKING		
Do you practice the basic steps in the decision-making process?	( )	( )
Have you made routine two or more decisions that you make frequently?	( )	( )
QUANTITATIVE METHODS		
Have you used quantitative methods to design a decision rule?	( )	( )
Can you name a practical application for the following techniques: simulation, linear programming, queuing?	( )	( )
FUNCTIONS OF MANAGEMENT		
Do you follow the seven basic steps in the planning process?	( )	( )
Do the four basic tenets of classical organization theory provide a beginning for your organization?	( )	( )
Do adequate control systems exist in your company:		
Standards set at all critical points?	( )	( )
Standards set for overall controls?	( )	( )
Periodic reports to measure performance?	( )	( )
Corrective action taken for deviations?	( )	( )

*A YES answer to any of these questions may indicate that obsolescence is setting in.

	Yes	No

MANAGEMENT INFORMATION SYSTEMS

Are quantitative techniques used for design of decision rules?   ( ) ( )

Does MIS support decision making rather than clerical reporting?   ( ) ( )

Does MIS provide for planning premises?   ( ) ( )

Does MIS support the organizational structure?   ( ) ( )

Does MIS provide for control of operations?   ( ) ( )

information and the systems approach to management

4

"To be a planner today takes the qualities of a Hebrew prophet, a first-class barrister, and a ward politician."

—Henry Boettinger, Director,
Corporate Planning, AT&T

The above comment reflects the dependence that managers have upon information, and also the most common complaint of managers—inadequate facts and data for decision making. If there is a problem in the organization, the chances are good that no one determined what kind of information was needed to prevent the trouble or took the time to organize a system to provide the information. Although data and information are frequently abundant, they are sometimes not enough of the right kind for setting objectives, evaluating alternatives, making decisions, anticipating problems, and measuring results against plans.

Although the great need for information systems should appear obvious to most managers, it is necessary to underscore their importance. Without information, a business simply cannot survive. This importance has been stated by Professor George A. Steiner of UCLA's Graduate School of Business Administration: "Information flows are as important to the life and health of a business as the flow of blood is to the life and health of an individual."

It has been said that the recipe for a good decision is "90 percent information and 10 percent inspiration." Information is the catalyst of management and the ingredient that coalesces the managerial functions of planning, organizing, and controlling. The manager depends on one specific tool, *information,* and although he "gets things done through people," his tool for achieving this is the spoken or written word.

In Chapter 3 we identified the major tools or techniques of management and discussed the three managerial functions of planning, organizing, and controlling. We then added the additional component of a *management information system* to provide information for decision makers at all levels of the organization. The MIS was one of the several integral resource flows and the essential element for the integration of the *management system.*

In this chapter we are concerned with the *systems approach* to the foregoing managerial functions and how these are facilitated with information. This understanding is essential if information systems are to be designed for managerial functions.

Many managers make the basic mistake of thinking that a management *information* system can be designed or made operational without the backup of an adequate *management* system. An adequate management system includes the organizational arrangements, the structure and procedures for adequate planning and control, the clear establishment of objectives, and all the other manifestations of good organization and management. Given this management structure, this framework of good management practices, an information system can be designed upon its foundation. Only then can the information system provide the manager with the information he needs in the form, place, and time that he needs it in, in order to help him perform his job according to the specifications of the *management* system.

PLANNING AND INFORMATION

Corporate planners have not always enjoyed good reputations or acceptance in the organization. Many have been accused of consulting crystal balls and operating out of think tanks and ivory towers. In the mid 1970s the planner came into his own. Ironically, what brought him back were the crunching corporate problems that no one could foresee; the energy crisis, recession, inflation, war and near war, interest rates, gold price fluctuations, and raw material shortages.

Planning is the most basic of all management functions because it involves the selection of organizational and departmental objectives and the determination of the means to achieve these objectives. Essentially, planning is the same whether applied to an entire organization or to any hierarchical level in it.

In Chapter 3 we identified the steps in the planning process and listed *establish planning premises* as an essential one. It is evident that this step and all subsequent steps depend entirely upon the availability and utilization of critical planning information. It is hard to imagine the manager trying to develop any of the major types of plans by function, level, purpose, or time element, without first gathering information (planning premises) that would permit an adequate evaluation of alternative courses of action to achieve the plan.

The planning information needs of an organization can be classified into three broad types: (a) environmental, (b) competitive, and (c) internal. Conceptually, these can be viewed as shown in Figure 4-1.

Environmental information is concerned with the external environment of the firm and is frequently of a strategic nature or used in long-range planning. *Competitive* information concerns those factors affecting the operation of the firm within an industry and includes data concerning industry and firm demand as well as data on competitors.

Because *internal* premises affect the planning decisions of so many levels in the organization, they are in some respects more important than

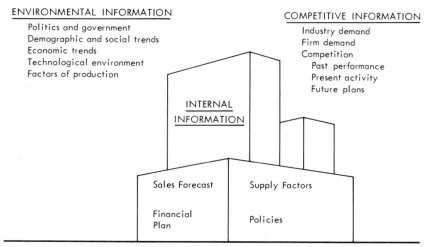

ENVIRONMENTAL INFORMATION
Politics and government
Demographic and social trends
Economic trends
Technological environment
Factors of production

COMPETITIVE INFORMATION
Industry demand
Firm demand
Competition
  Past performance
  Present activity
  Future plans

INTERNAL
INFORMATION

Sales Forecast

Financial
Plan

Supply Factors

Policies

Figure 4-1   Planning Premises

external information. Though the business environment and premises surrounding competition are no doubt very important, these categories of information are, after all, considered necessary for decision making by relatively few managers in a firm, mainly top managers and marketing executives. However, internal planning premises are vital and necessary for subsidiary planning at all levels in the organization. Therefore, the vast majority of information contained in information systems is internal in nature.

Internal data, as they relate to the total planning process, are aimed at an identification of the organization's strengths and weaknesses—those internal constraints that, when viewed in the perspective of external information, are vital decision-making premises that help managers shape future plans.

Perhaps the sales forecast and the financial plan are the most frequently used internal planning premises. The allocation of the entire company's resources is a function of the sales plan, sets the framework on which most other internal plans are constructed, and can therefore be regarded as the dominant planning premise internal to the firm. The financial plan, frequently called the *budget,* is second only to the sales forecast in importance. It represents a quantitative and time commitment of the allocation of the total resources of the company (manpower, plant, capital, materials, overhead, and general and administrative expenses). Properly constructed, the financial plan involves the entire organization, and when completed provides subsidiary planning information for a variety of subplans throughout the company.

THE SYSTEMS APPROACH TO PLANNING: STRATEGIC PLANNING

Short-range planning (frequently called operational, annual, or financial planning) is almost always financial in nature; that is, it expresses goals and performance standards in financial terms. The basic notion behind this type of planning is to develop an overall financial, or operational, plan (Figure 4-2) and to decentralize profit responsibility to profit centers, where standards of performance for sales, turnover, cost of sales, and other

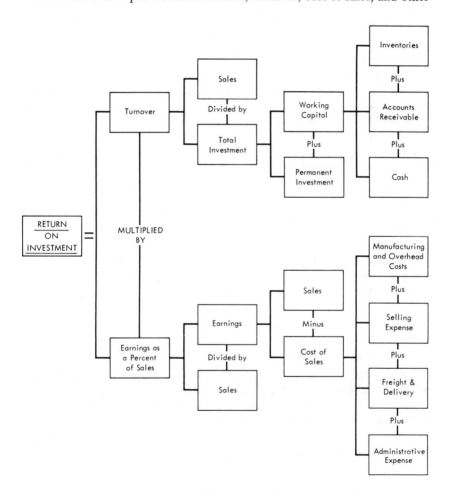

Figure 4-2   Elements of a Financial Plan (Return on Investment)

elements of the plan are established. In turn, those elements are broken down into measurable and controllable components such as investment (fixed assets, inventory, accounts receivable, cash, etc.) and cost of sales (direct labor, overhead, selling, transportation, and administration). This process is conceptualized in detail in the previous figure.

Short-range financial planning makes identification and control of profit determinants of separate organizational entities easier. Its use as a common denominator for comparison purposes, as a yardstick of performance, and presumably as a motivator has been widespread. However, as a *systems* (integrative) approach to planning, it has significant shortcomings. Generally, these fall into the following classes:

Non-Integrative. Although it would appear on the surface that the financial plan integrates the subsystems of the organization, it frequently fails in reality to do so. The major reason for lack of integration is that most managers are concerned with their individual, department, or unit goals at the expense of company-wide objectives. The accountant views his job as the preparation of the cost control report, whereas his real job is to improve production planning and cost control. The engineer designs the product without regard for product policy or subsequent manufacturing cost. The sales manager pursues his objective of increasing sales without regard for market segmentation, customer or product group profitability, or corporate strategy. The common tendency is to seek solutions in terms of individuals or departments, because positive feedback and rewards are given on this basis.

Inaccurate Costs. The financial plan is based on accounting costs, which are historical and rarely reflect current or replacement costs. It is very difficult to assign the costs in the financial plan to specific individuals.

Short-Range Approach. The focus of the financial plan by definition, is on annual financial results. Therefore, both the structure of the plan and its subsequent operation tend to focus on short-range objectives at the expense of longer-range company objectives.

Beating the System. Deferring maintenance, postponing research and development, firing staff personnel, and a variety of creative bookkeeping measures are available to the manager who wants to make sure that he looks good during the term of the current financial plan.

> A classic case of "creative bookkeeping" involved the bankrupt Penn Central Railroad. During the six-year period prior to bankruptcy, the railroad paid out $292 million in dividends while net income for the same period was a mere $2 million. These financial results, and the money to pay dividends, were possible through blatant delay and outright cancellation of basic road and equipment maintenance.

Strategic Planning is Integrative

If there is one single attribute that distinguishes a well-managed and profitable firm from a poorly managed and unprofitable one, it is strategic planning. A strategy is essential; it not only provides a *unified sense of direction* for all members of the organization, but it provides that foundation, that reference point, to which developmental and operational plans can relate.

> Year after year the correlation between good results and strategic planning has been proven. Witness the failure of the conglomerates (except for a few notable exceptions such as IT&T and TRW); they chose pyramidal growth over profitable operations as a strategy. Witness also the success stories attributable to correct strategy. Among them are Xerox (aggressive marketing and go-go-go attitude), IBM ("we sell solutions, not just computers"), Disney (find a need and fill it), Eastman Kodak (product reliability), Sears (customer is king), and J. C. Penney (upgrade, innovate, research).

What is a strategy? Simply stated it has three parts:

1. *Product/Market Scope.* A definition of what business you are in; your predominant product/market concentration by customer, product, distribution channel, and price/quality policy.
2. *Competitive Edge.* A definition of your distinctive competence; that company strength that will differentiate your product or service so that the customer will buy from you rather than the competition.
3. *Objectives.* A quantified statement of major organizational goals.

Given this statement of strategy and an accompanying strategic plan, everyone in the organization can relate his day-to-day decisions to a larger scheme of things to come. Integration is further enhanced by the fact that follow-up plans for development and short-range operations can be prepared in furtherance of the long-range strategic considerations. This is shown conceptually in Figure 4-3.

It is clear that strategic planning is integrative and encourages the systems approach. First, it places the emphasis on the decision-making aspects of planning wherein various levels of management become involved. Second, a major benefit of strategic planning lies in the involvement in the planning process as opposed to the development of an isolated document entitled "The Five-Year Plan." In other words, the *process of planning is as important as the plan itself*. It serves as a valuable communication device for getting agreement on objectives and courses of action.

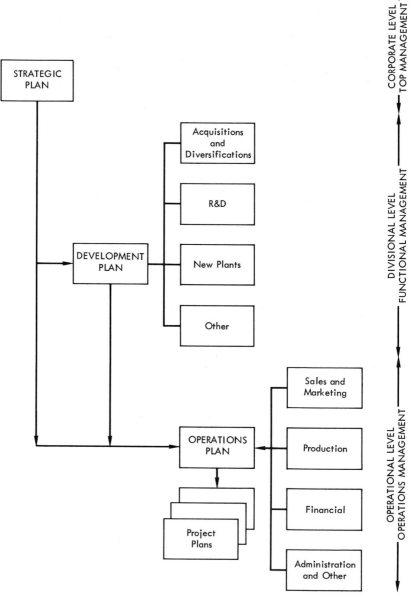

Figure 4-3   The Systems Approach to Planning

Finally, strategic planning is investigative and exploratory in nature as opposed to the short-range profit plan, which is oriented to short-run control of performance standards. Financial planning is not likely to release the innovative thinking and environmental research that is characteristic of strategic planning.

The Strategic Planning Process

A structured, sequential, step-by-step approach to strategic planning is not desirable, because the process is iterative and feedback is constant. However, a variation of the approach outlined below is recommended. It has common acceptance and ensures that all bases are covered.

1. *Analyze Past Performance.* A careful analysis of past performance will provide a measure of the success of previous strategy and help point out weak areas for the analysis to follow. One approach to evaluation is shown in the following matrix.

COMPARISON OF PAST PERFORMANCE

YARDSTICK	With Own Past Performance	With Management's Target	With Competition
Size and Rate of Growth (measured by sales, assets, net worth, etc.)			
Market Share and Rate of Change (measured by percent of market by customer, industry, area, end use)			
Profitability and Trend (measured by $ profit, return on investment, earnings per share, etc.)			
Survival Capacity (measured by capital, management depth, ownership breadth, etc.)			

Question: How effective has past strategy been?

2. *Conduct an Environmental Analysis.* This analysis is conducted to identify the existing and future environmental factors that have or may

have an influence on the company. It is also necessary to identify future opportunities and risks. Factors to consider include:

Economic. Monetary, fiscal, and general business conditions; health and growth of the economy; GNP and disposable personal income; major shifts in demand; foreign competition; labor force and rates.

Competitive. Future of your industry and firm relative to other industries and firms; potential inroads and competitive hazards.

Technological. Major technological trends that will offer both opportunities and ideas for new products and avoidance of obsolescence; capital requirements and availability of production factors.

Government. Prospects for regulation, intervention, subsidy; impact of government on foreign competition.

Market. The prospective market for existing and proposed products and services.

> *Question: What major environmental changes in the next 5–10 years will have a significant impact on our strategy?*

3. *Evaluate the Resources of the Organization.* Identify and evaluate the company strengths and weaknesses that exist in the environment as forecast in step 2. This analysis and assessment should include:

Marketing. Marketing policies, product policies, sales force, distribution channels, and other marketing forces that are available.

Production. Plant, labor force, capital equipment, location, and stability of production level.

Finance. Capital structure, ability to attract necessary capital at acceptable cost, financial policies.

Research and Development. The talent and organization required for the necessary R&D involved in new products and processes.

Management. Numbers and quality of managers available to achieve a strategy that takes advantage of opportunities in the environment.

> *Question: What strengths and weaknesses exist in company resources and how do these relate to opportunities and risks in the environment?*

4. *Identify Opportunities and Risks.* Following the environmental and resource analysis, certain opportunities and associated risks will become apparent. These include new products, innovations to existing products, and new services, markets, or customer groups.

> *Question: What major profitable product/
> service opportunities should be pur-
> sued or developed for the future?*

5. *Define the Competitive Edge.* Given the opportunities and the risks identified above, define a competitive edge that can best exploit the opportunities. Some of the competitive edges that might be identified would in-include:

Strong market position
A technological edge
Strength in raw material supply
Physical resources such as plant
Financial strength
Personnel relationships
Reputation
Personnel competencies

> *Question: (1) How can I lead from strength?
> (2) How can I concentrate resources
> where I can best gain a competitive
> advantage?*

6. *Define the New Product Market Scope.* Determine what business you are going to be in over the near- and long-term period of five to ten years. Define products and services, markets, customers, and geographic areas. The rule is to select the narrowest scope consistent with resources and market requirements and the one that best takes advantage of your competitive edge.

> *Question: What should be my future product/
> market scope?*

7. *Set Company Objectives.* Establish quantifiable and verifiable objectives in those areas considered vital to company success. These will be subsequently translated into measurable objectives throughout the organizational hierarchy. Some areas for consideration in objective setting include growth, profitability, market penetration, new products, innovation, survival capacity, cost reduction, employee development, social responsibility, etc.

> *Question: What are my major quantifiable
> objectives?*

8. *Define the Strategy and Develop the Strategic Plan.* All of the foregoing steps lead to the definition of the new strategy and the implementing plan. The skeleton format for this plan might take the following form:

The Strategic Plan

I STATEMENT OF STRATEGY
   Product/Market Scope
   Competitive Edge
   Objectives
II SUPPORTING POLICIES
   Market
   Product/Service
   Distribution
   Pricing
   Investment
   Production
   Financing
   Key Personnel
III RESOURCE/PROCUREMENT ALLOCATION
   Timetable of Strategic Moves
   Funds Flow Analysis
   Manning Table
   Organization

It should be obvious from the foregoing discussion that strategic planning is concerned with forecasting *future* conditions. Unfortunately, many planners attempt to forecast the future based solely on extrapolative forecasts of past patterns. This approach is not good enough. Consider three examples where it failed. First, there were the many firms caught napping on transistor technology that rendered the vacuum tube obsolete. Consider also the disaster experienced by the many banks that jumped on the credit card bandwagon without doing their strategic homework. Then there are the many universities that operated in isolation from their environment and experienced a rapidly falling demand for their research, educational programs, and graduates, because they didn't foresee change.

Strategic Planning Information

The increasing emphasis being given to strategic planning as opposed to operational planning has created a need for a new class of information that is long-range and external in nature. In general, information systems for strategic planning decisions have somewhat different characteristics than those for operating or short-range purposes. These characteristics can be explained:

1. *Information needs* are much more difficult to define because strategic planning and control systems are not structured or defined in a formal way, such as historical variance reports and other classical reporting systems.

2. *Information channels* are informal and ill-structured because of the newness of the information system and the wide variety of users of such data.

3. The *sources* of information are usually external to the organization; hence, it is more difficult to obtain, store, and retrieve. Because the sources are external (e.g., government, associations) and beyond the control of the using organization, much of it is unreliable.

4. The *time horizon* for the information is futuristic as opposed to historical as is the case with operational systems. This makes the strategic system doubly difficult due to the tenuous nature of the forecasting techniques as well as the unreliability of much of the data.

ORGANIZING AND INFORMATION

Organizational structure and information needs are inextricably interwoven. If we can draw an analogy between an organization and the human body, we can compare the organizational *structure* to the human anatomy and the *information* of the organization to the nervous system.

The systems view of the organization takes into account the integrative nature of information flows. This concept is demonstrated in Figure 4-4, where each organizational entity is seen as an information system with the components of input, processor, and output. Each is connected through information and communication channels, and each organizational entity becomes a decision point.

Information also affects organizing by the manner in which information systems are designed. They should conform to the organizational structure and the delegation of authority within the company. Only then can each organizational unit's objective be established and its contribution to company-wide goals be measured. This means that organizations must be designed around information flow and those factors of information chosen to plan and control performance. It is frequently the case that organizational structure and performance reporting do not coincide. In these cases, information systems cannot truly reflect plans and results of operations.

Another major cause of organizational and information mismatch is the lag between organizational changes and the information systems needed to

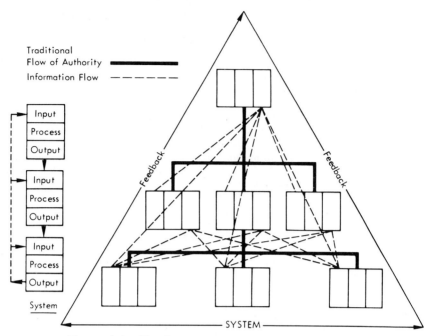

Figure 4-4   The Organization as an Information System

support them. As needs, structure, and managers change, the information system should be changed to support them. Rarely does one find a change in informational systems that matches changes in organizational responsibilities and the needs of managers. The result is often an "information lag."

THE ORGANIZATIONAL IMPACT OF MIS

Aside from the rather obvious impact resulting from the replacement of clerical employees and the restructuring of the jobs of "information handling" personnel, MIS and the computer are having more profound changes in job structure and organizational relationships. Some of these changes are still evolving. Others are not well understood. Further research and experimentation are necessary. However, certain patterns are discernible.

1. *Information and Decision Structures.* Historically, organizations have been structured around decision centers, and this is the way it should be.

These centers were frequently located where the best information was available; usually the chart of accounts. With the advent of computer-based MIS (and particularly teleprocessing), the locus of information is being shifted, and it becomes necessary to revise the organizational structure according to the shifting decision centers.

2. *Decision Making.* Improvements in management science (resulting in programmed decision rules) and the availability of the computer have caused a number of decisions, which were formerly judgmental in nature, to be programmed for the computer and made routinely. Making decisions routine has the effect of downgrading some managerial jobs and upgrading others.

3. *The Organizational Structure.* Because of the shifting information focus and making many decisions routine, many organizations are becoming "flatter," with fewer management levels than before. The result has been the elimination of the traditional "up the pyramid" ladder of advancement. In many cases a new style of manager is taking over, one who is comfortable with the man-computer relationship.

4. *Decentralization.* Computer-based MIS has heightened the debate of decentralization versus centralization. On one hand, the improved availability and rapidity of information encourages more decentralization. On the other hand, the consolidation of computing power at central locations as a result of third and fourth generation data communications means that managers at lower levels must give up control of their internal data processing.

> The dichotomy of centralized computing accompanied by decentralized authority can be illustrated with two cases. One involves the store managers of a national retailing chain whose computer services are performed centrally in remote headquarters. The managers dread Monday mornings because the previous week's profit statements for each store are prepared on the central computer over the weekend and are reviewed by central management first thing each Monday. If results are poor, store managers can expect critical telephone calls from headquarters based on information that the store managers have not had an opportunity to see. Thus the store managers have no way to defend themselves.
>
> A somewhat different example exists in Rockwell International. The chief executive officer concludes: "Because of the timely visibility and control made possible by computerized information systems, we can confidently delegate more responsibility and authority to subordinate managers. This, in turn, gives them more latitude to exercise their ingenuity, thus making the most of the company's managerial talent. One result is that, through the decentralization permitted by information systems, a growing company such as ours can still maintain good management at all levels."

SYSTEMS APPROACH TO ORGANIZING

The classical, bureaucratic, or hierarchical organizational approach was described in Chapter 3. It is characterized by *structure,* ruled by procedure and directives, and has a chart (along with position description) that shows who are the order-givers and the order-takers.

We also concluded in Chapter 3 that, despite the shortcomings of the classical pyramidal structure, its basic form will probably remain much the same. The problem is to find some form of modification that will provide the synergistic effect we are seeking, some form that will overcome its *structural* disadvantages. This form—*a systems approach*—should *integrate* the subsystems of the organization and provide for accommodating change. There is a growing recognition that some form of task force or team approach can achieve this. A number of approaches are emerging.

The Organic Model

The organic approach to organizational design is behavioral in nature but goes one step further in that it addresses itself to the structure and the specialization of tasks—classic fundamentals. Warren Bennis, a leading organizational theorist, argues that classical structure is too rigid to adapt to the frequent changes caused by modern technology. He describes the approach thus:

> First of all, the key word will be temporary. Organizations will become adaptive, rapidly changing temporary systems. Second, they will be organized around problems-to-be-solved. Third, these problems will be solved by relative groups of strangers who represent a diverse set of professional skills. Fourth, given the requirements of coordinating the various projects, articulating points or "linking pin" personnel will be necessary who can speak the diverse language of research and who can relay and mediate between the various project groups. Fifth, the groups will be conducted on organic rather than on mechanical lines; they will emerge and adapt to the problems, solve the problems rather than the programmed role expectations. People will be differentiated, not according to rank or roles, but according to skills and training. . . . Though no catch phrase comes to mind, it might be called an *organic-adaptive structure.* [Italic added by author.]

Project Management

This form of "team" organization gets its name from the fact that several project managers exert planning scheduling and cost control supervision over people who have been assigned to their projects while the functional managers exert line control. Thus there is shared responsibility for the worker, and he must please two superiors. This form of organization is very widespread in the aerospace industry and is growing elsewhere. The project manager is essentially a "contractor" who hires his personnel from the functional organization. Upon expiration of the project, the members return to their functional groups.

This arrangement is frequently called *matrix management*. A variation of this style is also *line project management* and is distinguishable by the fact that each member of the project has only one home, the project to which he is assigned. Usually a number of projects are active in the organization, and the line project manager has complete responsibility for resources of both money and men. He contracts for auxiliary services and is held accountable for meeting planned time, cost, and technical performance goals.

Venture Teams

One leading consultant concludes, "The greatest challenge facing most corporations today is the development and marketing of new products or services that will produce a profit in the face of increased risk of failure." The venture team is a recent organizational innovation to meet the demand for a breakthrough in product marketing. It is somewhat like the project-matrix management approach in that its personnel resources are obtained from the functional departments and its effort is directed to the achievement of a single result—product development and introduction. The team may also have a flexible life span wherein a completion time is loosely defined by broad time and financial goals.

The Contingency Model

The contingency approach to organizational design suggests that the right structure is a function of the interaction of four variables, each of which must be balanced against the effect of the others and against the desired output of the organization. These four variables are:

The manager. Since organizations don't have objectives but people do, the value system, philosophy, and objectives of top management have an impact on organizational design. How do they view individual freedom to make decisions? How do they feel about normal authority channels? How do they view the interaction between the company and its external environment? These are questions that shape the views of managers and hence the organization.

The work. The nature of the tasks required to achieve organizational goals (the real reason for organizing) determines the shape of the structure. In a mature, single process industry, such as steel, there would be less need for an adaptive structure than there would be in an emerging technological industry such as aerospace.

The environment. Social, political, economic, and technological factors in the environment and the degree to which the company interacts with that environment will have an impact on the design of the organizational structure. The more complexity and interaction, the more impact it will have.

The individual contributors. The human element is an essential factor. Growing evidence indicates that increased productivity and other desirable organizational outputs can be achieved by adapting the structure to accommodate the needs of organizational members.

> A rapidly growing number of firms are moving to some variation of the team or project or systems form of organizational design. General Electric, always an innovator, recently reorganized the entire firm around 63 "SBUs"—Strategic Business Units. Texas Instruments has a similar structure. Motorola has pushed decentralization down to the plant level where product managers develop their own strategy and operational plans. Ralston Purina has local decision making work groups right on the shop floor to innovate in work standards and methods. All of these innovations are an attempt to break through the structure of the classic organizational design and achieve the synergistic effect of some form of teamwork.

CONTROL AND INFORMATION

If we accept the definition that control is (a) setting standards of performance, (b) measuring performance against the standards, and (c) correcting deviations, then by definition the control process cannot be performed without information. Standards of performance are a part of any good plan, and hence, determination of standards, like other aspects of the planning process, is dependent upon obtaining relevant information. It also becomes obvious that performance against the standard cannot be measured unless some type of communication, report, or information on actual performance is supplied to the controlling individual.

Information required to perform control is different in both type and characteristic from information needed for planning. Planning places greater emphasis on structuring the future; control is based more on the immediate past and specific trends. Control information can generally be classed into the following types:

1. *Market.* Information concerning the progress of the sales plan: quotas, territories, pricing, and the like. In other words, this information is basically that required to measure performance against the sales forecast and the related sales plan. Additionally, control information may be obtained in other areas of the marketing plan, such as product acceptance, advertising, market research, and distribution costs.

2. *Manufacturing.* Control information that basically measures performance against the manufacturing financial plan. This category covers control of quantity and quality of direct labor, materials, overhead, and inventories. Control is also concerned greatly with the time aspect in the production system.

3. *Personnel* and various control reports concerning performance of personnel as well as the personnel function (staffing, recruiting, training, etc.).

4. *Financial.* This type of control information is the most frequent of all and concerns performance against the financial plan (profitability, costs, etc.) and information surrounding cash flow (credits and collections, tax, cash budget, etc.).

5. *Research, Development, and Engineering.* Usually concerned with controlling the time, cost, and technical specifications of R&D or engineering projects.

SYSTEMS APPROACH TO CONTROL

The traditional approach to the control process (setting standards, measuring performance, correcting deviations) has a number of significant shortcomings. The major one is lateness. By definition, a control report is historical; it reports deviations *after the fact*. The problem here is obvious. Upon the receipt of the control report it is too late to *prevent* the deviation. The sale is lost! The labor budget has been exceeded! The production line is down for lack of raw materials! Accounts receivable standards have been exceeded! What is needed is some system of control that will report deviations *before* they occur so that it can be avoided. What is needed is *feedforward* control.

Feedforward Control

By definition, feedback is derived from the output of a system; the output is measured against a predetermined control standard and the deviation is fed into the system again as information input. Since the output, the past, cannot be changed, effective *feedforward control* must be aimed at preventing present and future deviations from plans. Except for a very few applications such as PERT/CPM and a limited number of modeling techniques, *feedforward control* has not been utilized. The idea, borrowed from engineering, is to anticipate the lags in feedback systems by monitoring inputs and predicting their effects on outcome variables. By doing that, action can be taken to change the inputs and thereby bring the system output into equilibrium with desired standards of performance *before* measurement of the output discloses a deviation from standard.

> During the roller coaster fluctuations in commodity prices during the mid '70s, the bakery industry fell on hard times, averaging less than 1% on sales. However, the Dallas-based Campbell Taggart, Inc. managed to maintain a margin of better than 3%. The company's chief executive reported: "The key ingredient of these increased profits is a control system that monitors costs and pricing so precisely that we can pass on cost increases—something the competition cannot do. We can spot trouble *before it hurts us*. It takes other companies a month or more to get the figures. By that time you may be dead and not know it." [Italic added by author.]

The approach to *feedforward control* is not difficult. Through a process of careful planning and analysis, the input variables of the system are identified and placed in their relationship to the desired end results (output). Then a model of the control system is developed to show how the input variables affect desired goals. When that relationship is clear, the inputs can be monitored and changed in order to achieve the desired results before they occur. In other words, instead of measuring *historical* deviation from standard, we *measure inputs and forecast outputs*.

The feedforward approach to cash budgeting is illustrated in Figure 4-5.

> To illustrate homeostatic, or feedforward control, imagine the hypothetical example of Ultimate Corporation, a chemical company dealing only in liquid chemicals that are processed in vats. The company has an automatic reorder system, so that when the level of the chemical in the vat gets below a certain point there is a sensor that detects this and communicates the information to Ultimate's computer. The computer then communicates the information to a vendor's computer that processes the order and starts pumping chemicals through a pipeline to Ultimate Corporation. The company has a sensor on the pipeline that meters the receipt of this chemical, and as soon as it receives the amount that it ordered, it sends that information to the bank. The bank transfers the money from Ultimate's bank account to the vendor's.

In addition to the concept of feedforward control, the systems approach to the control process should be constructed around three additional ideas:

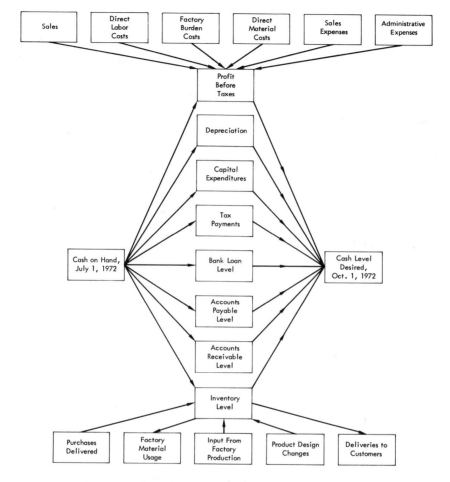

Figure 4-5   The Feedforward Approach to Cash Budgeting

1. *Integrate Planning and Control.* The central idea of integrated planning and control (IPC) is that each level of plans provides the standards of performance (objectives) for the next lower level of operations. This may take the form of a *management by objectives* program.

2. *Relate the Control System to the Organizational Structure.* The information system has usually been built around a financial chart of accounts, not decision centers. Moreover, the organization has not achieved synergism because the parts have not been related to the whole unified set of objectives.

3. *Design the System for Decision Making,* not historical reporting. The systems designer, accountant, or computer technician will usually design a variance reporting system in terms of "computerese" or some technical requirement rather than the needs of decision makers.

CHECK YOUR SYSTEMS APPROACH
TO INFORMATION AND MANAGEMENT

	Yes	No
MANAGEMENT SYSTEM		
Do you have the prerequisite management system to accompany your MIS:		
Organizational arrangements?	( )	( )
Planning and control systems?	( )	( )
PLANNING INFORMATION		
Does your planning system provide for adequate planning premises:		
Environmental?	( )	( )
Competitive?	( )	( )
Internal?	( )	( )
Sales forecast?	( )	( )
Financial plan?	( )	( )
STRATEGIC PLANNING		
Have you identified and disseminated a strategy:		
Product/market scope?	( )	( )
Competitive edge?	( )	( )
Organizational objectives?	( )	( )
Are you organized for strategic planning:		
Evaluation of past performance?	( )	( )
Environmental analysis?	( )	( )
Strengths and weaknesses?	( )	( )
Opportunities and risks?	( )	( )
A strategic plan?	( )	( )
Do you have a system to capture strategic planning information?	( )	( )
ORGANIZING AND INFORMATION		
Are the subsystems of your organization synergistically aligned with information exchange?	( )	( )
Have you assessed the impact of MIS on your organizational structure?	( )	( )
Can your classical pyramidal organizational structure be modified for improved synergism and productivity?	( )	( )
CONTROL AND INFORMATION		
Does adequate control information exist in all functional areas (marketing, financial, personnel, manufacturing, R&D, etc.)?	( )	( )

	Yes	No
Are all of your reporting systems historical reports or can some of them be designed for feedforward control?	( )	( )

Does you control system provide for the three essentials of the systems approach:

	Yes	No
Integrated planning and control (IPC)?	( )	( )
Control related to organization?	( )	( )
Designed to facilitate decisions rather than historical reporting?	( )	( )

the manager and the computer

5

In 1952 it cost $1.26 to do 100,000 multiplications on an IBM computer. Today, they can be done for a penny. Multiplications have gone from 2,000 a second to more than 2 million a second today.

—IBM Advertisement (1975)

Despite the increased speed and lower costs of computers, their benefits are not being realized. Herbert Grosch, editorial director of *Computerworld,* put the problem in perspective: "I submit that there is something wrong somewhere when you have a machine 100,000,000 times as fast as key-driven equipment and it still takes all morning to run a payroll. We only gained a factor of maybe tenfold in economics and we ought to have gained 10,000 times."

These are puzzling times for computer-using organizations and for managers in general. Many of them are confused and some of them are worried, feeling trapped on a treadmill and overwhelmed by a machine they don't understand. This confusion was typified by the head of a Wall Street firm that was having serious back-office troubles. He conceded: "Greek is a fine, flowing language to me compared to computer jargon."

Management information systems (MIS) are not new, only their computerization is relatively new. Instead of becoming confused with the techniques and technology of the computer, the manager-user would do well to remember that the machine is nothing more than a moronic device that handles data through repetitive digital algorithmic counting operations. His need for familiarity with the technology and operations is minimal; enough so that he can cut through the jargon and mystique of the

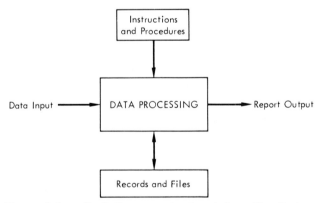

Figure 5-1a   Basic Components of an Information System

Figure 5-1b   Part of Differential Calculating Machine on which Charles Bab-
bage (English Mathematician) Worked for 37 Years. Com-
menced in 1823. Rejected for Patents by the Government.
Deposited in London Museum. Courtesy Bettman Archive, Inc.

technician and communicate his information needs. The purpose of this
chapter is to provide this minimal degree of familiarity.

DATA PROCESSING AND THE COMPUTER

An information system is composed of five basic components, as shown
in Figure 5-1. In a manual system, human beings perform the five basic
functions; in a computer-based system the functions are performed by
equipment. In either type of system the basic functions are: (a) entering
data into the system, (b) processing the data (rearranging input data and

processing files), (c) maintaining files and records, (d) developing procedures that tell what data are needed and when, where they are obtained, and how they are used, as well as instruction routines for the processor to follow, and (e) preparing report output. Man's knowledge and store of information is what can be acquired and stored in his memory or some peripheral source. The information must then be retrieved and manipulated in order to be useful. To augment his memory, man uses a variety of devices, including books, forms, and records. We are concerned here with the two major sources of storage and manipulation for information systems: records and the computer.

If it were not for records, the size and reliability of data storage would be restricted to what people could remember. Records were the earliest device for assisting in the data-processing task. Consisting first of pictures and marks, writing later relied on alphabets and numerals.* The "alphabet" for processing business data consists of ten numerals, 26 letters, and 25 special characters. This "alphabet" is represented by punched holes in cards (Figure 5-2) or paper tape and by positive and negative charges in magnetizable material. This electronic representation is necessary in order to provide a scheme that is efficient for processing purposes.

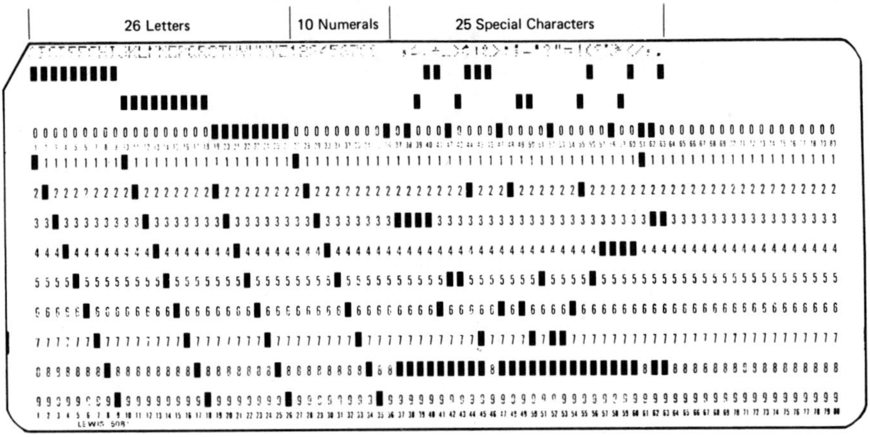

Figure 5-2   Business Data Input

Not since the discovery of writing, about 3000 B.C., has there been an advance as great as the computer for both the processing and the storing

---

*To appreciate the value of writing as a memory device, try to multiply two three-digit numbers without the aid of pencil and paper.

of information. Consider that in less than ten minutes, a low-cost computer ($3000 per month rental) can update an inventory file of 25,000 items with 5000 different types of transactions and print out the status of items that are over or under a predetermined limit. In the next decade the storage capacity of computers will be unlimited for most applications. It is estimated that holographic technology will provide the means for storing incredible amounts of information in condensed form—e.g., the entire Manhattan telephone directory on one 8- by 10-inch film card—and for erasing and replacing any single bit of information without disturbing others.

Both manual and computer-based information systems have the elements and attributes of systems in general and can be described in terms of these elements: input, output, and processor. Our examination of computer systems proceeds by analogy to make the transition from the easily understood manual system to a slightly more complex computer-based system. This transition and analogy between manual and computer system will accomplish two purposes. First, we will be able to see how a computer-based data processing system can become a vital adjunct to management planning and control. Second, by examining the system through its components (input, output, processor), we will be better able to understand how these components of an information system provide the framework for MIS design.

COMPONENTS OF A MANUAL INFORMATION SYSTEM

The human being is the earliest and still the most prevalent form of data processor. Despite the fantastic growth of computer applications, manual information systems still outnumber them in quantity of systems and information handled.

People receive input data by seeing or hearing them. These data are then stored in the brain, which also acts as a control and logic unit. The outputs from this type of information processing are oral or written reports and in some cases a variety of physical actions. The human mind, acting as a control and logic unit, can perform many operations on data: adding, subtracting, multiplying, and dividing; storing results; repeating the operations on different sets of data; comparing two items; outputting results in a prearranged manner and revising the processing operations as a result of changing instructions.

Despite his ability to perform the foregoing processing tasks, the human remains a slow and unreliable processor. The human mind is slow in performing the arithmetical computations required and is rather erratic in applying rules of logic. On the other hand, where judgment is required, the human mind is indispensable. Judgment is needed to make decisions in data-processing systems because of the difficulty of planning to handle all eventualities. In summary, human beings alone are inefficient data processors, but they become a vital element of all data-processing systems because of the need for decisions and judgment.

All the many information systems in the typical company (e.g., payroll, accounts receivable, billing, inventory, production scheduling, shipping, etc.) are fundamentally similar in that they possess the basic components of any system: input, processor, and output. It will make the understanding of such a system easier and facilitate the transition to a computer-based system if we examine a typical manual system. Figure 5-3 demonstrates an inventory clerk operating a manual information system. The fundamental elements of data processing, *manual or computer,* may be described in terms of this illustration.

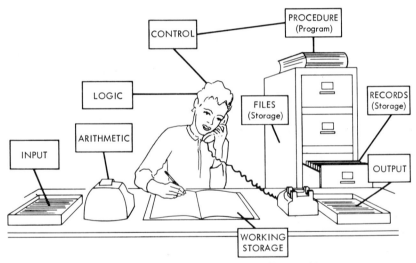

Figure 5-3a   Elements of Data Processing

Note that the components of this manual information system (Figure 5-3) are the same as those functions illustrated for an information system in Figure 5-1. These are also the same components we will use to describe a computer-based information system:

1.   Input
2.   Processor
      Arithmetic
      Control

3.   Storage
        Internal
            Memory
            Working storage
        External
            Records and files
4.   Procedure or program for instructing the processor
5.   Output

Figure 5-3b   Hollerith Tabulating Machines. Courtesy Bettman Archive, Inc.

In this chapter we will utilize the typical, elementary inventory accounting system to illustrate both the manual information system and the conversion from manual to computer-based.

Referring to Figure 5-3 we see that the *input* device for the manual
inventory processing system is the "in" basket of the inventory clerk. The
input to the system may be in various forms and media and is related to
information surrounding inventory receipts and issues. Inventory records
are updated with receipts on one hand and reduced with orders for the
item on the other. Receipts and issues may be recorded in writing by a
storekeeper, stamped on an invoice by a mechanical device, or punched
into a card. The resulting cards, invoices, receipts documents, issue papers,
shipping documents, and a variety of other input information affecting the
inventory system are entered into the "in" basket for processing and
ultimate preparation of output. *Output* can be (a) updated inventory

records, (b) an inventory status report, or (c) other reports and documents related to inventory.

From the standpoint of manipulating or processing the data, the *processor* of the manual system is the most important component. It is made up of a control element (contained in the inventory clerk's brain), which keeps the proper relationship between the other components of input, processor, storage, and output. An additional element of the *processor* is the calculator or the *arithmetic* element, which performs the four mathematical functions of add, subtract, multiply, and divide. The logic element of the processor, which is also in the clerk's brain, compares two quantities to see if one is equal to, greater than, or less than the other. It is surprising to most people to discover that these five operations (add, subtract, multiply, divide, compare) comprise the entire processing ability of the computer. However, this ability is a fantastic one, as we shall see.

The third element depicted in Figure 5-3 is the *storage*. There are two parts to the storage—the *internal* (internal to the processor) and the *external* storage. The internal storage in this manual system is the working storage represented by the pencil and whatever temporary record the processor (clerk) is working on. This internal storage is sometimes called *memory* because it is stored and is immediately available to the processor (clerk).

External storage is represented by the individual *records* for an item of

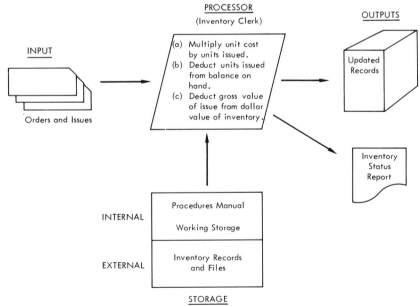

Figure 5-4a   Manual Inventory Accounting System

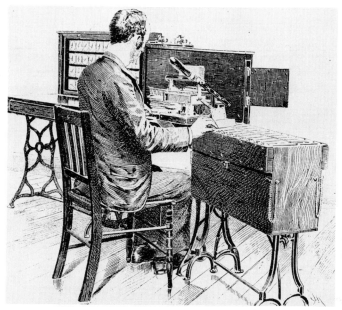

Figure 5-4b   Early Calculating Machine. Card is Removed from the Press
and Deposited in the Sorting Box. Census. Courtesy Bettman
Archive, Inc.

inventory. When these individual records are combined, they make up a
file. Prior to performing any processing or calculation upon external
storage, the processor (clerk) would have to retrieve the applicable records
from the appropriate file. The classification, structuring, and organization
of this external storage is very important to the design and operation of
any information system—manual or computer-based. As a general rule,
the costs of classification vary inversely with the costs of using and retrieving the information.

Another essential element of this manual system is the *procedure,* which
instructs the processor (clerk) regarding the manner in which calculations
are to be performed or the information processed. This is analogous to the
program of the computer. The procedures manual may, for example, instruct the processor to "(a) multiply unit cost by units issued, (b) deduct
units issued from balance on hand, (c) deduct gross value of issue from
dollar value of inventory." The clerk would then perform this processing
on the input information, update the inventory balance (external storage),
and prepare the required *output* report to go in the "out" basket. Preparation of the *output* is the final step of the information processing system.

A schematic diagram of the foregoing manual information system is
depicted in the two parts of Figure 5-4 on these facing pages.

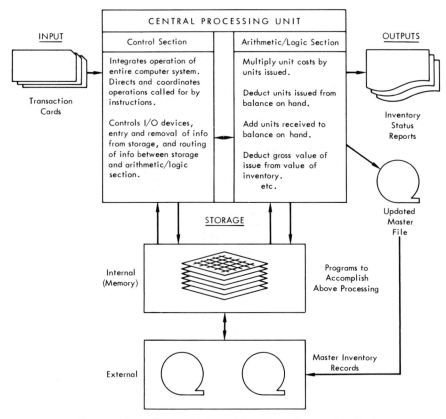

Figure 5-5a   Computer-Based Inventory Accounting System

COMPONENTS OF A COMPUTER SYSTEM

Despite the fact that many managers are awed and sometimes confused by the computer, its operation is essentially no more complex than the manual system just described. Indeed, if we make the transition from manual to computer-based system by drawing an analogy between them, the reader should have no difficulty in understanding the functions and operation of the computer. Following this description of the components of a computer system, we will want to make the conversion from the manual inventory system previously examined.

We saw in Figure 5-3 the elements of data processing and how data were processed manually by a clerk. The field of computers is called *electronic data processing,* and the computer is nothing more than an electronic data processor. Its components are the same as the manual system described; it accepts data in the form of alphanumeric (alphabetic and numeric) characters, as demonstrated in Figure 5-2. If we wish to convert our manual inventory system to computer, the input data would be the same for both systems; only its input form would be different. The computer *processes* these data. For example, it adds items received, deducts items issued, and updates the inventory record—but it does all this *electronically.* The alphabetic and numerical characters, normally in the form of punched cards or paper tape, are sensed and represented in electronic form within the computer. The subsequent arithmetic or processing operations are accomplished electronically; hence, the computer can be described as an *electronic data processor.*

The manual inventory control system previously discussed, when converted to computer application, might appear conceptually as in Figure 5-5, which will serve to illustrate the basic components of the computer system. A discussion of these components follows.

Figure 5-5b   The Original Eniac Computer (circa 1945). Courtesy Sperry Remington Corporation.

Input/Output Devices

The functions of entering data *into* the computer system and recording data *from* the system are performed by input/output devices. Data for input is recorded on punched cards, paper tape, magnetic tape, paper documents, and as direct input from keyboards. The input devices read or sense this coded data and make them available in a form acceptable to the computer. Whatever device is used, the data must generally be coded in a form compatible with the characters of Figure 5-2.

Output devices produce the final results of the data processing. They *record* information from the computer on a variety of media such as cards, paper tape, and magnetic tape. They *print* information on paper. Additionally, output devices may generate signals for transmission over teleprocessing networks, produce graphic displays or microfilm images, and take a variety of special forms. For the most part, the basic business-type applications take the output form of a paper printout.

The following list of commonly available input/output devices will provide a guide for assessing equipment alternatives.

Input Device	*Output Device*
Punched card readers	Magnetic tape units
Punched paper tape readers	High-speed line printers
Magnetic tape units	Cathode ray tubes
Remote inquiry/input terminals	Data plotters
Optical character recognition devices	Card punch units
Magnetic ink character recognition devices	Paper tape punch units
	Remote output terminals

Although, strictly speaking, the *mini computer* is not an input/output device (it is a computer system in its own right), its use to backup or supplement larger systems is accelerating. A Standard Research Institute study predicts a 400% market growth for minis in this decade alone. Major mini applications include tool scheduling/monitoring, control, automated quality assurance and assembly, instrument calibration/inspection/testing, total manufacturing control, and process control.

The Central Processor

The central processor is the most significant component of the computer. As in the case of our inventory control clerk in the manual system, it consists of a *control* section, which coordinates the system components, and the *arithmetic/logic unit,* which performs the same functions (add, subtract, multiply, divide, compare, shift, move, store) as the clerk-calculator combination of the manual system. However, the CPU (central processing unit) of the computer accomplishes these tasks with fantastically increased speed and accuracy. This meager processing logic accompanied by the five simple functions accounts for the almost infinite variety of tasks the computer can perform.

The control section of the CPU directs and coordinates all operations called for by the instructions (programs) to the system. It controls the input/output units and the arithmetic/logic unit, transferring data to and from storage, and routing information between storage and the arithmetic/logic unit. It is by means of the control section that automatic, integrated operation of the entire computer system is achieved.

The arithmetic/logic section performs the arithmetic and logic operations. The former portion calculates, shifts numbers, sets the algebraic sign of results, rounds, compares, and performs the other tasks of calculation. The logic section carries out the decision-making operations to change the sequence of instruction execution, and it has the capability to test various conditions encountered during processing.

Storage

Storage is somewhat like a huge electronic filing cabinet, completely indexed and accessible instantly to the computer. All data must be placed in storage before being processed by the computer. Storage consists of *internal,* which is a part of the processing component, and *external.*

Note the similarity between manual and computer systems. Internal storage, frequently referred to as *memory,* is the characteristic that permits the computer to store, in electronic form, data from input devices as well as lengthy series of instructions called *programs* that tell the machine what to do. These programs are similar to the procedures manual of the manual system. It is this memory facility that distinguishes the computer from devices such as calculators and bookkeeping machines. Although the latter devices have input, output, and processing capabilities, they do not have the capability of internally storing programs within the processing unit. It is the program that enables the computer to perform complex and lengthy calculations in order to process specific input data.

In order to understand how programs of instructions permit the computer to process data, it is necessary to examine the concept of *computer memory* and see how information and instructions can be stored within the computer. The information can be: (a) instructions (programs) to direct the processing unit; (b) data (input, in-process, or output); and (c) reference data associated with processing (tables, code charts, constant factors, etc.). Because the computer memory is the storehouse of this information, it is important to understand how it is represented in memory.

Memory is comprised of planes of magnetic cores, as shown in Figure 5-6. A magnetic core is a doughnut-shaped ring of ferromagnetic material

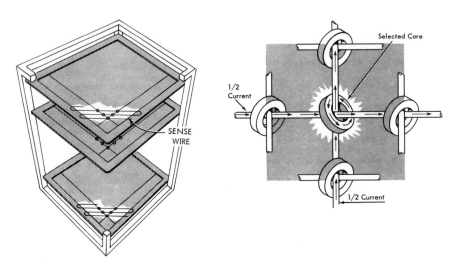

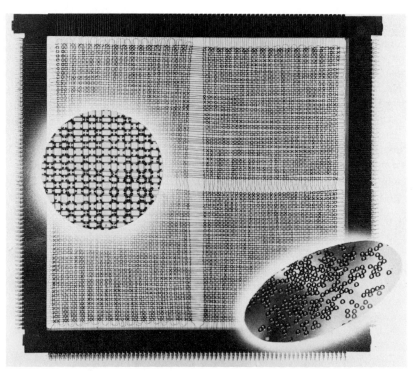

Figure 5-6a   Magnetic Cores. Courtesy IBM Corporation.

IBM tape drive. Courtesy IBM
Corporation.

Disk storage drive with removable cartridge and
magnetic tape drive in background.
Courtesy Mohawk Data Sciences.

IBM System/370 Model 145.
Courtesy IBM Corporation.

IBM disk drive.
Courtesy IBM Corporation.

Figure 5-6b   Input/Output Storage Devices

the size of a match head, capable of retaining either of two possible polarities—either 0 or 1—and this representation is therefore called *binary*. A current passed in one direction through the wires magnetizes the core; a current sent in the other direction reverses the core's magnetic state. One state represents a 1, the other a 0.

Since each magnetic core holds only one bit and can represent only two states, more than one core is needed to represent a number. Cores are arranged in planes (Figure 5-6) that may have 32, 64, or some other number of cores in each direction for a total of 1024 or 4096 cores. Modular construction of storage planes permits additional storage requirements to be met by "plugging in" additional units.

Unlike the decimal number system, where each position in a number represents a power of 10, the binary system of numbering represents each position by a power of 2. Moreover, in the binary numbering system we can use only 1's and 0's (which represent the polarities of our magnetic cores). Hence the binary number 1001 is $(1 \times 2^3) + (0 \times 2^2) + (0 \times 2^1) + (1 \times 2^0) = 9$. This is the manner in which numbers and characters are represented in the magnetic core of the *computer memory*.

Binary numbers from 0 to 9 can be represented by the table:

Binary	Decimal
0000	0
0001	1
0010	2
0011	3
0100	4
0101	5
0110	6
0111	7
1000	8
1001	9

Computer memory is made up of fixed units comprising a certain number of magnetic cores. We want to be able to represent in memory (see Figure 5-2): (a) ten decimal digits, (b) 26 alphabetic characters, and (c) 25 special symbols (comma, dollar sign, etc.). Binary schemes for representing these data vary, but all utilize a prearranged assignment of bits and groups of bits. This system of representation is important because of the need to arrange core storage and locate it by address.

The storage of computer memory is divided into locations, each with an assigned address. Each location holds a specific unit of data, which may be a character, a digit, an entire record, or a word. When a data item is desired, it is obtained from its known location in addressable storage units that are organized to obtain data when wanted. There are several schemes for using the processor to assist the programmer in keeping track of the storage locations. These schemes provide *data-names,* such as "update inventory" or "calculate net pay," to automatically refer to sections in the program designed to perform these calculations. Notice the similarity between these programs and the procedures manual of the manual inventory system described previously.

External storage (consisting of records and files, reference data, and other programs) is of two types:

1. *Direct access.* Disk, magnetic drum, and data cell devices providing random ordered mass storage that can be accessed without having to read from the beginning of the file to find the desired data.

2. *Sequential.* Magnetic tape that is sequentially ordered and must be read from the beginning in order to read or write a desired record.*

Summary

We have chosen the illustration of the inventory control system to make the transition by analogy from a manual to a computer-based system; these are compared in Table 5-1.

Table 5-1

Comparison of Manual and Computer-Based Inventory Accounting Systems

Component	Manual System	Computer System
INPUT	Various manual transaction documents	Punched cards
PROCESSOR	Inventory control clerk with calculating machine and human logic	Central processing unit
STORAGE		
Internal	Working storage of inventory clerk	Memory of central processing unit, which contains magnetic core
External	Manual inventory records and files	Master inventory file maintained on magnetic tape
PROCEDURE	Processing instruction contained in procedures manual	Program for processing data contained in memory of internal storage
OUTPUT	Manually prepared status report and updated master file	Automatic preparation of status report and updating of master file

---

* Magnetic tape storage can be compared to a home tape recorder, since the tape media of each are physically almost alike. If we wish to play song number 5 of the tape, we must play through songs 1, 2, 3, and 4 to reach the fifth song. So it is with tape storage for the computer. Conversely, random order storage can be compared to the phonograph. Information is recorded on grooves in a disc, and if we wish to play song number 5 we can place the needle in the proper groove immediately. So it is with disc storage for the computer.

There is nothing very complex about the computer components, a greater understanding of which can be obtained by comparing the components of the manual and computer systems. Both have the basic components: input, processor, storage (internal and external), programs or procedures for processing data, and outputs. A major consideration of the computer system is the structure of data storage in computer memory so that this information can be more easily and readily retrieved.

CONVERSION OF MANUAL TO COMPUTER-BASED SYSTEMS

To further our understanding of computer-based management information systems, we continue our transition from manual to computer system by describing those steps involved in making a conversion or changeover from the inventory accounting system of Figures 5-3 and 5-4. The various steps involved in making the conversion are listed as follows:

1. System description
2. Input documents
3. Output documents
4. File design
5. Program flow chart
6. Computer assembly
7. Computer program
8. Program operation

System Description

The system description is in narrative form and is usually prepared after preliminary investigation and definition of the problem. The description is essentially a statement of the major inputs, outputs, processing operations, and files needed. The purpose is to show the logical flow of information and the logical operations necessary to carry out the particular design alternative chosen. After a narrative description of the system, it is almost always depicted in flow chart form.

The *narrative* form of our inventory accounting system could take the following level of narration:

> The activity is concerned with an inventory control *accounting* system for finished-goods inventory. Transactions (receipts and issues) are read from punched cards, the relevant magnetic tape master record is found and updated, and the new inventory status report is printed.

The *flow chart* puts in symbolic form what has been described in narrative form. It facilitates a quick analysis of the job being performed and provides a general symbolic overview of the entire operation. The flow

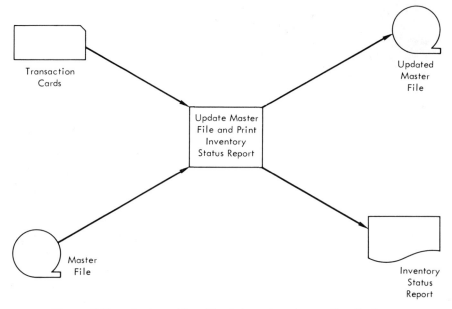

Transaction
Cards

Updated
Master
File

Update Master
File and Print
Inventory
Status Report

Master
File

Inventory
Status
Report

Figure 5-7a   Systems Flow Chart, Inventory Accounting System

chart for the narrative description of our inventory accounting system appears in Figure 5-7. The flow chart of the elementary accounting inventory system (Figure 5-7) should not be taken as representative. A more appropriate flow chart for a computerized inventory control system containing decision rules is shown in Figure 5-8. A typical flow chart for order entry is shown in Figure 5-9.

Input Documents

After the system description is completed, it is necessary to specify how the information will be structured in acceptable form as computer input. Volume of information, frequency, accuracy and verification requirements, and the handling of the information are considerations surrounding the selection of input format. Sometimes inputs have to be accepted in the form in which they are received from the outside. In this case the task of conversion is merely one of preparing input to machine-usable form.

IBM 1403 printer.
Courtesy IBM Corporation.

IBM 2540 card read punch.
Courtesy IBM Corporation.

IBM CRT. Courtesy IBM Corporation.

Silent 700 ASR terminal (with magnetic
tape cassette off-line storage). Courtesy
Texas Instruments Corporation.

Figure 5-7b Input/Output Devices

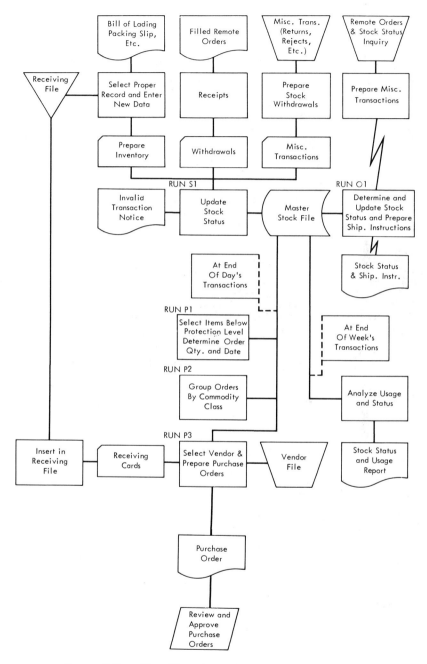

Figure 5-8a   Flow Chart for an Inventory Control System

Point-of-transaction terminal in use at hospital. Courtesy NCR Corporation.

Terminal key sta-
tion and tape drive.
Courtesy   Mohawk
Data Sciences.

Point-of-sale terminal operating under control of mini computer. Cash-
ier passes packages over a small
glass panel in the check-out stand,
exposing the universal product code
to the scanning device. Courtesy
NCR Corporation.

Figure 5-8b   Remote Terminal Operations

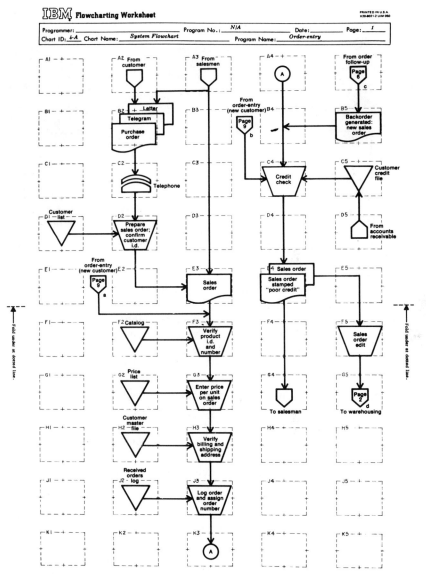

Figure 5-9a   Order-Entry Flow Chart

The exact layout of input documents is necessary because the computer program is an exact and precise sequence of steps that operates only when data is located in prescribed positions. In our example, the input format is determined to be punched cards. The holes in these cards are interpreted

Figure 5-9b   Medium/Large Computer. IBM System/370 Model 168. Courtesy IBM Corporation.

by the input device of the card reader, converted into computer-readable form, and stored in computer memory for processing.

The card input layout for our inventory accounting example is shown in Figure 5-10. The item number of inventory is represented by an eight-digit numeric field. A separate card is prepared for each transaction. The quantity involved in the transaction is represented by an eight-digit field indicating the amount of each transaction. The type of transaction is indicated by the last field on the card, which has an eight-digit code representing the nature of the transaction (this could be transaction by price, territory, customer, etc.).

The system provides four major groups of operations: (a) updating stock status (run S1), based on actual transactions; (b) response to inquiries (run O1) from auxiliary warehouses and central warehouse; (c)

Item Number	Quantity	Transaction Code	
1.......8	9.......16	17.......24	

Column Number

Figure 5-10a   Layout for Input Transaction Card

reorder analysis (runs P1, P2, P3) including purchase-order preparation; (d) weekly analysis reports (run S2) to show slow moving items, major changes in usage rates, behind-schedule deliveries, economic lot sizes, etc.

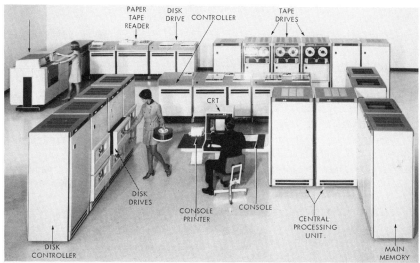

Figure 5-10b   Components of a Medium/Large Scale Computer System (NCR Century 300). Courtesy NCR Corporation.

Figure 5-10c   Components of a Small Computer System (NCR 101). Courtesy NCR Corporation.

An examination of the input document will reveal that it provides us with all the relevant information contained in the system description. The typical *item description* normally associated with inventory is not contained in the input document because it is already filed in storage.

Output Documents

Outputs are subject to much the same considerations as input documents. Also, the output format should be treated with additional care because it represents the purpose or objective of the entire operation. It is the output document with which management is almost exclusively concerned. Because of its critical nature, care should be taken in its design.

The output layout in our example is shown in Figure 5-11. Although the computer is capable of printing much more complex reports than our example, we show the minimum information required to meet the specifications of our system description and output requirements.

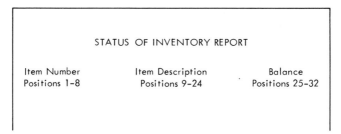

Figure 5-11a   Output Report Format

Figure 5-12 shows an output from an automated purchasing system.

File Design

The logic required to control the flow of data through the system is a part of systems design. This flow is in turn dependent upon the design of data files. These two steps are closely associated and should be considered in conjunction with type of equipment, storage capacity, input and output media, and format.

The character-by-character contents of every record are specified by the file record layouts. Since magnetic tape files are already specified for our example, we are concerned with the tape input layout. This is shown in Figure 5-13.

The item number is an eight-digit field the same as that on the punched card of the input document. The item description comprises two eight-digit fields making up sixteen alphabetic characters. This description is an integral part of the inventory file maintained on tape; there is no reason to include it on the input punched card representing individual transactions. The file design of the magnetic tape is completed by the eight-digit item balance field. For the sake of simplicity we have not included several other elements of file design such as price, unit costs, weight, minimum and maximum inventory limits, etc.

NCR Century 50/MOD I,

NCR 299

Figure 5-11b   Small and Mini Computers   Courtesy NCR Corporation.

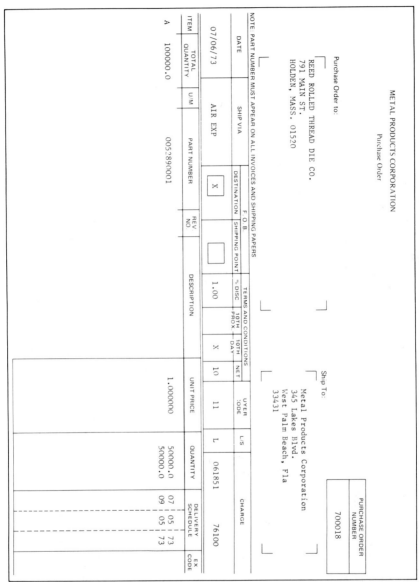

Figure 5-12 Output from Automated Purchasing System

106

Frames	1.......8	9.......24	25.......32	
	Item Number	Item Description	Item Balance	End of Record Gap

Figure 5-13   Layout of Magnetic Tape Records

The Program Flow Chart

The program flow chart is the programmer's logic of the detailed step-by-step representation of how the computer program will accomplish the job. It is the "blueprint" of a program and is used to marshal and organize the facts for examination on paper; to outline problems, logic, and solutions; and to deal with the whole problem in systematic steps. The flow chart of our conversion from manual to computer inventory accounting might appear as shown in Figure 5-14.

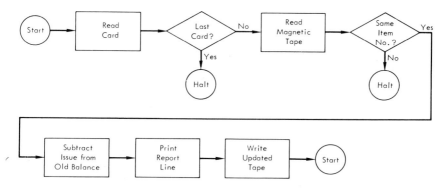

Figure 5-14   The Program Flow Chart

The flow chart symbols for both programming and system flowcharting are shown in Figure 5-15. By comparing these symbols with the decisions and actions depicted in our flow chart for the inventory accounting system, we can see how the computer will perform the logic of the application. After the program writes out a new updated master record on tape (Figure 5-14), it loops back to read another card, and so on, until all cards (transactions) are processed.

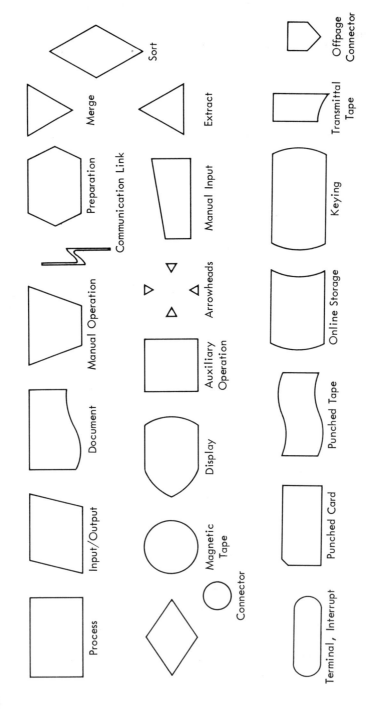

Figure 5-15   Program and System Flow Chart Symbols

Computer Assembly

Computer processing units can operate only from instructions expressed in machine-readable form—binary numbers. For example, the instruction to add regular pay to overtime pay giving total pay would look like this:

$$10 \qquad 100 \qquad 101 \qquad 200$$

The 10 indicates the ADD instruction, the 100 and 101 are addresses of storage locations for the numbers representing regular and overtime pay, and 200 is the location for the sum, total pay.

Obviously, it is too tedious for a programmer to instruct the computer in binary form, so assembly programs are written that allow the instructions to be written in alphanumeric notation and "assembled" into binary form for storage in the computer.

Computer Program

After data are transcribed to an input medium, and prior to assembly of the program into binary notation for computer use, the procedural steps that are to take place within the computer system must be defined precisely in terms of operations that the system can perform. Stated another way, the flow chart of Figure 5-14 must be written as an instruction that can be "run through" the assembly and converted into machine-readable format.

A series of instructions pertaining to an entire procedure is called a program. The program is stored internally and the processor has access to the instructions as required.

The details of computer programming are complex, specific, and beyond the scope of this brief investigation. We are concerned only with the general nature of how the processor is instructed to perform its operation on the input data in order to produce the output data in the desired format. For this general descriptive purpose we can refer to the programming description provided by a leading computer manufacturer:

Instructions

The computer is directed to perform each of its operations by an instruction—a unit of specific information located in main storage. This information is interpreted by the central processing unit as an operation to be performed.

If data are involved, the instruction directs the computer to the data. If some device is to be controlled—a magnetic tape unit, for example—the instruction specifies the device and the required operations.

Instructions may change the condition of an indicator, shift data from one location in storage to another, cause a tape unit to rewind, or change the contents of a counter. Some instructions can arbitrarily, or as a result of some machine or data indication, specify the storage location of the next instruction. In this way, it is possible to alter the sequence in which any instruction or block of instructions is followed.

An instruction usually consists of at least two parts:

1.   An operation part that designates *read, write, add, subtract, compare, move data,* and so on.

2.   An operand that designates the address of the information or device that is needed for the specified operation.

Operation	*Operand*
Select	Tape Unit 200
Read	One record into storage positions 1000–1050
Clear & Add	Quantity in storage location 1004 in accumulator
Subtract	Quantity in storage location 1005 from contents of accumulator
Store	Result in storage location 1051
Branch	To instruction in storage location 5004

During an instruction cycle, an instruction is selected from storage and analyzed by the central processing unit. The operation part indicates the operation to be performed. This information is coded to have a special meaning for the computer. For example, in a System/360, the letter A is interpreted as "add," the letter C as "compare," SIO as "start input/output," and TR as "translate." Other computers use different coding and numbers of characters or positions to define an operation.

The operand further defines or augments the function of the operation. For example, to perform arithmetic, the storage location of one of the factors involved is indicated. For input or output devices, the unit to be used is specified. For reading or writing, the area of storage for input or output records is indicated or fixed by machine design.

Because all instructions use the same storage media as data, they must be represented in the same form of coding.

In general, no particular areas of storage are reserved for the instructions only. In most instances they are grouped together and placed, in ascending sequential locations, in the normal order in which they are to be executed by the computer. However, the order of execution may be varied by special instruction, by recognition of a predetermined condition of data or devices within the system, by unpredictable interruptions from outside the system (teleprocessing input), by hardware conditions that require servicing from a special set of programs, or by other programs that require unusual priority.

Program Operation

After the program has been written and run through the assembly process, it is placed in memory in binary or "machine-readable" form and is ready to process the input cards, update the master file tape, and print the required report. The computer will execute the instructions of the program in sequence until the program comes to a halt.

Summary of System Conversion

We have gone through the complete cycle of converting a manual inventory accounting system to a computer-based system. Included were the eight steps in making the conversion, the steps that described the operation of the components of the computer system.

The reader should now have a very good idea of how information needs are translated into the language and operation of the computer. However, we have taken the simplest form of inventory accounting system to illustrate this conversion. Few, if any, applications are as simple and straightforward as the one we have demonstrated by way of illustration. The reader may wish to take the more complicated inventory control system of Figure 5-8 and speculate on the steps involved in bringing this system through the conversion process we have just described for the simple inventory accounting system.

> The reader is cautioned that the conversion process just described is essentially a one-for-one changeover; the clerical syndrome that you were warned about in Chapter 2. You are reminded that during the conversion process an excellent opportunity is available for upgrading the system into a higher-level decision assisting tool.

> On the other hand, clerical automation is not to be sneezed at. Indeed, in some instances it is a justifiable reason for computer utilization. At Jones & Laughlin Steel Corporation the automation of payroll alone saved the salaries of 100 clerks in the payroll department, enough money to pay for all the computers in the company.

THE DATA BANK CONCEPT

The concept of the data base provides one of the most fascinating aspects of computer use. Part of this concept is the notion that the data base (information) of the firm is a resource to be managed just the same as the plant, personnel, raw material, or money.

Many persons will argue that you cannot have a *management information system* without a data base; that the data base distinguishes the MIS from other types of information systems. This infers that the operation of the system depends on a data base that provides information about suppliers, customers, current inventories, costs, plans, past performance, and other data relevant to managing the organization. Whether you agree or not with this concept, the fact remains that the organization/operation of the firm's data base remains one of the most difficult technical aspects of MIS design and one with the greatest potential.

The point has been made repeatedly that the most basic element of a management information system, and indeed, the element that is vital to the management process, is knowledge: information about the goals and objectives of the organization, its policies, resources, operations, and environment. Yet an individual's personal knowledge is only what can be acquired and stored in his memory and then retrieved and manipulated as necessary. Despite the fact that many managers insist on operating only with the information stored in their personal memory, it is essential nowadays to augment this capacity with other storage media. Books, magazines, forms, records, and a variety of other media assist us in storing information until it is needed. However, in today's complex managerial environment it is becoming more and more necessary that the organization turn to the computer as a device for storing, processing, and retrieving information. In developing an information system to serve the diverse needs of today's organization, knowledge and information relative to the management and operations of that organization can be stored in the memory of the computer. This knowledge can be described and labeled as a data bank.

To understand the concept of central storage and acquisition of information from a data bank, it is helpful to review an elementary example of storage under a manual system.

Information Storage—Manual System

Today's complex organizations are plagued with a combination of problems, not the least of which is information handling. The ratio of clerical workers to production workers continues to rise and there appears to be no end in sight to the increasing volume of clerical operations performed in modern companies. Yet despite the growth in clerical workers and clerical operations, one out of four production workers in manufacturing is handling paperwork, and the percentage is much higher in nonmanufacturing industries.

Managers embroiled in paper have no time for planning and evaluation, and their working hours become more crisis-oriented. Most of their time is spent searching for information to handle various crises that arise in addition to the normal work flow. Add this cost of underutilization of management manpower to the rising cost and complexity of information handling, and the conclusion emerges that the gathering and dissemination of information is usually the company's most difficult problem. Information is voluminous, scattered, and often difficult to obtain.

Generally, dissemination of information falls within one or more of five categories: (a) replies to inquiries, (b) standard routine reports, (c) exception reports, (d) shop or operational paper, and (e) special reports. Costs and complexities surrounding the maintenance of manual information systems for these types of reports usually result from two factors:

1. The maintenance of separate conventional record files containing the same information in two or more departments.
2. Problems associated with *integration* of decentralized planning and operating departments.

The natural inclination of people to hoard duplicate information relating to their jobs, plus the tendency of departments to recognize only some of the costs associated with information, results in duplication of record files in many departments.

The integration of planning, operating, and controlling between departments through the medium of information is a problem of even greater importance. Departments tend to recognize only some of the costs and information important to them and frequently fail to recognize the interaction of their operations with other departments in the company. The sales department is well aware of customer service and the need for substantial inventories of finished goods, yet is unaware of the planning and resources involved in maintaining optimum inventory levels. The production department is concerned with utilization of employment, overhead, and facilities, yet is not totally aware of how these actions influence the marketing effort. Finance, on the other hand, watches over excessive inventory and carrying costs, fearful of cash drains and their effect on the profit picture. It is essential that the efforts of these decentralized departments be integrated.

How can today's manager possibly digest all the extraneous detail in a dynamic company? How can he maintain his information files at a minimum and at the same time ensure that the many departments within the company are integrated into a total system? The answer in both cases appears to lie in the proper design and implementation of a management information system. Yet this is difficult if not impossible with a manual information system. Experience has shown that if today's company wishes to improve its operations, it can do so with (a) a central information system, and (b) a framework to facilitate mechanization. These two attributes are part of the data bank concept.

Information Storage and Retrieval—Data Bank

The corporate or organization data bank can overcome the two primary objections to the manual system mentioned. In other words, the accumulation of information in an information center where "one set of books" is maintained avoids the maintenance of separate record files and also has a tendency to *integrate* the separate functions and departments of the company.

The data bank, or the central data base as it is sometimes called, is constructed to store and retrieve the information used in common by the various subsystems of the company. Using modern information-processing technology, a high-speed, random access, mass storage device is used to store large volumes of data concerning the various aspects of the firm and its environment. All relevant information about the company's operation is contained in one readily accessible file, arranged so that duplication and redundancy are avoided. Moreover, since only one set of records is necessary, it will be easier to maintain their accuracy.

Owner & Sons — Purchase Order			
Quantity	Stock Number	Unit Cost	Total
120	74B 34916–z	3.60	432.00

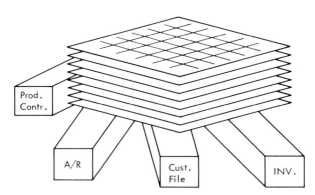

Figure 5-16   Integration of Separate Record Files into One Data Bank

Taking the example of the customer purchase order used to demonstrate our manual system, Figure 5-16 shows how the four separate files maintained in four departments can now be combined into one central data bank. Data is captured once, validated, and placed in the appropriate location in the data base.

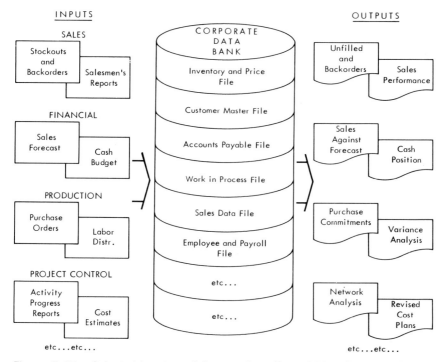

Figure 5-17   Selected Inputs and Outputs from Typical Manufacturing Company's Data Bank

Figure 5-17 is a more comprehensive illustration of the data bank concept and illustrates how more, but by no means all, of a typical manufacturing company's information files can be integrated into the central data base. In the usual case the data base is organized around the major information subsystems required to run the business. These are: (a) general accounting files, (b) inventory file, (c) customer and sales file, (d) vendor file, and (e) personnel file.

It is essential that the data base system satisfy the requirements of each user, otherwise he will continue to maintain his own system and thereby defeat the purpose of the central data base. The key element in this concept is that each subsystem utilizes the same data base in the satisfaction of its information needs. If this is done, an additional significant advantage will accrue: the integration of departments and functions. Figure 5-18 demonstrates conceptually how each organizational entity is integrated into a whole through its access and interface with the total information resources of the company. This integration provides a greater understanding and appreciation of how its actions and plans affect others throughout the organization.

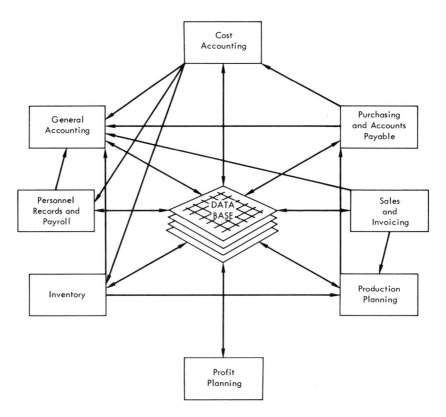

Figure 5-18   Integration of Functions and Departments Through the Integrated Data Base

A major side benefit to be achieved from the organization of a central data base is the simultaneous review of company structure, information needs, and management that naturally accompanies the comprehensive review required. The development of the data base may act as a catalyst in highlighting such problems as communication, organization, planning, and control.

Potential problems surrounding data-base construction are generally those connected with interdepartmental coordination and agreement. These might include: (a) the possibility of invalid input of information by a unit wishing to maintain *information security;* (b) the "multiplier effect" of erroneously entered data, which has an immediate influence on other departments utilizing the data; (c) the *time dimension* of input data, which requires that using departments agree on the time during which a transaction should be reflected by data input; and (d) the interdepartmental agreement required for the determination of the degree of detail to be included in data elements of the data base. Unless some common ground for agreement and solution of these problems is found, organizational units tend to maintain their own system for their peculiar needs. This, of course, defeats the purpose of the central data base.

DATA COMMUNICATIONS

There is no doubt that the move to data communications begun in the sixties and advanced in the seventies will continue to accelerate. The availability of new types of remote terminals has become commonplace and their use more widespread. The data communications system allows geographically dispersed users to communicate with centrally located computers. The sophistication of these systems will advance as fourth-generation hardware becomes generally available and as better data bases are developed to provide data-base oriented applications.

The dominant configuration in the past has been the central processor, which has accommodated a variety of remote input/output devices. This is changing to systems that will use inexpensive satellite (mini) computers to perform local functions and to communicate with the central system where the data base resides. The central system will employ highly cost-effective random access storage, advanced software for data-base management, and optimal performance of different kinds of concurrent jobs. A central data base provides the heart of this kind of MIS. Such a configuration is shown conceptually in Figure 5-19.

TYPES OF COMPUTER-BASED APPLICATIONS

An insight into the design of management information systems can be gained by considering three types or classifications of applications. We are not concerned with the many classifications by function or process (e.g., payroll, purchasing, inventory control, etc.), but with those where batch (cyclical) processing is used—applications that utilize the on-line or real-time capability of modern equipment, and applications that are designed primarily for making or aiding decisions.

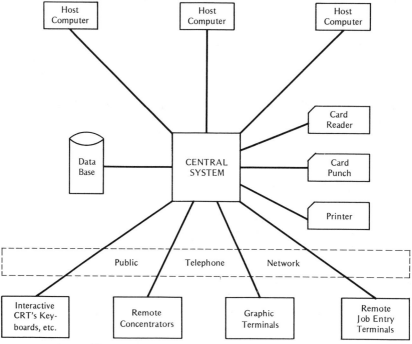

Figure 5-19   Data Communications System

The state-of-the-art in these applications and the effectiveness of each in providing management assistance for planning, operating, and controlling are important factors to consider when designing or modifying a management information system. The characteristics of the three types of application can be compared:

Type of Application	Degree of Implementation	Greatest Use	Orientation	Integration of Data Base	Decision Making
BATCH	Greatest	Operations	Historical and Accounting	Very Little	Limited
REAL TIME	Few	Control	Remote	Moderate	"Preset" Decision Rules
DECISION MAKING	Very Limited	Planning	Decision Assistance	Limited	Poor

Batch-Processing Applications

Batch processing is the classical method of processing data and is far and away the most frequently used MIS application. It entails the cyclical processing of input information in "batches." The time it takes to process the data and receive an output is known as *turnaround* time.

The batch processing of checking accounts in commercial banks is a good illustration of this type of application. The turnaround time, or the minimum unit of time in processing checks, is one business day, since a depositor's account is considered satisfactory if it has a positive balance at the close of the business day. Thus, checks received from all sources are proved and sorted for processing against customers' accounts. The checks are "paid" by posting after they are sorted to the accounts on which they are drawn. Any checks that cause an overdraft by reason of insufficient funds may be charged back to the source from which received.

Most applications in the batch-processing category involve the automation of routine functions, deal primarily with the data of the accounting system, and are oriented to record keeping and historical information. Most, but by no means all, of these systems are used for (a) payroll, (b) accounts payable, (c) customer billing, (d) general ledger, and (e) accounts receivable.

Since most of the cost associated with maintaining information in a company relates to the batch-processing type of application, these systems offer perhaps the greatest potential for reduction of information handling costs. Because of the relatively larger amount of experience with these applications, considerable advancements have been made in such large volume, self-contained applications as payrolls, inventory control, accounts payable, and customer billing.

Some of the more advanced work on improving batch-processing applications involves the integration of separate but related applications, such as the integration of production scheduling with personnel skills forecasting and the integration of inventory control and purchasing. Additionally, considerable work and advancement has been made in the data-base concept of these applications whereby multiple applications are obtained from single-source, single-file integrated data bases.

Real-Time Applications

Compared with batch processing, the real-time applications are very few but are highly publicized because of their exciting nature and because of the great potential for the future. These applications feature the use of the exciting capability of the computer for direct and instant access in which a dialogue is carried on between computer and user.

Most current real-time applications are little more than on-line versions of previous systems, and most are primarily application-oriented with little integration between subsystems. Characteristically, this type of application features remote terminal access with data transmission through telephone lines or some other means. Illustrative of real-time applications are systems for airline reservations, room reservations, work progress control in plants, inventory status ordering and reporting for geographically dispersed distributors, and credit status interrogation for a variety of users.

Real-time operation can be defined as "paralleling data processing with a physical process in such a fashion that the results of the data processing are immediately useful to the physical operation." This definition causes some difficulty because of the varying elapsed times required to *complete a transaction* and the varying time required for data processing to be *immediately useful.* To illustrate, we can say that real time in the case of an airline reservation system involves the processing of an answer while the customer is on the phone. On the other hand, we have systems that scan and match workers' identification badges and job tickets on a real-time basis but wait days or weeks to process paychecks.

Generally speaking, real-time systems have these three characteristics: (a) data will be maintained "on-line," (b) data will be updated as events occur, and (c) the computer can be interrogated from remote terminals or other devices. There is some doubt whether managers really need this capability in more than a small fraction of their daily information needs. As a practical matter, more systems with real-time capability utilize both the batch processing and real-time modes for their operations.

Decision Applications

Although spectacular breakthroughs have been made in computer applications for command and control decisions, similar uses for management problems are few and quite limited. Nothing approaching decision systems such as SAGE (Semi-Automatic Ground Environment) Air Defense System or the one that guides Apollo flights to the moon have yet been designed for business use.

Computer applications that make and execute low-level, routine decisions are relatively frequent. Examples are inventory reordering and certain types of production scheduling. However, for higher-order top-management decisions, available applications involve much interaction on the part of the decision maker with the computer. This type of man-machine interface may be called *computer-assisted decision making.*

The primary reason for lack of progress in higher-level decision making by management information systems is the difficulty of defining decision rules for business problems. Although management science techniques have been successfully applied to discrete parts of business activity, the application of these techniques to higher-management decision processes is still an item for further research. Indeed, applications at these levels are the forthcoming frontier to computer applications.

With regard to computer-assisted decision making, conclusions reached by several surveys indicate that the effectiveness of current and near-term applications in assisting management is, at best, below average. However, the majority of firms plan to devote a major share of computer effort to computer-assisted decision making for management in the future.

One of the most rapidly growing applications for computer-assisted decision making is the simulation or model. The corporate model enables management to: (a) reduce the time required to react to change, (b) evaluate alternative courses of action with a full knowledge of all pertinent factors, and (c) take longer looks into the future. By posing "what if" questions to the model, the decision maker can explore different alternatives and weigh the consequences of each. In other words, he can simulate the effects of many decisions without having to wait for the results of the decisions in "real life."

Figure 5-20 demonstrates a simulation utilized very effectively by Moore-McCormack Lines, Incorporated, for scheduling and routing cargo vessels. Two alternative means of varying inputs will illustrate the model. Assuming that some parameters are fixed (i.e., current fleet, freight rates, commodity volumes, origin and destination patterns, operating costs, etc.), the following inputs can be varied to determine their effect upon operations: schedule patterns, vessel assignments, and decision rules. On the other hand, the decision maker can assume that modes of operation are fixed, and he can then vary the following inputs to determine their effects: freight rates, annual volumes, operations costs, and origin and destination patterns. Under each of the foregoing assumptions and variations of fixed parameters and inputs, one valuable output from the model is a financial statement indicating the performance of each individual vessel based on the assumptions put into the model.

WHAT KIND OF COMPUTER DO I NEED?

The answer to this question is, of course, contingent upon a number of variables and a comprehensive treatment is somewhat beyond the scope of this book. However, some generalizations may help in answering the question and avoiding MIS "overkill."

It is generally recognized that most companies are overcomputerized. This situation has resulted from a combination of overzealous computer manufacturers and their salesmen plus the past reluctance of executives to ask whether or not they were getting their money's worth from the hardware, software, and personnel they were accumulating. Today, the tide is turning. Many top executives are now saying that EDP departments should justify their high cost by proving their value in dollars and cents. This is further explored in Chapter 8.

A second generalization regarding computer configuration is *keep it simple!* Don't get the most complicated hardware and software that the manufacturer offers. The more complex a system, the harder it is for one person or a few persons to go through the debugging and operational pro-

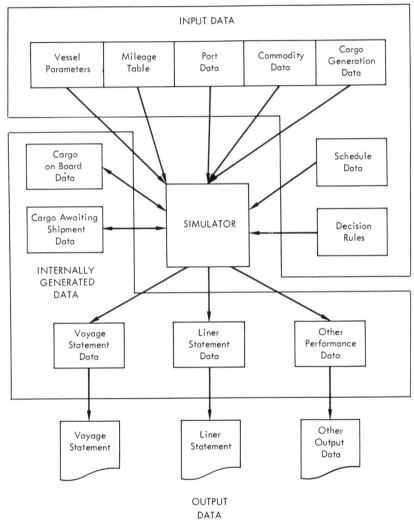

Figure 5-20   Simulation Model. Courtesy Moore-McCormack Lines, Inc.

cesses. This caution will be harder to observe in the future as more sophisticated and technologically complex generations of equipment are unveiled. Just remember—for most users, the old-fashioned equipment they now have is years ahead of their ability to design the information systems to utilize it. The problem is not hardware but "brainware"; design talent.

A *general* idea of computer needs can be gained by taking an approach somewhat like that in Table 5-2 overleaf. Here you can list frequent or planned applications, along with file medium, record size, processing frequency, and other *determinants* of computer needs. From this a general estimation can be made.

Finally, if you suspect that computer expenditures are exceeding what you think is reasonable, you should be aware of the existence of monitoring techniques for evaluating and improving the performance of existing equipment. This can lead to possible savings from these sources:

Elimination of underutilized and unneeded equipment
Deferment of installation or replacement of additional equipment
Reduction in working time to complete computer workload
Shortening of response time in data communications systems
Decreasing program running time, thereby increasing overall capacity

SUMMARY

In this chapter we have made the transition by analogy from a manual information system to one that is computer-based. Using the example of the inventory accounting system, it was shown that the components of both systems are the same: input, processor, storage, output, and procedure. Although in the manual system the operations are performed manually or with minimum mechanical assistance, the computer system processes data electronically. Hence we call it an electronic data processor.

In first establishing a computer information system or modifying a manual one for computer use, the programmer and designer go through the steps of system description, design of input document, output documents, file design, flowcharting the program, writing the computer program, and making the program operational.

The concept of a central data base has several advantages over the notion of individual departmental files. The data bank is constructed to store and retrieve the information that is used in common by the various subsystems of the company. This centralization avoids the cost of duplication involved in the maintenance of separate record files, but more important, the integrated data base tends to integrate the functions and subsystems of the organization.

Table 5-2

Applications approach to computer configuration.

Application	Master File Medium—Key	File Size Records—Characters	Processing Frequency	Transactions Per Run	Average Run Time (hr.)
ORDER ENTRY	Disk-order no.	10,000—150	Daily	1000	1
SALES ANALYSIS	Tape-cust. no.	2800—90	Weekly	7000	1½
INVENTORY	Tape-prod. no.	2500—120	Daily	7000	2
DISTRIBUTION SCHEDULE	Network program		Daily	—	1
PRODUCTION SCHEDULE	Linear program		Weekly	—	2
PAYROLL	Tape-employee no.	6000—400	Weekly	10,000	6
ACCT'S RECEIVABLE	Tape-cust. no.	3000—260	Daily	500	¾
OTHER APPLICATIONS AS REQUIRED					

Of the three types of applications (batch processing, real time, and decision), batch processing is far and away the most numerous and advanced in degree of implementation. Operational real-time systems are few in number but of great potential for advancing the boundaries of managerial decision making and control. Applications for top-management decision making are practically nonexistent, although those systems designed for computer-assisted decision making are growing in number and degree of sophistication. Modeling appears to offer the greatest potential for decision assistance in the future.

CHECK YOUR COMPUTER READINESS

	Yes	No
Can you communicate with the technician? (Or is it Greek to you?)	( )	( )
Can you describe existing and planned MIS in terms of the basic components of data processing?	( )	( )

Can you make the transitional analogy between manual and computer systems:

	Yes	No
Inputs/Output?	( )	( )
Processor?	( )	( )
Storage?	( )	( )
Programming?	( )	( )
Can you name the components and devices of a computer system and the characteristics of each?	( )	( )

Can you perform the steps in a manual to computer-based conversion:

System Description

	Yes	No
Narrative?	( )	( )
Flow chart?	( )	( )
Design the output?	( )	( )
Design the input?	( )	( )
Design the file?	( )	( )

Data bank concept

	Yes	No
Can you list the advantages of a data bank over non-integrated files?	( )	( )
Can you design the structure of major files in your operation?	( )	( )
Can you design the file structure so that interdepartmental files are integrated?	( )	( )
Can you provide a conceptual design for a data communications system for your organization?	( )	( )
Can you describe the pros and cons of different type applications (Batch, Real-Time, Decision) and recommend the optimum for your operation?	( )	( )
Can you evaluate the configuration of your existing or planned computer system?	( )	( )

chapter **6**

basic information
systems

6

Any organism is held together by the possession of means for the acquisition, use, retention, and transmission of information.

—Norbert Wiener

In this chapter we are concerned with basic (i.e., popular, widely used) *operational* information systems. Some writers like to describe the environment of the manager as one in which he has a cathode ray tube (CRT) on his desk or built into his telephone with immediate access to the "big brain" or the company data base. He is an expert in information retrieval and simulation techniques, asking "what if" questions on a real-time basis for his entire world of problems and decisions. This scenario is desirable, and just possibly attainable, but in the real managerial world the bulk of information systems remains in the somewhat pedestrian categories discussed in this chapter.

Over time the typical company has developed or is in the process of developing the many, somewhat independent *operational information systems* shown in Figure 6-1. In most cases, these represent basic data sources and have familiar names: personnel, payroll, order entry, billing, accounting, etc. These systems support the organizational structure shown in Figure 6-1 and can be categorized: (1) product development, (2) operations/manufacturing, (3) marketing, (4) finance and administration, and (5) supporting systems.

In most companies, these systems are characterized by heavy demands for *interfunctional* communications. They are not separate and distinct; they connect, interact, and otherwise tie together with information flows the operating systems that they represent. It is clear, for example, that order entry is very closely tied to order processing in manufacturing, that the personnel system is closely related to a payroll system, and so forth. These notions of *interaction* and *integration* are central to the design of management information systems. It is known as *subsystem integration,* and the concept is demonstrated in Figure 6-2. Notice how one subsystem's output provides input to another subsystem whose output provides input to yet another subsystem, and so on.

Many smaller firms shy away from computer-based information systems because they are under the impression that only the large firm can benefit. This is not the case. One such smaller firm attributed to the computer their growth in five years from $3.3 million in sales to \$16 million. This midwestern firm, which is engaged in designing, printing, and marketing greeting cards, says their increased sales and profitability resulted directly from their order processing, inventory, and sales forecasting systems. For example, the order processing system permitted expanded mailings plus the capture of data that is vital to the operation of other subsystems.

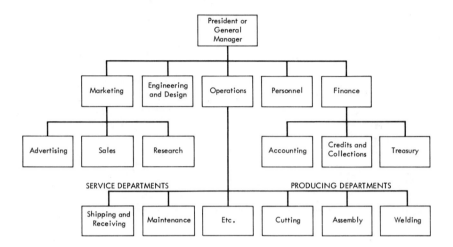

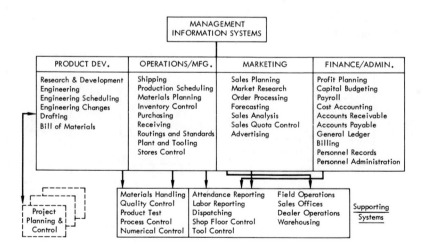

Figure 6-1   Basic Operational Information Systems

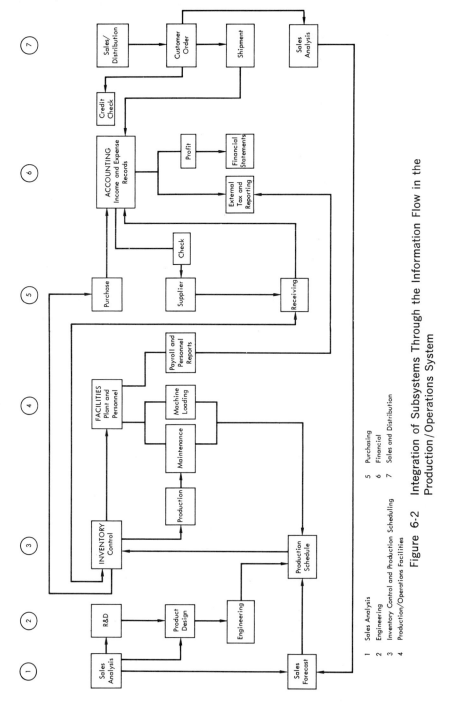

Figure 6-2   Integration of Subsystems Through the Information Flow in the
Production/Operations System

1   Sales Analysis
2   Engineering
3   Inventory Control and Production Scheduling
4   Production/Operations Facilities

5   Purchasing
6   Financial
7   Sales and Distribution

FINANCIAL INFORMATION SYSTEMS

All companies have some kind of financial information system, however rudimentary, and this category of information is the most widespread in use today. The basis of the system is the flow of dollars throughout the organization, and if they are designed correctly, the profitability and responsibility accounting systems reflect the organizational structure.

These systems involve large amounts of data that are concerned primarily with historical and internal information, although in some areas of financial planning and budgeting, the system does provide the futuristic look associated with systems planning and feedforward control.

The financial system is probably the most important single management information system in the company, and in most companies it is the oldest and best developed. The major problem with this system is the difficult design actions that are necessary to make it a vital tool for operating and planning rather than mere record keeping. This means that financial information must be something other than historical, as it has so frequently been in the past.

By and large, the conversion of a manual *financial* system to a *computer-based* system is subject to less improvement as a managerial device than other types of information systems. From a data-handling and cost point of view, financial systems are usually the first candidates for conversion, but there has been less opportunity to improve the quality of the information system during this conversion. This is because of the nature of the operations reflected by the information system, which is usually concerned primarily with budgetary control and promptness of reporting rather than upgrading information for operating decisions.

Profitability System

Management periodically approves some type of financial plan (e.g., the master budget) that assigns responsibility for maintaining operations and costs within certain limits. The construction of such a plan and the accompanying information systems are shown conceptually in Figure 6-3. This plan and related subsystem then become the basis for periodic reports on performance against plan, and these reports become the device by which control is exercised. Major problems in such a system involve: (a) determining equitable control standards; (b) determining when action is required; (c) obtaining rapid up-to-date information on variances, or better yet, *forecasting variances* before they occur. It is unlikely that the automation of financial records will improve the information associated with the first problem, but financial information systems can materially assist in the second two provided the *systems approach* (feedforward) to planning and control is taken in the design stages.

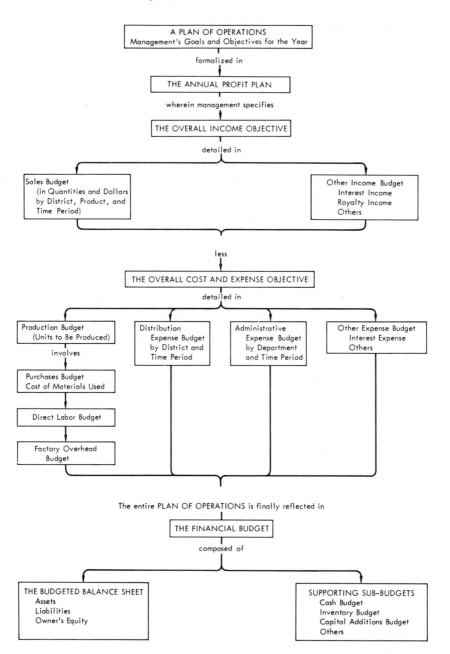

Figure 6-3   Development of a Financial Plan. SOURCE Glenn A. Welsch, *Budgeting: Profit Planning and Control,* 2nd ed. (Englewood Cliffs, N.J.: Prentice-Hall, Inc., 1970).

Some firms are moving in the direction of financial planning models, a mathematical representation of a particular aspect of an organization's operation. As an aid to corporate planning and decision making, a model allows a manager to prepare long-range or short-range forecasts of financial conditions under various assumptions. He can then ask "what if" questions such as: What will be the effect on divisional sales and profits *if* we hire six new salesmen? What will be the effect on inventory carrying costs *if* the prime interest rate advances by 1%? What will be the effect on product line profits *if* we raise the price by 5%?

> Robert Anderson of Rockwell International is one chief executive officer who believes in financial information systems. He says, "One of the best information systems for use by management in planning, monitoring, and controlling different functions is what we call our Financial Data System. It enables top management to identify the financial status of any important operation or program on almost a push-button basis. Through this system we can receive our periodic financial reports much faster, and are therefore able to take corrective action as needed on a very timely basis."

Accounting Systems

The art of management has been defined as the making of irrevocable decisions based on incomplete, inaccurate, and obsolete information. It is probably not too unfair to say that this lack of complete and current information has been due in part to the failure of the accountant to provide it. In the past, in accordance with the commonly accepted view of his activities, the accountant ceased activity beyond his involvement with record keeping and such related tasks as recording of costs and preparation of historical budgetary reports. Today, his job involves more—much more. Because of his background and training, the accountant has an excellent potential to stand in the forefront of the information systems explosion. This view is held by the American Accounting Association:

> "Essentially, accounting is an information system. More precisely, it is an application of general theory of information to the problem of efficient economic operations. It also makes up a large part of the general information expressed in quantitative terms. In this context accounting is both a part of the general information system of an operating entity and a part of the basic field bounded by the concept of information."

Properly designed accounting systems have the potential to provide essential management information for planning and control as well as becoming the vehicle through which other subsystems are integrated. This *integrative* attribute can be visualized in Figure 6-4. Notice how accounting information and subsystems flow through the operating systems, providing the mainstream of data for possible improvement in planning and control of the operating systems.

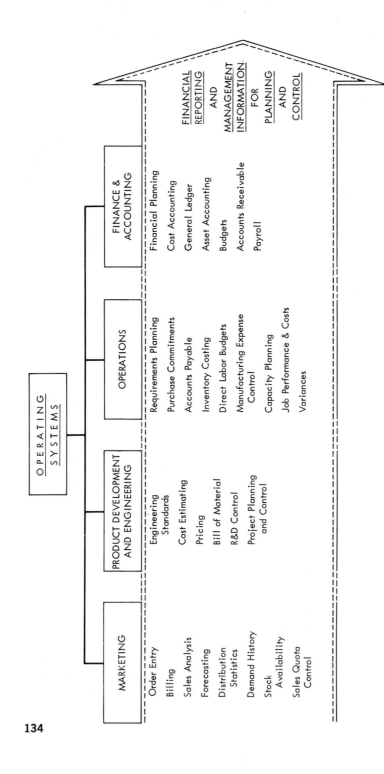

Figure 6-4 Integration of Operating Systems with Accounting and Financial Information Systems

Costing by line items during the billing operation provides gross profitability for analysis
by: customer
salesman
line
item

Objectives: Provide input to other subsystems
Improve cash flow
Maintain customer goodwill
Timely invoice processing
Keep salesmen informed

LAURENTIAN INDUSTRIES, INC.

SOLD TO
S. W. STAPLES
498 RIVERVIEW STREET
SAN JOSE, CALIF. 94067

SHIP TO
RODRIGUEZ DESIGN HOMES
DIVISION OF S. W. STAPLES
8363 OLIVE STREET
SUNNYVALE, CALIF. 95117

CUSTOMER NO. 430875

| DATE 09/15/-- | INV. NO. 138265 | ORDER NO. 717690 | SHIPPING INSTRUCTIONS VIA SMITH TRANSPORT | STATED TERMS 2% 15 DAYS NET 30 | | | SALESMAN G. PEREZ | |

QUANTITY ORDERED	QUANTITY SHIPPED	QUANTITY B/O	DESCRIPTION	UNIT PRICE	EXTENDED AMOUNT	DISCOUNT AMOUNT	NET AMOUNT	TAX-ABLE
40	40		B500 TWINLITE SOCKET B	.60	24.00	1.20	22.80	
350	100	250	B506 SOCKET ADAPTER BRN	.32	32.00	3.20	28.80	
200	150	50	C151C SILENT SWITCH IVORY	1.20	180.00	9.00	171.00	*
175	175		A210 PULL CORD GOLD	.42	73.50		73.50	*
60		60	1436 LAMP ENTRANCE	.50				
175	105	70	A200 FIXTURE 5 LIGHT	20.13	2113.65	211.37	1,902.28	
			FREIGHT CHARGE				18.95	
			PACKING CHARGE				45.00	

| TAXABLE 244.50 | TAX 12.23 | FREIGHT 18.95 | MISC. SPECIAL CHARGE 45.00 | | | | INVOICE AMOUNT 2,274.56 | |

Accounts receivable
Sales analysis
Tax reports
Commission statements
Shipping documents
Inventory

TO OTHER SYSTEMS

Figure 6-5 Customer's Invoice Output from the Billing System. Courtesy IBM Corporation.

Example—Billing

Billing is perhaps the most widely used data processing application. In its most common form, the billing function includes the selection and extension of prices, and the application of discounts, freight charges, and taxes. Despite the fact that the billing system is viewed as a somewhat pedestrian clerical function, the speed and accuracy of the operation can have a significant impact upon cash flow as well as customer good will.

A customer's invoice, the output of the typical billing system, is illustrated in Figure 6-5. Notice that in addition to the managerial objectives indicated in Figure 6-5, the customer's invoice can also provide valuable input to other subsystems. Here we see an example of how an otherwise routine clerical operation can be upgraded into higher-level decision-making systems. For example, the output from the billing system (the customer's invoice) can provide the essential input for a sales analysis system or a variety of inventory management systems.

Example—General Ledger

In many firms the general ledger is viewed as a source of historical accounting information without regard to how this may be used to plan and control. Putting a computer to work on the general ledger could provide current information to help analyze past performance, evaluate present conditions, and forecast future plans. Moreover, data processing can provide earlier closings, more frequent trial balances and other accounting reports at less cost in time and manpower. Some accounting reports that can be generated are:

> Journal voucher proof list
> Journal register
> General ledger report
> Income statement
> Balance sheet
> Summary ledger report (shown in Figure 6-6).

OPERATIONS/MANUFACTURING INFORMATION SYSTEMS

These systems are concerned with the information about the physical flow of goods or the production of goods and services. They cover such activities as production planning and control, inventory control and management, purchasing, distribution, and transportation.

```
 ┌─────────────────────────────────────────────────────────────────────┐
O│                    SUMMARY LEDGER REPORT                              │O
 │                                                                       │
O│                         3/31/--                            PAGE 1     │O
 │  ACCOUNT NO.              ACCOUNT DESCRIPTION           ACCOUNT BALANCES
O│  MAJ.    MIN.                                        THIS YEAR TD  LAST YEAR TD │O
 │  111     000   CASH ON HAND AND IN BANKS              36,710.23      25,893.26  │
O│  112     000   ACCOUNTS RECEIVABLE    NET            122,273.47     117,762.80  │O
 │  114     000   NOTES RECEIVABLE                        8,000.00       4,000.00  │
 │  116     000   INVENTORIES                           703,402.65     590,808.40  │
O│  121     000   LAND                                  500,000.00     500,000.00  │O
 │  122     000   BUILDINGS                           1,850,000.00   1,800,000.00  │
O│  123     000   DEPRECIATION RESERVE FOR BUILDINGS     49,000.00      48,000.00  │O
 │  124     000   EQUIPMENT AND MACHINERY               450,850.00     425,465.00  │
 │  125     000   DEPREC RESERVE FOR EQUIP AND MACH      79,456.00      76,305.00  │
O│  221     000   NOTES PAYABLE                          40,000.00      35,000.00  │O
 │  321     000   SURPLUS                                75,203.76      50,397.73  │
 │  411     000   SALES                               1,075,113.85     950,675.33  │
O│  412     000   COST OF GOODS SOLD                    375,819.10     255,839.19  │O
 │  421     000   SELLING EXPENSE                       185,615.25     195,267.48  │
O│                                                                       │O
 └─────────────────────────────────────────────────────────────────────┘
```

Figure 6-6   Summary Ledger Report. Courtesy IBM Corporation.

Because the quantities of data are so large and the timing of information so essential, the operations/manufacturing systems are the most adaptable to automation and yield the largest benefits in terms of immediate solution of critical and costly problems.

The type of information that lends itself best to computer use usually has these characteristics:

A number of interacting variables.

Reasonably accurate values.

Speed as an important factor.

Repetitive operations.

Accuracy as a requirement.

Large amounts of information.

Because the information needed for effective management of operations/manufacturing has all these characteristics, these systems are probably the most adaptable to automation of any in the company. Moreover, because of the requirement for timeliness in handling large quantities of data, the greatest advances in improvements and economy are likely to be made in this area.

These systems, particularly in a manufacturing company, are unquestionably the most important from an operating standpoint. They cross all subsystem boundaries and have an effect throughout the company. Yet despite this importance, these systems have had less management involvement and consequently less development than the financial system. This is unfortunate, because in most companies this area offers more opportunity for development, cost saving, and management improvement than any other. Indeed, much of the "total systems" activity in recent years

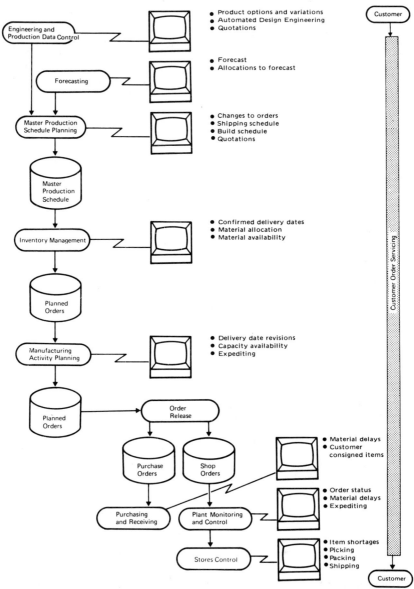

Figure 6-7   Customer Order Processing. Courtesy IBM Corporation.

has begun because of problems in the operations/manufacturing area and because once begun, an examination of this area leads to the design of related and integrated subsystems throughout the company. This attribute, the importance of these systems, and their impact on systems elsewhere in the organization was shown in Figure 6-2, which demonstated how the production subsystem interacts with all major functions of a manufacturing company. Note that the critical input to the system is the customer order. The activity of customer *order processing* is so essential that it is discussed below as an example.

Example—Order Processing

For many companies, particularly those with a large number of transactions involving customers' orders, the *order entry* and subsequent *order processing* systems are very central and crucial to operations. Delays or errors can cause a disruption in production or inventory management, excessive backorders, reduced cash flow, and a loss of customer good will.

Many companies begin their development of management information systems with order processing because it is viewed as a *lifestream* activity. This is true because the capture of customer data is important and because these data are needed subsequently by so many other subsystems. It can provide the central stream of information around which other subsystems can be integrated. The central role of order processing can be appreciated by an examination of Figure 6-7.

Although Figure 6-7 depicts the operation of order processing in a manufacturing company, the system is equally as important in such service industries as banks, hospitals, educational institutions, and in utilities and transportation.

United Stationers Supply Company of Forest Park, Illinois, sells over 23,000 items of office supplies and equipment from a 280,000 sq ft warehouse. The computer system starts in the telephone order department utilizing 14 on-line cathode ray tube terminals and a WATS (Wide Area Telephone Service) hook-up to customers. The system feeds sequential information to order takers, runs credit checks, extends prices, bills, prints picking orders, and maintains inventory control as well as a variety of planning and control reports. It also guarantees order shipment within 48 hours.

Example—Materials Planning

The materials planning subsystem handles parts and subassemblies for which a demand is generated from a production schedule for end-products.

The system must also determine exactly when the parts and/or subassemblies are required. The objectives of the system can be stated as:

Plan and control parts from a predetermined production schedule.

Reduce time and costs of determining and ordering requirements.

Prevent disruptive schedules to occur in production.

Forecast future needs for ordering material.

Forecast changes in material requirements resulting from production schedule change.

(*Figure 6-8 illustrates outputs from the materials planning system.*)

Example—Purchasing

Raw materials and other purchased material represent a very significant expense to most industrial companies, and the proper operation of the purchasing function can lower costs and increase profitability. The more automation that can be brought to the design of the purchasing system, the more time the buyer or purchasing agent has for his primary job of negotiating with suppliers and seeking out new and better sources of supply. Therefore, in addition to the objective of automating the routine clerical functions, the system has these additional objectives:

Determine economic order quantity to purchase.

Reduce clerical costs.

Monitor buyer performance.

Identify high volume vendors in order to negotiate discounts.

Determine supplier performance by identifying late deliveries and poor quality.

(*Figure 6-9 illustrates outputs from the purchasing system.*)

Example—Capacity Planning and Operation Scheduling

Production management needs information for capacity planning and operation sequences, for overtime planning, subcontracting, and rescheduling of shop orders. Some objectives of this subsystem would be:

Identify work center loads for future time periods and those that are over- or under-loaded.

Evaluate alternatives of subcontracting or overtime to meet delivery dates.

Identify orders to be rescheduled in order to level the load.

Forecast time and location of equipment and tooling needs.

End product requirements

Stock no.	Description	Six month projection					
		1	2	3	4	5	6
1016H	ENGINE	100	0	100	50	100	100
6094HD	ENGINE	50	0	50	50	0	75
4377L	POWER UNIT	60	60	0	120	60	0
3355LD	ENGINE	0	50	0	25	0	25
3355B	ENGINE	0	25	25	25	25	25
9774AB	POWER UNIT	125	75	125	0	50	100

Requirements planning report

Item no.	Description	Stock	10/08	10/22	11/05	11/19	12/03	12/17
A300-9965	FILTER	50						
	GROSS REQ.		337	196	231	175	372	563
	NET REQ.		287	196	231	175	372	563
	PLANNED ORDERS			700	700		700	700
	LEADTIME OFFSET		500					
A403-4773	GAUGE	150						
	GROSS REQ.			600		300	265	
	NET REQ.			450		300	265	
	PLANNED ORDERS			500	250	250	250	500
	LEADTIME OFFSET		500			250		

Figure 6-8   Materials Planning Reports. Courtesy IBM Corporation.

141

Open Purchase Order Status

By P/O □   By Supplier ☒   By Part □   Date 02/03

Purchase order no.	Part no.	Mat. code	Supplier no.	Supplier name	Qty. on order	Qty. rec'd	Balance date	Delivery date	Value outstanding $	Action
140562	201610	924	0021	BAILY & CO.	220		110	03/06	200	
144250	222521	924	0021	BAILY & CO.	25	110	25	04/05	47	
146402	368065	924	0021	BAILY & CO.	200		200	04/03	634	
									881	
136781	179923	801	0027	ACTION INC.	4,000	3,500	500	01/03	774	EXP.
144548	474149	801	0027	ACTION INC.	800		800	03/06	175	

Vendor Delivery Performance Report   10/06

Buyer	Vendor name	Vendor no.	Total value open orders	Open orders	Orders behind	Percent behind	YTD purchase percent behind	YTD orders behind
CA	GENERAL MFG. CO.	19080	792.00	16	4	25	15	27
CA	POWER DESIGN CO.	40001	2,103.75	2	1	50	25	8
CA	CENTRAL TOOL CO.	56012	301.20	10	1	10	2	50
	BUYER TOTAL		3,196.95	28	6	21	7	85
TK	ORIN FORGE CO.	49045	3,115.00	30	6	20	20	50
TK	LAKE MILLING	73111	603.00	23	0	0	4	30
	BUYER TOTAL		3,718.00	53	6	11	12	80
	DEPT. TOTAL		6,914.95	81	12	15	9	165

Figure 6-9   Purchasing Reports. Courtesy IBM Corporation.

Compute start dates for shop orders in order to meet delivery dates.

Forecast skills and trades required.

Forecast order release dates.

(*Figure 6-10 illustrates outputs from this system.*)

MARKETING SYSTEMS

Systems theory and practice indicate that the basic areas of the marketing function that lend themselves to improvement through information systems include: (a) forecasting/sales planning, (b) market research, (c) advertising, and (d) operating and control information required to manage the marketing function. This conclusion tends to agree with a survey of 122 marketing vice-presidents. Their top four choices for utilizing their companies' computers were: forecasting sales, customer services, predicting markets for new products and services, and sales analysis and control.

Marketing information is one of the most important information systems to most businesses, yet it is the one most often overlooked. Few marketing executives use information effectively on their jobs; most of them rely on intuition as a basis for decisions. The vast majority of firms tend to maintain information only about sales records or orders and shipments. What is needed is a system to give marketing managers information that will help them make better decisions about pricing, advertising, product promotion policy, sales force effort, and other vital marketing decisions. Such a system should also take into account the vital need elsewhere in the organization for information concerning marketing, information that affects other subsystems in the company.

The effectiveness of marketing information systems depends to a large extent on feedback from the marketplace to the firm, so that the firm can judge the adequacy of its past performance as well as appraise the opportunities for new activity. Despite this need, many firms consider their marketing information system to be some type of "sales analysis" activity that has been superimposed onto an accounting system. Yet there is no reason why this vital area of management activity should not take an approach similar to other areas of the firm where information needs are designed around the managerial functions of planning, operating, and controlling.

Table 6-1 summarizes some of the more important types of information systems applications in the marketing area and indicates selected outputs that are useful for market planning, market research, and marketing control. The nature of these three types of marketing systems is summarized:

Work center load summary

07/15 Machine shop A

Dept. no.	GRP no.	Description	No. of mach.	Wk.	Capacity	Load	Available capacity	Overload
1	01	BENCH MILLS	5	1	136.0	130.0	6.0	
				2	170.0	150.0	20.0	
				3	170.0	165.5	4.5	
				4	170.0	179.0		9.0
				5	170.0	162.3	7.7	
				6	170.0	185.1		15.1

All the individual labor operations that are needed for planned shop orders are summarized by time period for each machine group.

Shop load schedule

07/15

Mach./GRP	Hrs./day	Scheduled Day	Hr.	Part no.	Job	Oper.	Priority code	Order qty.	Claimed qty.
1609-01	7.50	622	.0	461235	3422	020	1	2,100	210
		622	4.50	461747	6343	035	5	1,988	
		623	5.50	461396	4211	020	5	113	
1207-01	15.00	622	.0	537141	3762	055	2	2,759	500
		622	6.25	537593	4727	030	3	457	
		623	13.40	537547	3249	040	5	637	

Shop supervisors use this report to schedule jobs and optimize the use of men and machines.

Tooling list   Date 07/15

Part no.	Job	Oper.	Dept.	Mach./GRP	Scheduled Day	Hr.	Tool no.	Tool code	Description
131634	1700	0040	018	1610–01	624	11.1	31665	B	FIXTURE
							1021545	B	CUTTER
133195	1800	0045	005	1609–02	622	.0	1000555	B	VISE JAWS
133694	6601	0090	011	1400–01	622	8.7	153310	D	INDEX GAUGE
							151347	D	COMP. CHART
							95601	B	COMP. FIXT.

This report, supplied to the tool crib, lists the tools required by each operation and makes it possible to pre-pack tools.

Figure 6-10   Three Capacity Planning and Operation Scheduling Reports. Courtesy IBM Corporation.

1. *Control systems* provide monitoring and review of performance against plan; also provide information concerning trends, problems, and possible marketing opportunities.

2. *Planning systems* provide information needed for planning the marketing and sales program. A good system provides information to permit the marketing manager to weigh the effects of alternate plans in trade promotion, pricing, and other variables in the forecasting equation.

3. *Market research systems* are used to develop, test, and predict the effects of actions taken or planned in the basic subsystems of marketing (pricing, advertising, etc.).

Table 6-1

Selected Applications and Outputs of a Marketing Information System

Application	Output
MARKET PLANNING	
Forecasting	Parts requirements and production schedule based on demand for industrial goods.
Purchasing	Automatic optimization of purchasing function and inventory control based on decision rules.
Credit Management	Automatic computer processing of credit decisions.
MARKET RESEARCH	
Pricing Policy	Policy based on historical analysis of past.
Advertising Strategy	Strategy based on sales analysis of a variety of market segment breakdowns.
Advertising Expenditure	Correlation by numerous market segments of sales and advertising expenditures.
MARKETING CONTROL	
Marketing Costs	Current reports of deviation from standard and undesirable trends.
Sales Performance	A variety of data to help discover reasons for sales performance and correct deviations.
Territorial Control of Sales, Distribution, Costs, etc.	Timely reports of performance on territorial basis to permit reallocation of resources to substandard areas.

Example—Sales Analysis

The sales/marketing function has historically been serviced with information contained in month-end sales reports. Generally, these have been clerical in nature and did not contain the sales analysis needed for decisions. Basic questions that should be answered by a sales analysis report would include:

Which are the small accounts? Can we afford to service them?

Are salesmen spending disproportionate time on marginal accounts?

Which are our high-volume/high-profit accounts?

What is the gross profit contribution by item and line?

Are salesmen specializing in too many "pet" items?

Where are the potential sales improvements by customer, line, item?

The basic sales analysis reports shown in Figure 6-11 are easily obtained and can provide answers to questions similar to those asked above.

Example—Inventory Management

Because so many businesses have a large part of their assets tied up in inventory, it is very important that proper inventory control systems be maintained. Too much stock results in excessive carrying costs and the risks of obsolescence. Too little stock can mean lost sales or expensive rush orders. Two typical inventory management reports are shown in Figure 6-12. These are:

Distribution-by-Value Report. Items are shown in sequence by sales dollars, so that the item with the largest annual sales comes first and the item with the smallest annual sales comes last. Percentages are also shown. Notice that the top 1% of items accounts for almost 18% of sales. Six items account for nearly one-fifth of sales. The top 20% of items account for 70% of sales. This type of information could lead to a variety of inventory management decisions.

Distribution-by-Value with Item Movement. This report permits four basic types of analysis: (a) life cycle analysis, (b) segmentation of inventory to allow concentration on high investment items, (c) establishment of order quantities and order points, and (d) life cycle analysis of vendor lines.

MANPOWER/PERSONNEL SYSTEMS

Manpower planning, personnel management, and their accompanying information systems are significantly less advanced than other operating systems. This is largely because top management, and hence personnel managers and EDP managers, have been relatively unconcerned with applying MIS techniques to managing the predominant cost of doing business—the human resource cost.

LAURENTIAN INDUSTRIES, INC.

COMPARATIVE ANALYSIS OF SALES BY ITEM

PERIOD ENDING 10/31/--

ITEM NO.	DESCRIPTION	CURR. PERIOD QUAN. THIS YR	LAST YR	PCT CHG	YTD QUANTITY THIS YR	LAST YR	PCT CHG
624634	D20068 OVERHAUL GASKET	10	14	29-	90	98	8-
624832	17D0011 BELT DYNAMIC FAN	190	150	27	1,820	1,905	4-
624901	DMK6448 HUB ASSEMBLY J2	1-	5	120-	18	18	0

LAURENTIAN INDUSTRIES, INC.

SALES BY ITEM CLASS

MONTH ENDING 03/31/--

ITEM CLASS	CLASS DESCRIPTION	SOLD THIS MONTH	GROSS PROFIT	PROFIT PERCENT	SOLD THIS YEAR	GROSS PROFIT	PROFIT PERCENT
1	ABRASIVES	2,720.19	271.36	10	9,900.17	907.60	9
2	ACIDS AND CHEMICALS	1,216.27	170.27	14	3,139.68	408.07	13
3	BRASS	6,220.83	435.45	7	16,341.47	1,143.87	7

LAURENTIAN INDUSTRIES, INC.

COMPARATIVE SALES ANALYSIS

BY ITEM CLASS FOR EACH CUSTOMER

MONTH ENDING 05/31/--

PAGE

CUST NO	ITEM CLASS	CUSTOMER/ITEM CLASS NAME	MONTHLY SALES THIS YEAR	MONTHLY SALES LAST YEAR	PRCNT CHG	YEAR TO DATE SALES THIS YEAR	YEAR TO DATE SALES LAST YEAR	PRCNT CHG
3310		TARDELL HARDWARE						
	11	BUILDER HARDWARE	103.19	91.31	13	515.92	729.43	29-
	12	ELECTRICAL SUPPLIES	87.58	85.02	2	435.57	375.29	16
	13	GIFTS AND SUNDRIES	63.01	.00		315.09	490.36	35-
	14	HOUSEWARES	198.05	150.23	32	990.32	1,123.19	12-

LAURENTIAN INDUSTRIES, INC.

COMPARATIVE SALES ANALYSIS BY CUSTOMER

FOR EACH SALESMAN

PERIOD ENDING 07/31/--

PAGE

SLMN NO.	CUST. NO.	SALESMAN/CUSTOMER NAME	THIS PERIOD THIS YEAR	THIS PERIOD LAST YEAR	YEAR-TO-DATE THIS YEAR	YEAR-TO-DATE LAST YEAR
10		A R WESTON				
	1426	HYDRO CYCLES INC	3,210.26	4,312.06	10,010.28	9,000.92
	2632	RUPP AQUA CYCLES	7,800.02	2,301.98	20,322.60	11,020.16
	3217	SEA PORT WEST CO	90.00CR	421.06	900.00	593.10
		SALESMAN TOTALS	10,920.28	7,035.10	31,732.88	20,614.18
12		H T BRAVEMAN				
	0301	BOLLINGER ASSOCIATES	100.96	0.00	100.96	0.00

Figure 6-11   Sales Analysis Reports. Courtesy IBM Corporation.

LAURENTIAN INDUSTRIES, INC.
ANALYSIS OF INVENTORY ACTIVITY

12 MONTH PERIOD ENDING 7/1/--

STOCK LOCATION	STOCK NUMBER	DESCRIPTION	UNIT	DATE OF LAST ACTIVITY	NET ISSUES FOR PERIOD			BALANCE ON HAND		
					NUMBER OF TRANS.	QUANTITY	AVERAGE PER MONTH	QUANTITY	MONTHS' SUPPLY	VALUE
2715-237	127205	LIGHT RECEPTACLE	EA	7/--	2	4	.3	16	53.3	$ 4.32
2715-420	247389	SOLENOID. HEATER	EA	7/--	1	1	.1	7	70.0	4.48
2715-267	111462	SWITCH,STARTER	EA	8/--	1	4	.3	4	13.3	8.64
2715-601	896124	PINION STUD	EA	9/--	4	16	1.3	84	64.6	9.24
2716-234	59827	GASKET. MANIFOLD	EA	11/--	2	12	1.0	16	16.0	7.52
2716-320	614	WASHER, RUBBER	DZ	12/--	1	3	.2	14	70.0	2.52
2717-086	6213	BOLT, CARRIAGE	DZ	12/--	1	2	.2	27	135.0	32.40
2717-742	1032	BEARING, CLUTCH	EA	1/--	1	1	.1	9	90.0	34.83
2717-748	148722	AXLE	EA	3/--	1	1	.1	3	30.0	24.60
2719-147	2642	BRUSH, GENERATOR	EA	3/--	3	9	.7	42	60.0	7.14
2719-382	222649	REGULATOR	EA	3/--	4	4	.3	3	10.0	3.78

Item No	Cumulative Count		Annual Units	Unit Cost	Annual $ Sales	Cumulative Sales	
	Rank by $ Sales	%				$	%
411045	1	.2	104,578	.966	101,023	101,023	3.8
411118	2	.4	375,959	.246	92,486	193,509	7.3
411063	3	.5	40,602	2.012	81,693	275,202	10.4
411075	4	.7	69,570	1.123	78,128	353,330	13.3
411176	5	.9	133,534	.490	65,432	418,762	15.8
411381	6	1.1	106,651	.510	54,392	473,154	17.8
411368	110	20.0	90,191	.073	6,584	1,886,385	71.0
411425	111	20.2	7,513	.800	6,011	1,892,396	71.2
411263	112	20.4	1,820	3.286	5,983	1,898,379	71.4
411503	113	20.5	10,611	.553	5,868	1,904,247	71.6
411444	545	99.2	813	.145	118	2,657,997	100.0
411465	546	99.4	4,227	.022	93	2,658,090	100.0
411243	547	99.6	90	.715	65	2,658,155	100.0
411516	548	99.8	4	2.916	12	2,658,167	100.0
411541	549	100.0	0	0	0	2,658,167	100.0

Figure 6-12   Distribution by Value Report. Courtesy IBM Corporation.

The personnel information system deals with the flow of information about people working in the organization as well as future personnel needs. In most organizations, the system is concerned primarily with the five basic subsystems of the personnel function: recruiting, placement, training, compensation, and maintenance.

It is probably not unfair to say that many personnel managers are proving to be myopic in their conventional specialization and concern with personnel records for their own sake. Manpower management, as opposed to the traditional view of the personnel function, should be considered a total system that interacts with the other major systems of the organization —marketing, production, finance, and the external environment. Indeed, the primary purpose of the manpower management program is to service these major systems. Forecasting and planning the manpower needs of the organization, maintaining an adequate and satisfactory work force, and controlling the personnel policies and programs of the company are the major responsibilities of manpower management. Plant security is often an auxiliary function.

In order to achieve the foregoing, a *manpower system* is necessary. Like any system, it consists of a number of inputs and outputs, and a number of related subsystems, processes, and activities, all operating through the medium of information. Such a system is shown in Figure 6-13. Note that the output from the manpower subsystems goes to personnel staff specialists as well as to line operating managers. Many personnel managers mistakenly conceive of their information systems as a tool of the personnel

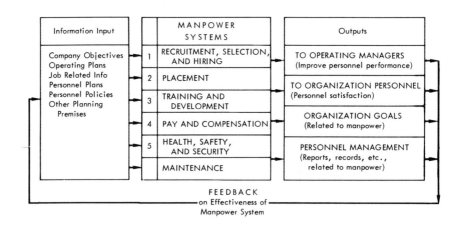

Figure 6-13   Manpower Information Systems

function alone rather than as the real reason for a manpower system—organizational effectiveness. A systems-oriented approach to manpower management interrelates and integrates the functions of the personnel manager with the duties of the operating personnel, who benefit most from a manpower information system.

Briefly, the six major subsystems of the manpower management system designed to accomplish these objectives are:

1. *Recruitment.* Properly managed, the recruitment system forecasts personnel needs and skills and recruits the personnel at the proper time to meet organizational needs. A properly designed information system will furnish information concerning (a) skills required for company programs and processes, and (b) inventory of skills available in the organization. Manning tables, job specifications, and other personnel data are also useful in this subsystem.

2. *Placement.* This system is perhaps the most vital of all personnel functions because it matches available personnel with requirements, and hence the effective use of manpower as a resource takes place within this system. A properly designed placement information system takes account of the latest behavioral tools and techniques to ensure that the capabilities of people are identified and placed with properly organized work requirements.

3. *Training and development.* As technological changes and demands for new skills accelerate, many companies find that they must necessarily develop much of their talent requirements from internal sources. In addition, a large part of the work force must constantly be updated in new techniques and developments. This task is the function of the training and development system. Basic information requirements include a continuing skills inventory of company personnel matched against a forecast of current and estimated needs for improved skills.

4. *Compensation.* The pay and other values (fringe benefits, for example) for the satisfaction of individual wants and needs and for compliance with government, union, and other requirements is the basic function of the compensation system. Information included in or required by this system is largely that associated with the traditional payroll and other financial records.

5. *Maintenance.* This system, largely for the benefit of operating managers, should be designed to ensure that personnel policies and procedures are achieved. It may extend to the operation of systems to control work standards, those required to measure performance against financial plans

or other programs, and the many subsidiary records normally associated with the collection, maintenance, and dissemination of personnel data.

6. *Health, safety, and plant security.* As the name implies, this system is concerned with the health of personnel and the safety of job practices and related operations. Plant security includes actions necessary to prevent theft, damage, or compromise of classified information.

Recently, a good deal of attention has been focused on the design and utilization of skills inventory programs. These are sometimes called "skills banks" or "manpower assessment programs." The objective of such programs is to identify and locate the talent resources of the organization in order to maximize their use. It is easy to see that such an objective could be essential in the engineering, research, or other firms where talent is the most costly and valuable resource.

Figure 6-14 depicts the conceptual operation of a skills inventory program. Notice that in addition to the regular report generated by the program, it may also include a computer simulation model. We can call this

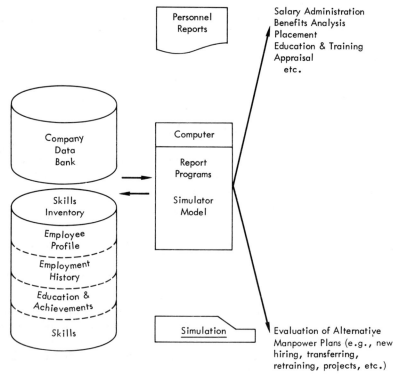

Figure 6-14   Operation of a Skills Inventory Program

the "personnel simulator" or the "work force simulator," or any other appropriate title. It is a valuable tool for gaining information about different manpower approaches under varying conditions.

INTEGRATED INFORMATION SYSTEMS

Most of us have experienced or witnessed the very small business operation that is managed by a single individual, the "one-man show." In this type of operation the entrepreneur (manager) has complete and immediate access to all the knowledge and information required to run the business. Moreover, he can immediately compute the impact of one subsystem (e.g., inventory) on others (e.g., cash flow). His information system is totally integrated, it is usually in a "real-time" mode, and decision-making procedures are limited to a whole unit.

By examining such an operation and information system and how it evolves into the more complex managerial environment accompanying bigness, we can better understand the need for information systems and their integration. After all, the basic purpose of an information system is to provide the decision maker with the necessary information to manage his operation much in the same sense as the "one-man show." (See Figure 1-1 on page 6.)

A management information system is, by definition, a set of *integrated subsystems*. And although integrated subsystems are less often the case in practice, the notion should be kept constantly in mind while designing for the future. Otherwise, patchwork systems and "islands of mechanization" will result. Moreover, an integrated approach is necessary if we are to provide the manager with the information necessary to plan and control his operations in the manner of the "one-man show."

An integrated management information system serves as a substitute or replacement for the "one-man show." It combines the roles of diverse disciplines, including marketing, engineering, R&D, manufacturing, accounting, data processing, and management sciences. It synthesizes a data base, using the most pertinent information available, to supply the information needed for making decisions.

An illustration of a somewhat sophisticated integrated system is the one recommended by IBM Corporation for manufacturing operations. It is called the Communications Oriented Production Information Control System (COPICS). Part of this system is shown in Figure 6-7 (order processing). The integrative nature of the data base is indicated in Figure 6-15, and Figure 6-16 depicts the relationship among the subsystems and the managerial functions.

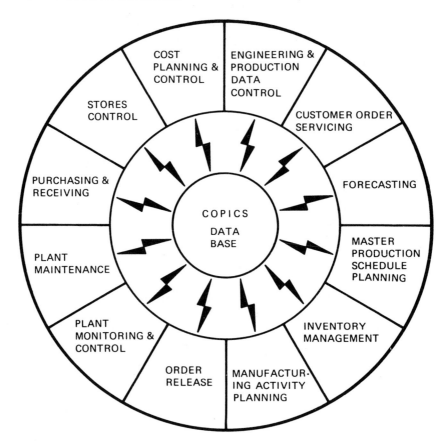

Figure 6-15   COPICS Data Base. Courtesy IBM Corporation.

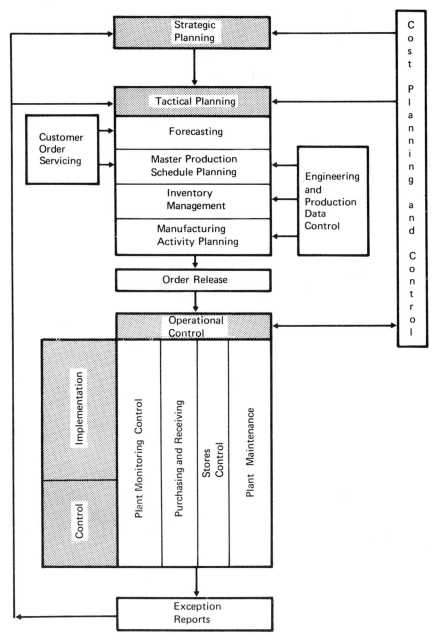

Figure 6-16   Relationship of Operating Systems, Information Systems, and Managerial Functions. Courtesy IBM Corporation.

CHECKLIST
FOR DIAGNOSING YOUR BASIC MIS
PROBLEMS

Problem	Yes	No	Cure
Do you feel that your existing information systems are incomplete in that they:			
(a) provide interfunctional relationships?	( )	( )	Take an *integrative* approach to design. Get a *master plan*.
(b) consist of "islands of mechanization"?	( )	( )	

FINANCIAL/ACCOUNTING SYSTEMS
Do you feel that your financial planning and control systems:

	Yes	No	Cure
(a) consist of little more than historical bookkeeping?	( )	( )	Adopt a financial planning rather than a financial reporting system.
(b) provide variance reports after it's too late to correct?	( )	( )	Design control systems with a feedforward approach.
(c) do not allow you to forecast the results of decisions?	( )	( )	Model the critical financial subsystems.
(d) are accounting oriented for the purpose of preparing nonmanagerial reporting data?	( )	( )	Integrate accounting and operating systems for mutual support.

Billing. Does the system:

	Yes	No	Cure
(a) maintain fast processing?	( )	( )	Automate billing with the objectives of fast turnaround time and optimum integration with related subsystems.
(b) improve cash flow?	( )	( )	
(c) keep customer goodwill?	( )	( )	
(d) keep salesmen informed?	( )	( )	
(e) provide input to other subsystems?	( )	( )	

Problem	Yes	No	Cure
General Ledger. Is it viewed only as a source of historical accounting information?	( )	( )	Put the computer to work to provide current information for analysis of performance and forecasting future conditions.

OPERATIONS/MANUFACTURING SYSTEMS

Problem	Yes	No	Cure
Have you taken a "total systems" approach to this system?	( )	( )	Design the operations system as the mainstream around which other systems integrate.

Is *order processing* resulting in:

Problem	Yes	No	Cure
(a) excessive errors and slowness due to clerical or edit steps?	( )	( )	Design the order processing as the central information stream, the *lifestream* activity.
(b) stockouts and backorders?	( )	( )	
(c) customer complaints?	( )	( )	
(d) production foul ups?	( )	( )	

Are the commonly accepted objectives being met in:

Problem	Yes	No	Cure
(a) materials planning?	( )	( )	Design these basic operations systems according to commonly accepted design principles.
(b) purchasing?	( )	( )	
(c) capacity planning?	( )	( )	
(d) operations scheduling?	( )	( )	

MARKETING SYSTEMS

Problem	Yes	No	Cure
Is the marketing function being managed largely by hunch and intuition?	( )	( )	Provide basic marketing information systems for planning, control, and market research.
Do you have the optimum customer/salesman/product mix?	( )	( )	Utilize basic sales analysis systems.
Do you have sufficient information on item and product line profitability to make good *inventory management* decisions?	( )	( )	Install standard inventory management reports for forecasting and control.

Problem	Yes	No	Cure

MANPOWER/PERSONNEL SYSTEMS

Is manpower management viewed as a records maintenance function rather than an essential job of managing the predominant cost of doing business?   ( ) ( )   Apply MIS techniques to the manpower management function.

how to improve decision making with the computer

7

"You don't know how you do it; you just do it."
"I don't think businessmen know how they make decisions. I know I don't."
"It is like asking a pro baseball player to define the swing that has always come natural to him."

—*Fortune*

The art of management has been defined as making irrevocable decisions based on incomplete, inaccurate, obsolete information. This tongue-in-cheek definition is about as useful as the above candid remarks about inability to analyze the process of decision making, as reported in *Fortune* magazine by some of America's most successful corporate chief executives. Business managers are by profession decision makers, yet for most of them the *process* of how they arrive at decisions is not well understood.

Despite the fact that decision making can be treated synonymously with managing, the literature and teaching surrounding decision making have generally focused on the *moment* of decision rather than on the whole lengthy, complex process of defining and exploring the many alternatives that precede the final act of deciding. For the systems analyst and for the manager who participates in or utilizes the management information system to aid in the decision-making *process,* the steps in problem solving and systems design are extremely important. Peter Drucker's comment that "over the next 20 years the emphasis in management will be on the understanding of decision making" reflects a growing need to formalize the process as a fundamental and necessary part of management and information systems design. And since information is the essential ingredient of management and decision making, the concept of the organization as an information flow process is growing as a basic tenet of management. Consider Norbert Wiener's comment: "Control is the art of decision and information is the measure of decision."

What has the computer to do with decision making? Professor Herbert Simon of Carnegie Tech, the current high priest of decision theory, views the computer as the fourth great breakthrough in history to aid man in his thinking process and decision-making ability. The first was the invention of writing, which gave man a memory in performing mental tasks. The remaining two events prior to the computer were the devising of the Arabic number system with its zero and positional notation, and the invention of analytic geometry and calculus, which permitted the solution of complex problems in scientific theory. Now the electronic digital computer combines the advantages and attributes of all these breakthroughs and makes them available for decision making and management of organizations.

We shall be concerned in this chapter with management information systems in their broad context, including the computer-based aspects in systems design, the use of management science techniques to improve programmed decision making, and the ways in which the problem-solving or decision-making approach to management can be vastly improved. The *information-decision* aspects of the MIS are emphasized in order to make the point clear that systems should be designed in light of (a) the decisions to be made throughout the organization, and (b) the managerial functions of planning, organizing, and control.

DECISIONS: THE OUTPUT OF MANAGEMENT INFORMATION SYSTEMS (MIS)

We have defined a management information system (MIS) as a communication process wherein information (input) is recorded, stored, and retrieved (processed) for decisions (output) regarding the managerial processes of planning, organizing, and controlling. If we now define decision making as the *process of selecting from among alternatives a course of action to achieve an objective,* the link between *information and decisions* becomes clear. Indeed, decision making and information processing, if not identical, are so interdependent that they become inseparable in practice. Therefore, considerations surrounding either information systems or decision making inevitably involve both topics. The magnitude of both is better appreciated when we consider that the output of all white-collar workers results ultimately in the end product of information for decisions.

What goes on inside the decision maker? What is the decision-making process, and what has it to do with information? These questions can be answered if we view the decision maker as the processor of management with inputs of information and outputs of decisions, as illustrated in Figure 7-1. Although the processor (decision maker) in this system is indescribably complex, we can understand something of the decision-making process if we consider briefly what goes on inside the decision maker. By reaching an understanding of this process, the manager can better design his information system for making both programmed and nonprogrammed decisions.*

---

*Technically, the information system (or computer component) cannot "make" a decision but it can compare data and follow instructions to the extent of its capacity. Thus the computer, when properly instructed (programmed), can compare inventory levels with a programmed decision rule such as economic order quantity (EOQ), print out a purchase order, and take several other actions previously performed by clerical decision.

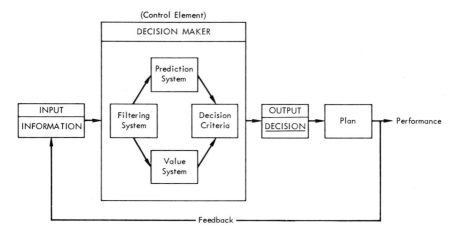

Figure 7-1   Management and the Decision-Making Process

The input to the decision maker of Figure 7-1 (and here we are describing a statistical decision maker) is information. The information goes into the predicting element, which yields a list of possible outcomes for each action and a probability associated with each outcome. The value element provides a second quantity associated with each outcome, the desirability. At this point we have (a) a list of possible courses of action, (b) a list of outcomes for each course, and (c) a probability and a desirability associated with each outcome. The decision maker then applies a decision criterion to obtain a recommended course of action or a *decision.* The manner in which the decision-making subsystem provides input to the management process is also sketched in Figure 7-1.

The foregoing operation of a decision-making process is directed to statistical decision making, where probabilities and desirabilities of various courses and outcomes must either be determined or estimated. In practice, although many managers may intuitively assign these probabilities, the decision is made with a nonprogrammed approach, as discussed later. For our purposes at this point it is important to become familiar with the *process,* the *approach,* and the *steps* in decision making. Despite the relative simplicity of the decision-making *process,* many managers continue to make snap judgments based on experience, intuition, or hunch.

It is interesting and important to note also that similarity between the processes of problem solving, planning, systems designing, and the scientific method. The steps in each are shown in Table 7-1. The basic and fundamental steps in each involve: (a) a clear definition of the problem and objective, (b) a weighing of alternative solutions based upon fact, and (c) the choice (decision) of an alternative based upon predetermined criteria for evaluating them.

Table 7-1

Steps in Decision Making and Related Processes

Problem Solving/ Decision Making	Scientific Method	Planning Process	Systems Design
Define the problem	Define the area of investigation	Define the objective	Analyze present system
Gather relevant facts	Develop a hypothesis	Develop planning premises	Develop model of present system
Define alternatives	Gather data	Define alternatives	Propose a new system
Weigh alternatives	Test hypothesis	Evaluate alternatives	Test new system
Choose best alternative	Reach conclusion	Choose best alternative	Install new system

The decision-making or problem-solving approach cannot be over-emphasized; it is fundamental to systems design. One view of business is that it consists of a collection of problems, and the raison d'etre of an information system is providing information to decision makers and problem solvers.

> The modern role of MIS for managerial decision making in a complex organization can be demonstrated by analogy with the military commander. For centuries, battles were fought with both sides deployed in full view of the opposing generals. Each positioned themselves on hilltops where they had direct and complete observation of the battlefield. In World War II, Rommel improved on this technique by racing from one front to another, remaining only long enough to plot current positions and plan local tactics. His total strategy was built by direct observation of partial situations. This is the style used by those managers who track operations by weekly communications with outlying sales offices, plants, divisions, and the like.

> The age we are moving into is like the SAGE Air Defense System where commanders have indirect, but total, observation and are able to manage their operation through a computer replica of the real world. So it is with the modern corporate executive.

ADVANCING THE BOUNDARIES OF MANAGEMENT DECISIONS

If the computer and MIS are to realize the potential claimed for them, it is clear that they must accomplish two essential tasks: (a) expand the frontier of applications, both in numbers and complexity, for which automated techniques are workable, and (b) improve and increase the applications and their usefulness in more areas of management concern and in higher levels of managerial decision making.

In Figure 7-2 four types of decisions are shown: programmed (automatic), semi-automatic, judgment, and unexplored. The programmed decisions of Type I are automatic in the sense that procedures or rules have been established for them. A major objective of MIS is to move the boundaries of this type of decision to the right. With the help and participation of managers, the systems approach combined with management science can devise decision rules and thereby delegate to computers the decision-making power that was once the prerogative of management.

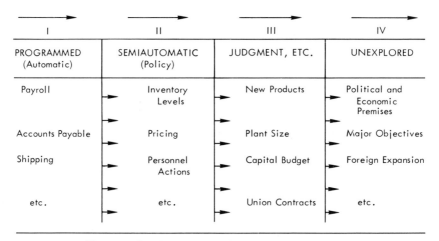

Figure 7-2   Boundaries of Management Decisions

The progress in moving those boundaries to the right has been slow. Computers and information systems thus far have been concerned largely with clerical applications. The proper design of computer-based management information systems can be the breakthrough that will move the boundaries to the right and program more and more of those decisions that now take so much time and effort.

THE FIRST STEP: UPGRADE EXISTING CLERICAL SYSTEMS

The first step to take in the utilization of the computer for improved decisions is to upgrade existing clerical systems. Although in a strict sense the clerical types of application are not oriented to decision making, it is entirely possible that they can be made to be so.

Most clerical applications are not advanced or sophisticated and are functionally similar to the punch card tabulating equipment that the larger EDP systems replaced. The great majority of small firms are just beginning to consider the use of EDP. Even in the largest firms the EDP applications are frequently and overwhelmingly of a clerical nature. One survey of applications by the 500 largest U.S. corporations showed the following relative frequency of application:

1. Inventory control
2. Payroll
3. Cost studies and reports
4. Production planning
5. Raw materials ordering
6. Parts ordering

The intention here is not to disparage the use of the computer for clerical applications. On the contrary, the clerical area offers immediate payoff in cost reduction as well as improvement of information. Moreover, much of the information furnished as output from clerical systems has decision-making applications at the supervisory level and elsewhere.

The illustrations in Figure 7-3 give insight into how some of the widespread clerical applications, normally used for administration and control,

ADMINISTRATION AND CONTROL		DECISION MAKING AND OPERATIONAL	
Application	Objective	Application	Objective
Ledger Accounting	Clerical Displacement and Control	Accounting	Cash Control Budget Control
Marketing Order Entry Billing	" "	Personnel Skills Inventory	Personnel Stability
Personnel Payroll	" "	Purchasing Replenishment Orders	Vendor/Buyer Relationship
Production Output Reporting	" "	Production	Cost Control
		Inventory	Optimize Inventory
Inventory Inventory Level	" "	Marketing	Customer Relations
		Distribution	Optimize Costs Customer Relations

Figure 7-3   Advances in Clerical EDP Applications

can be upgraded into decision making and operational applications. Notice particularly the transition from clerical operations to decision applications, which demonstrates how well the operations of the company are improved (e.g., customer relations, personnel stability, etc.).

The reader can make his own list of clerical reporting systems that are candidates for upgrading. Consider, for example, how sales reporting can be upgraded to sales analysis, inventory accounting to inventory management, and so on.

> One harried executive became unnerved with the continuing deluge of reports spewed out by the computer. He called a meeting of computer personnel and announced: "What I want [as he held up a matchbook cover] is a report that will fit on this! Then I can spend some time correcting the problem, not hunting for it through dozens of pages of data."

The potential payoff in upgrading existing systems can be demonstrated in the much neglected area of distribution. Although this is frequently considered to be a somewhat pedestrian system, the distribution function accounts for about 15 cents of each sales dollar in the average manufacturing company. Table 7-2 shows the potential for cost savings through better information upgrading.

Table 7-2

Potential Cost Savings With Better Information in the Distribution Function

Subfunction	*Savings*
Inventory	Pilferage loss Inventory turnover Investment in inventory Reduce obsolescence

Clerical	Reduction of paperwork
	Automation of order entry and
	    related systems (invoices,
	    order picking, bill of lading, etc.)
	Customer inquiry capability
	Credit check automation
	Leveling of workload

Freight	Reduce shipping dock delays Optimize shipments from alternative distribution points Minimize premium transportation Combine new orders and backorders
Warehousing	Reduce employees and equipment Improve order picking Automate weight calculation

PROGRAMMED AND NONPROGRAMMED DECISIONS

It is of the utmost importance to distinguish between two polar types of decisions: *programmed decisions* and *nonprogrammed decisions*. Naturally, these labels derive from the vocabulary of the computer trade where *program* is defined as a plan for the automatic solution of a problem.* Since few problems and decisions lend themselves totally to automatic solutions, we have few totally programmed decisions, and the labels assigned are not distinct types but a continuum from black to grey to white along a scale. However, the notion of programmed decisions becomes important for decision-making and information systems design because the major purpose of systems design is to program decisions for automatic solution, and failing this, to provide the optimum information to the decision maker who must solve the problem in a nonprogrammed fashion.

Decisions lend themselves to programming techniques if they are repetitive and routine and if a procedure can be worked out for handling them so that each is not an ad hoc decision or does not have to be treated as a new situation each time it arises. Naturally, the problems that lend themselves to programming are those that tend to be repetitive and occur frequently. Numerous examples of programmed decisions are available in almost any organization, the most familiar being the computation of pay in accordance with a union agreement, contract, company policy, regulation, etc. Hence the *program* or *decision rule* is contained in the agreement, contract, policy, or regulation. Other examples are pricing orders, credit checks, payment of accounts receivable, and those dozens of decisions made daily in accordance with company policy (decision rule).

Decisions are nonprogrammed to the extent that they are unstructured, new, of high consequence, involve major commitments, or are elusive or complex. Advertising budgets, new product decisions, acquisition and merger considerations, board member selection, and a host of other similar problems illustrate the nonprogrammed type of decision that cannot be automated.

Can we not say that the hypothetically ideal situation in an organization would be to have all decisions programmed? Without a decision rule to cover a situation, the manager must fall back upon the general problem-solving methodology, which depends so much on human judgment. The cost of solving the organization's problems in this manner is usually high, and solutions sometimes may be unsatisfactory. One of the goals then of

---

*Other definitions may include: a set of instructions or steps that tells the computer exactly how (a) to handle a complete problem, (b) to plan the method of attack for a defined problem, (c) to plan the whole operation from input to output and set the control section to handle it, etc.

MIS design is to devise decision rules for those problems that lend themselves to solution by decision rule and the programmed approach.

The major reason for distinguishing between these two types of decisions is to arrive at some classification of decision-making methods. This is done in Figure 7-4, which classifies two types of decisions, programmed and nonprogrammed, and two general approaches, old and new, to the techniques involved.

TYPE OF DECISION	METHODS OF DECISION MAKING	
	OLD	NEW
PROGRAMMED Repetitive and Routine	Habit Standard Operating Procedure Organization Structure Policy etc...	Management Information Systems (Includes Management Science Techniques and the Computer)
NONPROGRAMMED One-shot, Ill-structured	Judgment, Intuition, Insight Experience Training and Learning	Systematic Approach to Problem Solving & Decision Making

Figure 7-4   Methods of Decision Making

Making Programmed Decisions

The great majority of business decisions are repetitive and routine. One survey found that routine decisions comprise about 90% of management decisions. If this is true, then an overriding need exists to automate or *program* these decisions so that the executive can get on about his true task, the design and the plans for improved organizations and operations. If the manager's job is primarily that of decision making, he should get away from short-term tactics and routine, place these types of decisions in the programmed category, and have them made by one or more techniques of programmed decisions. To draw an analogy, there is no reason why we should not standardize information for mass production of programmed decisions in much the same way we do in standardization for production of products.

Some of the traditional ways of making programmed decisions are shown in Figure 7-4. The most general and most pervasive way is by force of habit. We go to the office, make decisions regarding the disposition of the "in" basket correspondence, and take dozens of actions daily that are "programmed" through force of habit. These habits and skills are valuable to the organization; one of the major costs in personnel turnover is involved in having new people acquire the habits of the organization and the job.

Following habit, the most prevalent technique for programming decisions is with the procedure—written, oral, or understood. Standard operating procedures provide a means for indoctrinating and training new personnel and for guiding old personnel in the performance of specific tasks. The procedure has the additional advantage of forcing a certain amount of detailed planning, because it cannot be adequately designed, reviewed, or implemented without careful thought. In a strict sense, the policy could not be classified as a programming technique because by definition it provides only a general guide to action. However, it becomes clear that the decision-making process in the organization is vastly improved by the establishment and communication of clearly understood policies.

Finally, the organizational structure and the manner in which it is documented and communicated become a technique of programming decisions. If the organization is charted, position descriptions written, and authority delegated, these programmed characteristics establish guidelines and expectations regarding decision-making levels and categories of problems to which various levels of persons should address themselves. The structure also determines information flow to some extent and otherwise reduces the time necessary for determining who is to make what decision. The organization provides the information system (manual or computer) and decision centers for decision making. The flow of information to decision authority centers is the lifeblood of the decision process.

MIS and Programmed Decisions

Future prospects for programming the decisions of the organization through the proper design of an MIS are enormous. If we include (as we will in this chapter) the *computer* and *management science* as integral parts or tools of computer-based information systems, the prospects for a revolution in programmed decision making are very real. Just as the manufacturing process is becoming more and more automated, so is the automation of programmed decisions to support this production and other information needs throughout the organization.

How will this revolution come about? What is there about management information systems that will program so many of our routine decisions? The answer lies in three basic considerations surrounding the design of an MIS:

1. The problem to be solved, the decision process to be programmed, or the process for which information is desired. The essential element in programming the decision is the *decision rule* (e.g., reorder if inventory declines below X level).

2. Management science. We shall take liberties with the term to the extent of including as subsystems: operations research, associated

mathematical tools, and the scientific approach to problem solving. Management science, thus defined, gives us the techniques to design the *decision rules.*

3. The computer is a fantastic device for processing information and "making" programmed decisions in accordance with predetermined decision rules.

Schematically, the management information system will operate as shown in Figure 7-5. The importance of this concept of making programmed decisions by management information systems cannot be overestimated. It is at the heart of good systems design.

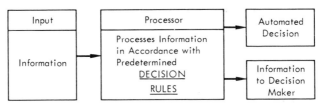

Figure 7-5 Making Programmed Decisions with a Management Information System

The programmed system is theoretically the ultimate in systems design and application because discretion is removed from the human decision maker and turned over to the information-decision system. In the "never-never land" of total systems, the complete automation of decisions will have been accomplished and the organization will remain in dynamic equilibrium by means of self-correction obtained by means of cybernetic feedback.*

Figure 7-6 illustrates schematically the notion of programmed information systems. The objective is to design the information in such a way that the computer automatically "makes" the decisions. This is accomplished with these steps:

1. Analyze the problem by means of the *management science* approach and design a *decision rule* that solves all applications.

2. Program the *decision rule* for the computer.

3. Design the input and output of the computer information system to provide for automatic decisions by the computer.

---

* In cybernetic terms we might call the organization "a homeostatic machine for regulating itself through feedback." Despite the fact that thousands of examples of this kind of control exist for mechanical systems (machines), economic systems (Keynesian theory), biological systems (human brain), etc., it is difficult to think of the company or the organization in these terms. Yet the fundamental design idea is the same.

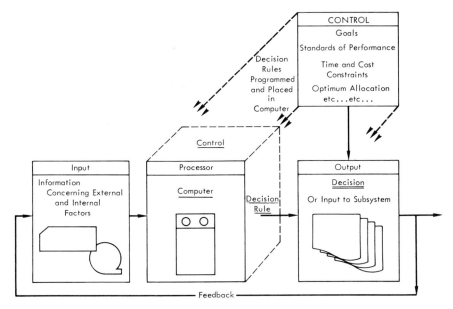

Figure 7-6   Automation of Decision Making—The Programmed Decision System

Note that under the decision rule concept of programmed decision systems (Figure 7-6), the control component of the information system now becomes a part of the processor (the computer), and the human judgment formerly required in control and decision making is now accomplished automatically by computations performed in the computer. This concept is essential for an understanding of how programmed decision systems are designed for computer-based information systems. A word of caution, however: in actual practice the complete removal of human intervention for management applications is unlikely due to the need to *periodically review the decision rule*. So in the sense that the decision rule is subject to change, for whatever reason, the system is not 100% programmed.

Figure 7-7 illustrates some programmed decision systems in manufacturing, planning, and control. From this illustration it can be seen that the systems that are totally programmed are, for the most part, somewhat primitive, consisting primarily of applications that automate the paperwork involved in clerical operations and output decisions formerly supervisory in nature and made by humans. Decisions regarding accounts receivable, payroll, inventory quantity determination, order placement, customer billing, shipping schedules, and a host of other decisions formerly programmed by standard operating procedure for manual processing lend themselves admirably to absorption in a programmed decision system.

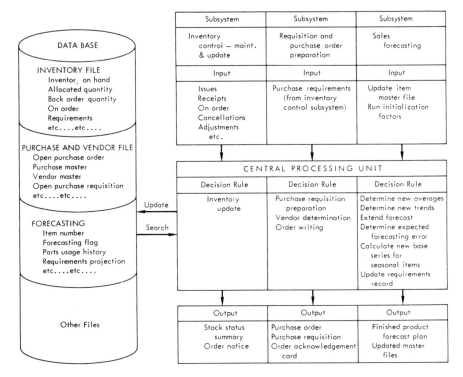

Figure 7-7   Examples of Programmed Decisions in Manufacturing Subsystems

Figure 7-8 illustrates a much more sophisticated distribution logistics model (sometimes called distribution management, physical distribution control, or rhochrematics) that, in its more advanced stage, treats the entire logistics of a business from sales forecast through purchase and processing of material and inventory to shipping of finished goods. The objectives of this system include the optimization of total costs while meeting established constraints such as capital cost and customer satisfaction.

From the model illustrated in Figure 7-8 it can be seen that the system is not only exceedingly complex but can be a fine instrument of planning and control. It shows the system as a group of subsystems that are integrated, interrelated, and connected in a total system of distribution. It goes without saying that such a system requires constant review to insure that the quantification of the inputs as well as the decision rules have been and remain correct. In this sense it is not truly a fully programmed system.

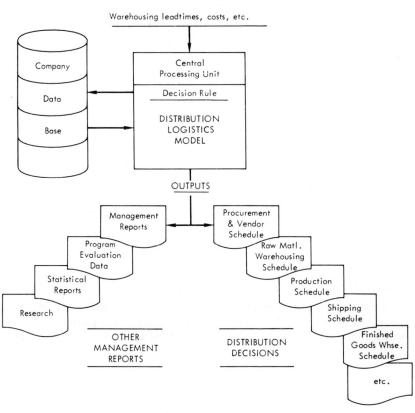

Figure 7-8   Programmed Distribution Logistics System

In practice, the totally programmed decision system is rare except for the clerical operations involved in paperwork. The expansion of the applications in the programmed area is unquestionably one of the most fruitful fields for research and offers the greatest payoff in the future for designing better information systems. Moreover, *and this is important,* the general lack of totally programmed systems for middle- and top-management use does not invalidate the approach. Indeed, the approach is vital because the management science techniques involved in the design of decision rules are fundamental and necessary for improving the *decision information systems* that promise to revolutionize management in the very near future.

A major caution to be observed in the programmed decision system is the time and expense of design and programming—costs that are constantly accelerating. Don't forget that when information is processed manually by humans, all kinds of exceptions can be accommodated as the work is done. The range of human decisions in performing simple tasks is much greater than the computer. For example, in a manual payroll system a clerk would not likely process a time card for the single employee who reported 160 hours of work in one week. It is not necessary to establish a decision rule for this procedure. But in programming a computer for the payroll application, unless the programmer builds in a decision rule saying, "Do not pay anything over 100 hours per week," the computer will simply process the transaction. But what happens if for some reason an employee works 101 hours in a week? The program says not to pay him. The moral is that it is expensive and time consuming to program decision rules for even the simplest application.

MIS and Nonprogrammed Decisions

System architects (and computer salesmen) originally envisioned the ultimate MIS as fully integrated with a large data base of information containing all the information that the company would ever want. Mathematical techniques would be used to provide simulations, forecasting models, decision trees, and the like as revolutionary aids to management decision making. The problem has been that management decisions aren't that easy, and more often than not the techniques have proved ineffective because the specific facts needed to make realistic models have not been available.

So the problem—and the potential—remains—how to furnish as much accurate information as you can to help the manager make the *nonprogrammed decision.* You might call the vehicle for doing this the *decision-assisting MIS.* It is characterized by the fact that it concentrates on the information required by the manager as a decision maker to distinguish it from the programmed application where the computer "makes" the decision. The information may be furnished to the manager independently (as in output reports) or in an interactive sense where there is a man-machine relationship in a problem-solving network. Figure 7-9 demonstrates conceptually how the integrated MIS could provide both programmed decision outputs and *decision-assisting* information. Notice that in this illustration:

1. Some outputs are decisions; the computer has "made" a decision in accordance with a *programmed decision* rule. (The shipment routing order.)
2. Some outputs are secondary information in the form of reports to be used by a subsequent human decision maker. (Variance analysis.)
3. There are provisions for man-machine type interactions in the sense that the manager/decision maker can "model" his decisions prior to commitment.
4. *Optimum* solutions are provided by management science decision rules.

Simulation Models

A special case of the *decision-assisting* application is the simulation model. Here are some examples:

Arkwright-Boston Insurance Company builds fires on the computer. Mathematical models of plants are constructed and by varying the air flow and the ignition and the construction of the building, they are able to forecast how bad a fire would be under varying circumstances. This information is used for setting rates and fire protection policy.

American Airlines (the same people whose modeling flair brought us SABRE, the first successful on-line reservation system) has its AAIMS—An Analytical Information Management System whose primary use is as an analytical tool that easily and rapidly generates reports and/or plots. A typical "what if" question might be: "What if the overhead can be reduced from 120% to 115%? What will happen to pretax profit?"

Executives of a large utility gather in the "command control center" to model their decisions on a time-sharing terminal. The president comments, "The greatest advantage of this type of system is the fact that the data can be obtained and mistakes made without the need to commit expensive manpower and equipment."

Contrary to public opinion, a model doesn't have to represent the economy or the entire firm to be useful. These simulations are somewhat spectacular but in general are too expensive for the average company. What is needed are models that are simple and represent routine activities that have widespread application to many decision makers. Indeed, from

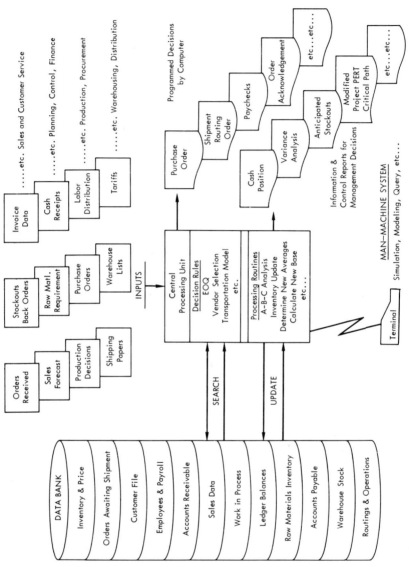

Figure 7-9   Integrated Manufacturing Information System

a cost/benefit standpoint, the best applications may result from providing assistance to employees making many routine and relatively low-level decisions.

Here is a list of suggested application programs and analytical routines that are inexpensive and relatively easy to implement:

Asset payback schedule.
Direct-indirect labor cost by job.
Product break-even analysis.
Job-costing analysis.
Depreciation schedule.
Installment note payment schedule.
Financial statement ratios.
Forecasting trends.
Accounts receivable analysis.
Cash flow analysis.
Security portfolio analysis.
Inventory valuation.
Inventory turnover analysis.
Personal financial planning.
Time series analysis.
Statistical analysis.
Graphic analysis.

MANAGEMENT SCIENCE AS A TOOL FOR INFORMATION SYSTEMS DESIGN

The ordinary manager, unless he has received a graduate degree in business administratior within the last five years, is likely to view the management science approach to running a business with either alarm or suspicion. This is understandable, because it has been only during the last half of the 1960s that the techniques and approaches advanced by management science have had any wide degree of acceptance. The prediction must follow that the coming decade in the management sciences is going to witness even more rapid and exciting progress than the decade just past.

The Approach of Management Science

Let us remove some of the fear of the label *management science* by defining the term and its use in the context of designing decision rules for management information systems. Most managers equate the term with operations research and the quantitative techniques related to this term. This is generally acceptable because operations research and management science are really two names for the same thing: the science of decision and its application. Many management scientists would include *cybernetics,* the science of control systems, as integral to the toolbox of theories, principles, and techniques applicable to management science. However, for our purposes, the term *management science* has a broader meaning, one that the practicing manager will find easier to grasp. First, we are concerned with the scientific approach to the definition and solution of management problems. This may or may not require quantitative techniques, but it does require the gathering of data concerning alternatives in a problem and the utilization of decision making as a central approach to its solution. Second, management science does include the mathematical tools of operations research but is much broader in concept. Herbert Simon recently summarized what management science was about when he wrote: "Gathering empirical data about behavior in organizations, building and testing theories in collaboration with the other behavioral sciences, using decision making as a control concept for organizing the analysis, employing quantitative and mathematical techniques . . . are the warp and weft of the increasingly successful endeavor to create a genuine science of management, and an art based on that science."

The bench marks of the approach and the progress to management science are:

1. *Empirical Data.* The conceptual and analytical approach to management and management problems based on *facts,* not personal experience or unchecked individual observations as has been the case in the past when we have developed management principles or undertaken the solution of problems.

2. *Theories.* The construction of sets of propositions or principles that describe, explain, and predict the complex interrelationships among elements of systems. Contrast this to the recent situation when management theory consisted largely of a set of unrelated principles that attempted to formalize organizational structure with no regard for the human element.

3. *Decision Making.* Management science is characterized by the constant demand for a decision-making point of view in the approach to all aspects of the managers' jobs. This, of course, is overwhelmingly the case in the considerations surrounding management information systems.

4. *Quantitative Tools.* Progress in the development of a management theory and progress in improved management decisions in practice are inextricably interwoven with the quantitative techniques of observation,

experiment, and decision making. These techniques should not frighten the manager into an avoidance of their use. The housewife does not understand the workings of the "program" of her washing machine and the manager does not understand the firing order of the pistons in his car. Lack of understanding is no bar to the use of quantitative techniques in business. Today management frequently makes use of simulation, linear programming, and a variety of other tools without the need to understand how they work.

To repeat, our major concerns with management science, as this approach affects the design of management information systems, are (a) the need to adopt the structured, scientific, decision-making approach to problem solving, and (b) the need to utilize the quantitative tools of management science. Both of the needs are for the purpose of designing information systems for *problem solving* and for designing *decision rules* for making programmed decisions. Enough has been said of the scientific approach to problem solving. Let us turn our attention to decision rules designed by the use of the quantitative methods of management science.

A Management Science Decision Model

At the certain risk of oversimplifying the use of quantitative techniques in management science solutions to decision problems, a general model will be described for purposes of orientation only. However, since we are concerned with a general familiarization with the topic, perhaps the general model will suffice. It is shown in Figure 7-10.

The manager's decision problem usually involves the selection of the one alternative he can use from among all the alternatives he is considering. In management science problems, the number of alternatives is usually very large, and the problem is usually, but by no means always, the selection of the alternative that *optimizes* the goal (e.g., minimizes inventory cost, optimizes sales, maximizes profit, etc.).

The alternatives in the problem are represented as A, B, C, etc., in Figure 7-10 and the problem is to choose the one that best represents our goal. Notice that the alternatives are controllable (the decision maker can choose any one he wishes) and are dependent variables because the value each takes depends on the values of the other variables in the system. Hence, the farmer can plant wheat, corn, cotton, or barley (his alternatives), and his choice is *controllable* but *dependent* upon the values assigned to the other variables. Typical managerial problems include those involved with inventory levels, production scheduling, lot sizes, assignment of salesmen, and a host of related problems.

The *independent* variables in the system consist of those factors that are *internal* to the firm and therefore *controllable,* and those that are *external* to the firm and *noncontrollable.* The internal factors represent those resources and decisions internal to the firm and therefore controllable by the decision maker. His decision will consist of the selection of the use of one or a combination of these resources. The farmer has a fixed amount of land, equipment, and capital. From these determinants, he may be able to control other variables such as seed and fertilizer application or yield per acre. In addition to the specific assignment and utilization of the resources of the firm (personnel, capital, equipment, inventory, organization, etc.), other internal variables over which the manager may have control include pricing, advertising, research, product mix, maintenance, output, scheduling, and other internal factors affecting the achievement of most objectives.

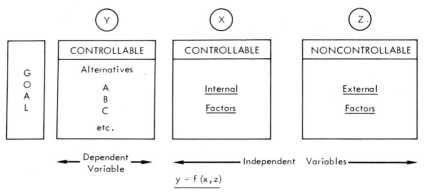

Figure 7-10   A General Model of the Management Science Solution to Decision Problems

The decision maker has no control over *external* factors, the vagaries and intransigence of society and nature and the competitive decisions and actions of his rational opponents. Thus, the farmer cannot control the weather nor the decisions of his competitors, which affect the price of the product. The manager's decision to capture a larger market share by reducing price may be frustrated by his competitors' actions, factors over which he has no control.

We can now write a mathematical description of the relationship between these variables: $y = f(x, z)$. Thus y is our goal (usually the "optimum" alternative), and if we can assign values to x and z, the equation can be solved, or to say it another way, a decision can be made. *An important point*—if the equation defies quantification, it is still useful because important information is conveyed by the equation itself. To illustrate, we can say that a salesman's effectiveness is a function of his education, his time with the company, his age, his base salary, and the per capita income of his territory. Although this model lacks quantification, it provides a systems view of the relations, an important byproduct of management science and the approach to be taken in problem solving and the design of management information systems for making programmed decisions.

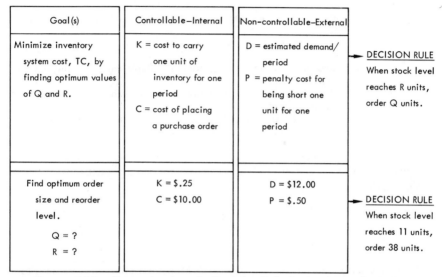

Goal (s)	Controllable–Internal	Non–controllable–External	
Minimize inventory system cost, TC, by finding optimum values of Q and R.	K = cost to carry one unit of inventory for one period C = cost of placing a purchase order	D = estimated demand/ period P = penalty cost for being short one unit for one period	DECISION RULE When stock level reaches R units, order Q units.
Find optimum order size and reorder level. Q = ? R = ?	K = $.25 C = $10.00	D = $12.00 P = $.50	DECISION RULE When stock level reaches 11 units, order 38 units.

Figure 7-11   Determination of a Decision Rule for Inventory Control

Figure 7-11 illustrates a situation involving decisions that can be solved with the management science model. More important, a *decision rule* is determined, a decision rule that can be programmed for computer use so that the computer can "make" the reorder decision. Two very important considerations should not be overlooked in using the quantitative techniques related to this approach. First, the external factors are noncontrollable by the decision maker, hence the *values assigned to these variables must be estimated,* predicted, or forecast by the decision maker. For example, the estimated annual demand ($D = 16$ units) in the economic lot size problem of Figure 7-11 must be estimated. The techniques of probability and statistics are available for assisting the decision maker to predict the values of the *noncontrollable, external factors.* A second important consideration involves the assignment of values and relationships between the controllable internal factors, particularly cost, price, and volume relationships. In many cases, the accounting system doesn't yield this kind of information, and care should be taken to determine actual (not necessarily accounting) costs, the allocations of these costs, and the relationships between them. Finally, the restrictions that limit the value of internal factors must be stated. There is no reason, for example, to solve our economic lot size problem of Figure 7-11 for values that exceed the capacity of our warehouse, because this capacity is a constraint or restriction on the variable involved.

The operations involved in this sequence of the management science approach can be summarized:

1. Define the goal and specify its dimension and value (usually to optimize).
2. Define and develop the relationships between the independent variables.
3. Distinguish controllable from noncontrollable variables and develop predictions or forecasts of the values.
4. Develop the functions (equations) relating the independent and dependent variables.
5. State the restrictions that limit the values of the variables that provide the best alternative or optimize the goal.

Table 7-3 identifies some of the techniques available to assist the manager-user, as well as the systems designer, in making decisions and designing decision rules.

Table 7-3
Basic and Advanced Techniques for Decision Making

Basic	Advanced
Economic and Financial Analysis	Maximum-Minimum Value Problems (e.g., inventory control, warehousing)
Cash flow analysis	
Breakeven analysis	
Capital budgeting analysis	Monte Carlo models
Ratio analysis	Decision trees
Marginal analysis	Queuing models
Incremental analysis	
Return on investment analysis	Optimization Problems (Resource allocation and sequencing)
Forecasting	
Trend extrapolation	Linear programming
Correlation analysis	Dynamic programming
Regression analysis	Transportation methods
Input-output matrices	Assignment methods
Exponential smoothing	
Probability distribution	Cost Benefit Analysis
	Systems simulation
Project Planning, Scheduling, and Control	Systems analysis
PERT/CPM and PERT/Cost	Program budgeting
Line-of-balance charts	
Gantt charts	
Network analysis	

EVALUATE THE DECISION POTENTIAL
OF YOUR MIS

	Yes	No
Is your MIS designed:		
(a) for decisions?	( )	( )
(b) for planning and control?	( )	( )
(c) for selection of alternatives?	( )	( )
(d) in light of decisions to be made throughout the organization?	( )	( )
Do you view decision making as a process?		
Problem defined?	( )	( )
Relevant facts gathered?	( )	( )
Alternatives defined?	( )	( )
Alternatives evaluated?	( )	( )
Best alternative selected?	( )	( )
Are you advancing the boundaries of:		
(a) existing MIS applications to higher-level decisions?	( )	( )
(b) judgment decisions to semi-automatic?	( )	( )
(c) semi-automatic decisions to programmed?	( )	( )
Have you upgraded *clerical* systems to *decision* systems?		
Accounting	( )	( )
Order entry	( )	( )
Billing	( )	( )
Personnel	( )	( )
Production reporting	( )	( )
Inventory	( )	( )
Program planning and control	( )	( )
Other	( )	( )
Have you programmed major clerical applications?		
Sales forecasting	( )	( )
Production planning and control	( )	( )
Purchasing	( )	( )
Inventory	( )	( )
Shipping	( )	( )
Sales analysis	( )	( )
Shop floor control	( )	( )
Project planning and control	( )	( )
Variance analysis	( )	( )
Other	( )	( )

	Yes	No
Do your nonprogrammed applications provide *decision-assisting* information?		
Problem solving routines	( )	( )
Analytical routines	( )	( )
Applications programs	( )	( )
Models/simulations	( )	( )
Are you utilizing the *management science* approach:		
(a) for designing decision rules?	( )	( )
(b) for constructing decision models?	( )	( )
(c) for utilizing management science techniques?	( )	( )

the economics of MIS

8

"I am strongly opposed to the notion that the mere accumulation of information in computer files should be treated as having some general economic value apart from the specific uses to which the information may be put. The aimless accumulation of marginally useful information, in fact, strikes me as being one of the more serious economic problems associated with the computer age."

—Vice-President, MIS
Major Automobile Manufacturer

It is estimated that up to 90% of the work involved in most white-collar jobs involves the seeking and obtaining of information. This applies in the technical functions of accounting, marketing, finance, production, and engineering operations as well as in the general management processes. If we think of 90% of man-hours and salaries going into information processing, it is easy to see why managers seek improvements in the design and application of information systems and how the automation of this information becomes important.

The impact of information costs is enormous. Over ten years ago, Adrian McDonough estimated in his book, *Information Economics and Management Systems,* that 10 million individuals are directly concerned with the production and processing of information and that at least 50% of the cost of running our economy is information costs. In the mid-seventies, the data-processing and data communications industries alone split about $60 billion in annual revenue, and this amount is increasing at about $7 billion per year.

Despite the accelerating impact of *information* on the operation of our economy, the *management* of this resource is an embryonic discipline at best. This lack of maturity can be attributed to two major reasons.

First, *the management of information systems* is not a structured discipline (or art, or science) such as we have developed over the years in the technical managerial functions of industrial engineering, accounting, marketing, or finance, or in the general management functions such as planning, organizing, or controlling. Although white-collar, or information-handling, workers now outnumber blue-collar, or production, workers, the industrial engineering approach that we have historically taken to manufacturing or shop operations has not yet been taken to office work or to the general problem of information handling. What Frederick Taylor did for industrial operations in his *scientific management* approach to shopwork, we now need to do for the information systems function.

188

The second basic reason for the failure to develop a discipline of MIS management is the *lack of managerial involvement*. It is commonplace for the ablest and toughest managers to demand greater productivity from plant managers and shop foremen, lay it on the sales force for increased quotas, make cuts in the staffs of purchasing departments, and involve the entire organization in a cost reduction program. Yet when these same managers are faced with productivity in the data center or related operations, they stumble to a halt, baffled by the jargon of the technician and the uncertainties of their own MIS knowledge. Their frequent comment is something like this: "I just can't get a handle on that operation."

THE PROBLEM OF INFORMATION VALUATION

What is information worth? One authority suggested that an inch of computer printout is worth about $75 if you take into account all of the input that is involved. Therefore, if your office has 10 feet or more of printout that is unusable, a small fortune is going down the drain. However, cost is not necessarily representative of utility.

At one time, in the "pre-MIS" days when the accountant prepared most reports, he viewed the objective of his activity as the preparation of "true and fair" reports. Today, it is widely realized that reports are of little value for their own sake but are part of a larger *managerial process* and must therefore be evaluated not merely on the basis of truth, but more importantly on the basis of the report's potential use in improving management and the decision-making process. In other words, it must contribute to the objectives of the enterprise. But the problem remains; how to measure this contribution and how to put a value on the information contained in the existing or proposed MIS.

In normal business practice the evaluation of proposed computer-based information systems usually takes one or a combination of these three forms:

Cost-Justification. This approach requires that all projects be justified by auditable cost savings. The idea is that the expected value of the proposed change will exceed its expected cost and that the particular change proposed will provide the highest expected increase in value. The problem with this method is that the development of evaluation techniques has been very limited and it has been almost impossible to accurately estimate the costs of the project at the outset. Widespread experience has shown this to be so, although the variance between actual and estimated costs declines with experience drawn from similar systems.

Payback or Return-on-Investment (ROI). This has been the most widely used approach, and it involves the application of capital investment analysis techniques to a proposed project. Since it causes MIS proposals to be compared with other alternatives in competition for financial resources, those companies that have used this approach generally have concluded that they were able to "afford" their expenditures for computer-based systems. It has the additional advantage of preventing commitment to a grandiose or infeasible project that can't be justified on a pay-off basis.

Despite the widespread use of the ROI method of valuation, it has two important drawbacks. First, it is based on the assumption that both costs and benefits of an MIS project are known and are subject to quantification at the outset. We know that this quantification is very difficult and impractical except in limited cases such as clerical savings. The second drawback is the basic assumption of the ROI method itself that cost savings should be used to set priorities for computer-based projects. This assumption may lead the manager away from the mainstream of the business into less important issues that, on the surface, appear to be more important. For example, the information needs of production, marketing, inventory, and finance may be rated as secondary, because the cost-savings measures of ROI will always bias priorities toward the clerical savings available from an accounting system.

The lesson to be remembered is that the quantification fallacies of the capital investment approach may lead to a misallocation of time and money because the approach leads to a false sense of security and good management. In reality, the mainstream of the business and the related information that is valued by other measures can be more important than the variables in the ROI analysis.

Intangible Value. This approach places the emphasis on *qualitative* measurement. It assumes that senior management is well-equipped by training and experience to deal with qualitative variables, because this is what senior management does every day.

> Each year every major Ford Motor Company activity (division or major affiliate) develops a detailed systems plan covering the current year and the three years ahead. The review of these plans is accomplished at a meeting held with the top management of that activity, along with key staff managers and the executive director of the corporate systems office. This director reports on the qualitative aspects of proposed plans: "Both in this systems review process and also in the justification of individual systems projects, we provide for full consideration of 'intangible benefits' as well as direct financial savings. Some of our larger systems, in fact, have been justified primarily on the basis of their intangible value."

A PROPOSED APPROACH: COST/BENEFIT ASSESSMENT

Notwithstanding the difficulty of arriving at a conclusion based on measurable alternatives regarding project selection and information valuation, some method of assessing proposed information systems projects is necessary. The process described here represents a synthesis of available techniques and attempts to arrive at the best method for project selection. We are essentially concerned with the balance between costs and benefits. Conceptually, the approach can be shown in Figure 8-1.

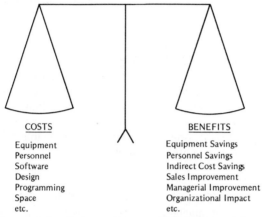

COSTS	BENEFITS
Equipment	Equipment Savings
Personnel	Personnel Savings
Software	Indirect Cost Savings
Design	Sales Improvement
Programming	Managerial Improvement
Space	Organizational Impact
etc.	etc.

Figure 8-1   Balance Between MIS Costs and Benefits

Costs

For most MIS projects, it becomes extremely difficult to estimate the costs prior to commencing the work. Nevertheless, some estimate must be made at the outset. After work has commenced, careful tracking of costs during the different stages of development will add further refinement.

Three approaches can be used. These are listed in ascending order of detail and difficulty:

The Preliminary Estimate. This somewhat cursory analysis can be used for initial estimates but can vary as much as 40–50% upon subsequent refinements in system scope (what it is supposed to do), design specifications, and priority resolutions. These refinements cannot usually be determined until system trade-offs are discussed at a secondary stage of development. Thus, for many projects, development may have advanced as much as 25% in both time and dollars before a firm estimate is available.

Estimate Based on Key Milestones. This involves the identification of specifications and the major milestones in the project development in rather specific terms regarding the results expected at each milestone. Then the cost estimates can be developed for the milestones and the total project.

Estimate Based on a Project Schedule. This involes the detailed development and layout of the work breakdown structure and accompanying detailed timetable for the completion of each task in the project. Although this provides a better estimate and a subsequent control document for project planning and monitoring, the costs of estimating are high.

Assessing Benefits

The following framework for assessing benefits is a general one; specific organizations may want to modify it to suit their own particular needs. However, it covers most cases. This framework (Figure 8-1) is arranged in descending order of *ease of quantification* but note that, in general, it is in ascending order of *importance,* lending further credence to the notion that top management's assessment of qualitative intangible factors may be more important than a purely quantitative approach to cost/benefit analysis.

Equipment Savings. The value of equipment that will be displaced by the system. Accounting machines, calculators, and slower, more costly computer equipment would be included.

Personnel Savings. The value of direct cost displacement resulting from savings in personnel replaced by the system. These savings are usually calculated in the clerical areas but could include report preparation, analytical computation, and work performed by middle management and staff personnel. It should be remembered that this type of benefit does not normally improve operations or have a significant effect on changing the mainstream of major company functions.

Indirect Cost Savings. Those profit improvements resulting from the proposed information system's capability to collect, store, and retrieve information better. Production planning and control, inventory management, distribution, purchasing, and accounts receivable are a few of the many subsystems that have impact on the profit and loss statement and that could achieve cost savings through MIS improvements.

Improvement in Sales. In addition to the traditional areas of sales planning and control, the information system can maintain and enhance sales by providing market intelligence such as sales analysis and market research. Additionally, feedback on the performance of the sales effort and the adequacy of product/market strategy is desired. Finally, there are a growing number of applications that are a direct part of the sales effort. Examples include the airline reservation systems and the many customer inquiry systems now in use.

Managerial Improvement. Computers can not only relieve managers from the time-consuming task of calculating and recording, but more importantly, can provide them with superior tools for planning and control. This is accomplished in three ways. First, the MIS, through more rapid dissemination of information and the utilization of planning models, can shorten the time required for developing a plan and can also provide many more alternatives for decisions regarding the development of a plan. Second, the MIS can provide reports and data bases to give managers a deeper insight into the critical variables of the business. Examples include sales reports, cost analyses, and the variety of "as required" studies that would not be available without the computer and supporting software. Third, the MIS can do all this with greater rapidity and accuracy than the manual system.

The assessment of these benefits is extremely hard to quantify. Consider these questions:

> What is it worth to reduce the information overload of the manual system and to provide a repository for information (that may be forgotten)?

> What is the increased value of information that is retrievable upon request, perhaps on an interactive basis?

> Is it worth the cost to collect and store information that may be useful in making some unspecified decision in the future?

> How much are profits improved by designing the MIS to provide information that may make the decision maker aware of alternative actions?

Organizational Impact. This final benefit refers to the change in organizational character, *the managerial climate,* resulting from implementation of computer-based information systems. Things have changed from the old days when a company bought a computer because the competition did it or because it was simply the thing to do.

In some ways, the impact of the computer is an organizational dichotomy. On one hand, the *programming* or routinization provided by the machine insures discipline and adherence to policies and procedures regarding information flow. It also provides a greater degree of organizational flexibility than the manual system, because the latter left the company somewhat at the mercy of those individuals who operated the system. On the other hand, the very discipline and structure of the computer system sometimes discourages change, innovation, and the flexibility to handle the exception. Moreover, the unyielding structure of the computer system sometimes has a dehumanizing effect on personnel, and there may be an occasional negative human motivational fallout.

On balance, the impact of the computer is a positive one *provided* managers become involved in systems design and *provided* these systems are viewed as management, not clerical, tools. Not only do many benefits accrue from MIS, once these are implemented, but the *process* of analysis and design leading up to implementation provides new insights and improvements in the management of the organization. In short, the examination and improvement of the *management system* can sometimes be as beneficial as the implementation of the *information system*.

CONTROLLING COSTS

If the typical manager took the time to conduct a survey of the reports he receives, he would be astonished at the large number of them and rather embarrassed at the small number that are of use in controlling his operation. If he were then asked the question, "Do you have a report or an information problem?" his answer would very likely be "Yes, I certainly do!" Most of us would conclude:

> We get *too many* reports.
>
> We get *too much data* and not enough information.
>
> We get *too little* of the information needed.
>
> We get the information *too late*.
>
> We pay *too much* for the information.

> There is an actual case on record of the bank employee (fired but not jailed) who transferred to his wife's account $100 from each of 41 different individuals' accounts. He knew that although this would be printed out in the daily exception report it would be ignored because of the sheer size of the report.

Control of MIS costs is a two part problem—controlling new or planned projects and controlling the costs of existing systems.

The secret to control of *new projects* or major modifications is heavy user involvement. Things should be set up organizationally so that the EDP manager, in the development process, establishes points where the user must "buy off" on major steps in the project. As a minimum, these steps should include: (a) the statement of the problem or system objectives, (b) the benefits to be derived from the system, (c) a preliminary plan, followed by, (d) a detailed design plan.

This preliminary plan will establish checkpoints to be approved by the user before the detailed plan is authorized. This responsibility on the part of the user can and should extend to accountability for both the results as well as the costs of the system. Project milestones can be spaced closely enough in terms of both time and effort so that minimum money is expended between them. This approach is sometimes called "the inchworm budget." When projects are finished, they may be audited by the financial area to see that they achieved their original objectives within estimated cost constraints. The whole idea is to avoid leaving the entire process of cost estimation, design, and implementation in the hands of the EDP manager.

In some respects, controlling the costs and growth of *existing* systems is more difficult than new projects. There is a natural tendency for reports to grow and expand, both in terms of numbers and volume of data. *More information is not necessarily good, but good information is necessary.* Unfortunately, many managers want everything in the computer but can't possibly use it.

> Probably the most frequent complaint of the EDP manager (after the lack of user involvement) is the one associated with changing people in jobs. Consider that the average job has had four incumbents since the original MIS was designed. The original incumbent, *A,* established the information needs for the original system. Upon his replacement by *B,* nothing was eliminated but new information needs were added. Later, when *C* filled the job position, he couldn't understand what *A* and *B* wanted with all that information, but he was afraid to eliminate it because he concluded that if *A* and *B* needed it, then he must need it too. *C* added additional information of his own. By the time that *D* comes along and fills the job, he won't be using much of the information he's getting, but you can never drive the scope of the system back down to *B* or *A*.

Controlling these expanding costs is very difficult because of the natural reluctance of people to give up information and the inability to get a handle on the cost/benefit equation of a system. Three approaches are currently being used: the systems review, organizational innovations, and transfer pricing of EDP services. The latter approach makes a profit center of EDP.

Most companies have a *periodic review* of existing systems during which they challenge the information needs of users. Frequency, scope, and design of MIS outputs and reports are reviewed to determine whether cost reductions can be made. In most cases, this review is considered to be "just another report" and results are disappointing.

A second technique involves *organizational separation* of systems designers from those who operate the computer center. The EDP manager can be instructed not to take anything operational until it is fully documented and debugged. This will reduce the natural tendency of computer center personnel to "print everything in the computer." These people sometimes view their performance in terms of volume of printout or the number of shifts for which the machine is used rather than the real value of the output.

The third approach, and one that seems to be growing, involves making a *profit center* out of EDP.

EDP as a Profit Center?

Many managers, frustrated at the difficulty of controlling costs, believe that good management principles should be used in running the computer end of MIS. They believe that the function lends itself to the same principles that a production manager applies in the factory. The basic idea is that MIS operations, normally a *cost center,* should be converted into a profit center by the introduction of transfer prices; essentially the user would be charged for the services by means of a charge-back policy. In principle, this would change the manager's objective from one of constrained cost minimization to a less constrained objective of profit maximization. If the user has to justify his MIS charges in his budget, he is unlikely to request services that cannot be justified on a cost/benefit basis.

The advantages and disadvantages of transfer pricing (charge-back) can be summarized:

Advantages	*Disadvantages*
Reduces nonessential and unjustifiable work requests.	Major systems expenditures cannot be justified because they require significant cooperation among many users (e.g., hardware, data banks, etc.).
Improves allocation of EDP costs on cost/benefit basis.	
Provides evaluation standard for both EDP and user operations.	
Encourages quantitative evaluation of MIS needs.	Transfer prices are difficult to establish fairly and may therefore fail to attain objectives.
Provides quantitative justification for additional computer resources.	
Helps control use of MIS resources.	

On balance, it appears that the advantages outweigh the disadvantages. The number of companies that are establishing EDP operations as a profit center are growing.

Two executives who do use transfer pricing are James A. Mages, director, MIS Department of Jones & Laughlin Steel and Herbert H. Blevins, vice-president, management information systems of Merck & Company. Here's what they say:

Mages: "We bill every department for our data processing services. Each has to budget for this expense and they have to justify their budget to their own management. They also have to justify any variance from budget. We bill most of our service to requesting departments at a standard hourly rate."

Blevins: "We have a different philosophy on this than any other company I know of. The MIS department has no responsibility for input. If a manager wants us to do a job for him, he supplies us with the cards and tapes. We run our computers strictly as a service—like a fast adding machine."

MANAGING MIS OPERATIONS

Alvin Toffler, in his book, *Future Shock,* warns of the dangers of irresponsibly-used technology and concludes, "The horrifying truth is that, so far as technology is concerned, no one is in charge." This conclusion is partially wrong, at least as far as computers and MIS are concerned, because the computer technicians are in charge. And therein lies a major problem in the management of MIS operations. Despite the rate of change in computer technology and the above-average difficulty of controlling operations, there is accelerating evidence that a well-managed EDP center can meet its commitments. The fundamentals of good management and supervision apply and are badly needed. Indeed, given the somewhat emergent nature of EDP operations, it is clear that somewhat better than average management is required.

We have not had management this good in the past. The technicians, egged on by the computer manufacturers, have dreamed up widening and more esoteric applications in order to build empires and improve power structures. And the manufacturers have one overriding motivation—sell more hardware.

Too many MIS operations are devoted to housekeeping functions and the design of clerical reporting systems rather than decision systems for management use. One executive was shocked to learn that his company's large computer was processing transactions only 6% of the available time. The rest was occupied by housekeeping functions, reruns, program development, and just plain waiting. One recent study indicates that 40–60% of every EDP staff dollar is devoted to maintenance of existing programs. Another study concluded that more than a 30% increase in productivity could result from additional management attention.

If better management will help, what are the areas to plan and control? Fundamentally, there are three: schedule, cost, and system performance. These may be somewhat different for the new project than for the existing operations but should include the basics shown below.

New Project	*Existing Operations*

Schedule

| Project document that shows when development starts and finishes with milestones for user sign-off as project unfolds. | Measures for meeting user deadlines.

Measures for quick response to user needs. |
| --- | --- |

Cost

| Report actual expenditures against those planned for each milestone.

Upon job completion, report on original estimate versus actual expenditures.

Set cost consciousness climate. | Set budget performance measurement.

Set standards of performance in major operational areas and provide cost control against these.

Set cost consciousness climate. |
| --- | --- |

Performance

| Project document that provides clear-cut statement of system objectives, purposes, improvements, and how overall company goals are enhanced.

Use specific performance yardsticks to measure or estimate before and after results of proposed system. | Provide cost/benefit analysis for new and existing operations.

Provide periodic appraisal of system results.

Check whether systems are meeting established objectives.

Check whether performance measures are achieved. |
| --- | --- |

CHECKLIST FOR MANAGING MIS

DO YOU HAVE THESE PROBLEMS?

	Yes	No
Do you feel that the information you are getting is not worth the cost?	( )	( )
Do you lack a formal approach to the evaluation and selection of MIS projects?	( )	( )
Do you feel you are getting too much data at the wrong time and at too much cost?	( )	( )

Are you having "overruns" on your MIS projects?

	Yes	No
Time	( )	( )
Cost	( )	( )
Performance	( )	( )

Are you experiencing any of these problems in the operation of the EDP center:

	Yes	No
Delays in getting work completed?	( )	( )
High level of job reruns?	( )	( )
Frequent overtime?	( )	( )
High personnel turnover?	( )	( )
High level of hardware failure?	( )	( )
Lack of planning and control?	( )	( )
Frequent requests for more resources?	( )	( )
Lack of orderliness in plant, procedures, or work flow?	( )	( )

Five or more YES answers suggest that significant improvement is needed.

HAVE YOU TRIED THESE CURES?

	Yes	No
Have you insisted on user involvement in MIS?	( )	( )
Do you have a cost/benefit assessment system for new and existing projects?	( )	( )
Do you estimate and measure costs? (Equipment, personnel, software, design, programming, space, etc.)	( )	( )
Do you estimate and measure benefits? (Equipment savings, personnel savings, indirect savings, sales improvement, managerial and organizational improvement)	( )	( )

Have you tried these cures?	Yes	No

Do you apply basic managerial principles of planning and control to MIS operations?

	Yes	No
Schedule	( )	( )
Cost	( )	( )
Performance	( )	( )

One NO answer suggests that significant improvement is needed.

chapter **9**

systems planning

9

Advocates of management information systems have seen their concept of computerized company-wide, fully integrated systems become the impossible dream.

—Financial Executive

There is little doubt that the increasing capability and capacity of modern computers are outracing the ability of the average company to properly utilize them. Survey after survey reveals that the *utilization* of the computer falls far short of its potential for improving management. Indeed, some companies and some executives are having second thoughts about the broken promises and unfulfilled potential.

> The chief executive of Aerojet-General, a high-technology corporation, has literally eliminated its centralized computer-based management information system (CBMIS). He says that the people doing the work at the grass-roots level weren't really using the systems, and those who did were swamped with reports that had become almost meaningless.

In almost every case of computer misuse and disillusionment, the underlying reason has been the lack of *systems planning*. Fourth-generation equipment is being used on first-generation systems. The *"Band-aid"* approach, installing a technical system as a short-run stopgap measure, has been the rule. In most companies, descriptions of "what we plan to do next year" shade into "what we are doing now" or "what we have done in the past."

The boundaries of the systems planning topic, as we will treat it in this chapter, are somewhat more limited than in the usual technical sense. Systems development activities and tasks may number in the hundreds and range from such initial actions as the recognition of a problem and its preliminary analysis to the final action concerned with the performance evaluation of an operating system. *Systems planning,* on the other hand, is the necessary first step in systems development and our discussion is limited to considerations of primary concern to the manager-user.

THE NEED FOR SYSTEMS PLANNING

Judging from the foregoing studies and what one observes in real-life applications, little more than lip service has been paid to the widely promoted notion of a "total" single system or to the goal of a highly integrated set of subsystems. What has apparently happened is the development of "islands of mechanization" that followed unrelated starts in quick payoff areas such as payroll and some clerical accounting functions. This patchwork approach has resulted in the development of unrelated and sometimes incompatible subsystems.

This patchwork or piecemeal approach to systems development, which has no unifying framework and is without a master plan, has several disadvantages. One of these stems from the unrelated nature of the subsystems developed. Frequently autonomous departments and divisions have developed individualistic systems without regard to the interface of such systems elsewhere in the organization. The result has been an inability to communicate between systems and the incompatibility of subsystems of a like nature throughout the company.

A fairly common example of failure to relate subsystems lies in the manner in which personnel information is structured. Frequently several departments (sales, production, accounting, personnel) will maintain employee files that overlap with other similar files but do not provide for interface between them. I have witnessed the development of critical engineering and labor skills shortages in one or more geographically separated divisions of a multidivision company. But despite the fact that these skills are available elsewhere in the company, no identification can be made owing to the lack of a common personnel skills information system.

A second, and serious, disadvantage is the cost involved: cost in time, resources, and money. The longer a master plan is put off, the more costly will be the inevitable need to overhaul, unify, and standardize the approach to integrated systems design. Many companies have invested in the automation of clerical records and subsequently discovered that a complete overhaul of the system is necessary when it becomes integrated with a larger effort. A popular one-for-one conversion in the past has been the materials inventory "tab" system, a system that frequently requires complete rework when a production planning and control system is implemented.

The questions arise: First, why has the piecemeal approach been allowed to develop? And second, what should and can be done to improve the design situation so that an improved integrated approach can be taken?

The answer to the first question is complex, but the major reason is probably that managers have generally failed to realize in the early stages of systems development the computer's scope, its investment value, and its potential impact on the operations of the business. Belatedly, many firms have realized the need for integration through the implementation of a master plan and are now undertaking massive efforts to correct the situation. The signs are favorable. Evidence seems to indicate that in the future, systems development will be characterized by four improving trends:

1. A much greater share of systems effort will be devoted to the planning and control of operations rather than the previous concentration on the clerical and routine paperwork of finance and administration. Operations, marketing, product or process development, and personnel management are among those areas that are expected to have increasingly sophisticated applications.

2. An increasing percentage of expenditures (of new plant and equipment) and an increasing percentage of sales will be spent on data-processing equipment and activities. This trend reflects primarily the growing recognition on the part of management that information systems are a vital resource. Moreover, increasing expenditures will be made on managerial applications, the surface of which has barely been scratched.

3. An increasing fraction of computer and related expenditures will be devoted to design and software as opposed to mainframe and hardware. This changing "mix" of systems expenditures reflects the relatively unsophisticated state-of-the-art in systems design in most companies and the recognition that greater efforts under a master plan are needed.*

4. There will be an accelerating tendency toward the integration of subsystems. Integration not only is economical but yields much more effective information for management planning, operating, and control. More and more companies are realizing this and are moving in that direction.

The answer to the second question, regarding the means to achieve an integrated approach to systems development, lies clearly in the adoption of a master plan. The case for working from a long-range blueprint is desirable; it is proven, and it is practical. Indeed, the same reasons that can be advanced for business planning in general can be advanced also as the argument for systems planning.

These four special reasons for systems planning are:

1. To offset uncertainty
2. To improve economy of operations
3. To focus on objectives
4. To provide a device for control of operations

Aside from the uncertainty of business operations and the resulting need for better forecasting information, the special need for a systems plan is evident because of advancing computer technology and its widespread effect on business operations. Both software (programming languages, systems design, etc.) and hardware (computers, related devices, data

---

*One estimate predicts that the cost distribution in a typical company in 1977 will be 80% software (design and programming) and 20% hardware (equipment). In 1957 the distribution was 90% hardware and 10% software.

transmission, etc.) have become so complex that the job of selection and utilization has been made more difficult. As a result, the majority of organizations have fallen far short of their potential to use computers to process the information necessary to effectively manage the company. A master plan may not remove this *uncertainty,* but it will almost surely place the firm in a better position to deal with the unknowns and to take advantages of developments as they occur.

Planning the overall approach to an integrated systems timetable is also *economical.* The prevailing pattern of design effort in most companies reflects the short-term approach of automating those clerical operations that offer an immediate payoff in terms of reduction of paperwork and staff. Customer billing, payroll, accounts payable, and inventory records (not inventory control) are favorite targets for automation of clerical tasks. However, experience has shown that in the long run this approach is likely to be more costly than proceeding under a predetermined plan. Once one job or function has been automated, the need for the design and automation of contiguous functions frequently becomes obvious. Take, for example, the well-designed production planning system whose inputs come from a manual sales order and forecasting system and whose outputs are largely ignored by purchasing and personnel. It becomes obvious that money can be saved and performance improved by an effective linking together of these neighboring functions through a good plan for integrated systems design. However, if adjacent or interacting systems are not considered under a plan, costly rework will almost surely result.

Economies surrounding organizational changes, personnel considerations, and equipment purchase or rental may also be realized by working toward a predetermined grand scheme rather than permitting systems applications to grow unchecked.

With any other organizational resource it is necessary to achieve some sort of economic balance. This balance with regard to information systems applies in two ways: first, an optimal use of resources allocated in information systems; second, an optimal balance between MIS resources and those resources allocated to other uses in the company. In other words, the organizational objective is to allocate the correct amount of resources to information systems development and design and to get the best systems possible out of those resources allocated to information systems. Here we see the economic principle of marginal utility at work. If no allocation were made to the gathering and dissemination of information, the company would likely go out of business. On the other hand, if all or a substantial amount of company resources went into information systems, there would be no product, and the same result would occur.

The practical problem, however, is rarely the allocation of resources to information systems vis-à-vis other uses, but rather where to apply the limited personnel, equipment, and dollars available for the systems effort. The obvious answer appears to be payoff, i.e., where the highest benefits can be obtained for the systems effort. This choice is easier said than made, however, and practical considerations of estimating benefits must be faced.

The benefits of any one or group of applications are not always self-evident. Many companies have taken the easy way out by automating the routine bookkeeping and clerical functions because these appear to be the obvious areas and because personnel replacement costs can be estimated. This approach is rarely the correct one, however. There are a few organizations (perhaps the Social Security Administration or Internal Revenue Service) whose clerical displacement savings outweigh the savings to be realized in the improvement of planning and control applications. Although the benefits in these managerial areas are intangible and difficult to measure, it is in these types of applications that system development effort has the most impact on costs and on company operations. Three areas in industry that consistently yield the greatest benefits are:

1. Planning and control of finished goods in the distribution network.
2. Planning and control of the use of materials, machines, and labor in manufacturing operations.
3. Planning and control of the material procurement function.

He also makes the point that precedence relationships of functions being automated should be followed. Precedence relationship is given by the time sequence in which related functions take place. For example, if materials planning is chosen to be automated, then forecasting or inventory control should be next because these functions are immediately adjacent to materials planning. The approach assures the most orderly growth with a minimum of costly system rework.

In short, the manager or systems designer should focus on an overall plan and those applications that provide the greatest payoff in terms of improved planning and control. In almost every case, this approach is more economical than concentrating on areas that offer a quick short-term payoff in terms of clerical savings.

A good plan for systems development also serves to *focus on company and systems objectives*. Conversely, firms that lack explicit organizational objectives and explicit plans for achieving them, or that prefer to respond after the fact to environmental factors rather than shaping their own environment, are unlikely to have formulated systems objectives backed by a plan for achieving them. The manager or the systems designer will have to ferret out business objectives as well as systems plans to support them. Indeed, if we review the fundamental process of planning, we discover that planning cannot proceed in any area of endeavor until adequate objectives have been set. It follows that the development of a master systems plan forces the examination and definition of objectives.

The question arises: What are the objectives of an information systems plan? Although we will discuss this in detail later in this chapter, it is appropriate at this time to point out that systems objectives must always be supportive to the objectives of the firm. If the organization's objectives are to be supported, those in charge of systems development will have to ask these questions: What will be the nature of the firm in the future, and what information will be needed to assist in the satisfaction of these needs arising from the management of the company in the future changing environment? What will be our products . . . our customers . . . our competition . . . our distribution channels? What kind of sales forces will be needed . . . what facilities . . . etc.? Only after these questions are stated can the designer begin to determine the objectives of the systems plan and the specifics of information needs and sources.

Systems development, implementation, and operations are among the most difficult activities to control within the company. The fourth major advantage of the development of systems effort under a predetermined plan is the manner in which such a plan provides a means for subsequent *control*. Plans and objectives also provide the means for measuring progress. If systems development activities and events are organized on a project basis with specific objectives (e.g., optimize cost of raw materials inventory) to be achieved within a certain time period and at a predetermined cost, then these goals can be used as yardsticks to measure subsequent accomplishments.

Yet despite the fact that the real reason for the development of management information systems lies in their use to improve the management of organizations, the planning and control of systems development efforts are frequently left to chance. Perhaps those responsible for this effort should take their own advice: "What you need is a system!"

> A large banking system set out to design its ultimate "total system," which it conceived of as six large integrated systems. Only one was eventually completed in the original form; the lost investment in the other five was estimated at $12 million. The conclusion was reached that many interim steps must be taken; many people trained, equipment planned, and the long-range plan developed *before* expensive systems are made operational.

OBJECTIVES OF MIS PLANNING

We have previously described the nature of planning by saying that "planning involves the development and selection from among alternatives of the necessary course of action to achieve an objective." This definition is but one of many, but when planning is defined, it is inevitably described in terms of the actions necessary to achieve an *objective*. The objective is therefore the essential prerequisite to planning, and planning can commence and be useful only when objectives are properly selected. The improper selection or failure to define objectives can result only in frustration and in failure of the entire planning process.

Although the preceding discussion relates to general business planning, there is no reason to believe that it does not apply to the more limited context of information systems planning as well. Indeed, the argument advanced here is that systems planning cannot proceed to a master plan or any other constructive scheme unless the objectives of the information systems plan are detailed and well understood.

We are not referring to specific *objectives* (e.g., explosion of bill of materials, requiring that stock orders be billed and shipped within twelve hours after receipt) of subsystems, but to the overall *systems planning objectives*—in other words, the characteristics of the information systems that should be developed for both the near-term and long-range effort. Included herein are objectives having to do first with the systems planning effort and second with how this effort will improve the allocation of resources and hence the profitability of the organization.

Systems Objectives

An excellent framework of objectives for the systems planning function has been developed by Blumenthal:

> The systems-planning function must therefore encompass the review of proposed systems in terms of planning criteria designed to minimize the number of systems, to broaden their scope, and to place them in the proper sequence for development. All these requirements can be expressed by the following list of systems-planning objectives:
>
> 1. To avoid overlapping development of major systems elements [that] are widely applicable across organizational lines, when there is no compelling technical or functional reason for difference.
> 2. To help ensure a uniform basis for determining sequence of development in terms of payoff potential, natural precedence, and probability of success.
> 3. To minimize the cost of integrating related systems with each other.
> 4. To reduce the total number of small, isolated systems to be developed, maintained, and operated.

5. To provide adaptability of systems to business change and growth without periodic major overhaul.

6. To provide a foundation for coordinated development of consistent, comprehensive, corporate-wide, and inter-organizational information systems.

7. To provide guidelines for and direction to continuing systems-development studies and projects.*

Organizational Objectives

With regard to the impact of the systems planning effort on the organization and how it can best serve the organization in the management process, planning objectives can best be stated in terms of how these *integrate* the organization; i.e., management integration, resources integration, and integration between management levels.

Integration of the Management Process

The ideal management information system should provide for the integration of the functions of management at and between the various levels as well as laterally throughout the organization by providing for:

1. *Planning*—integration of related information created in the various prime steps of the management cycle, i.e., plans and programs (requirements, forecasts, allowances, allocations, budgets, projects, etc.). This implies the proper design of content as well as data flow to insure that everyone involved is aware of planning information. An illustration of this might be the plan for distribution expense, which provides planning information vertically throughout the sales organization as well as laterally to finance any operations whose own plans may be affected thereby.

2. *Direction*—the use of information systems design to communicate, coordinate, and give direction to plans at various levels. There is no reason why the information system (structure and outputs) could not be the vehicle through which plans are implemented and controlled. For example, a PERT/CPM schedule, once adopted as a plan, may be the communication device that can thereafter achieve coordination of all organizational elements.

3. *Operations*—integration of information concerning plans, direction, and necessary data concerning the transformation process of taking inputs (personnel, money, materials, equipment, etc.) and processing these into outputs. Figure 6-2 illustrates this approach to the design of the manu-

*Sherman C. Blumenthal, *Management Information Systems: A Framework for Planning and Development* (Englewood Cliffs, N.J.: Prentice-Hall, Inc., 1969), p. 13.

facturing information system. Unless some integrative approach is taken toward the separate operational elements (manufacturing, engineering, shipping, distribution, finances, etc.), these functional units will tend to focus on their own objectives at the expense of the firm's.

4. *Control*—integration of information concerning progress of plans against standards so that plans, programs, and operations can be corrected to achieve desired output. To the extent that it is feasible, automatic control should be built into the information system, not for automatic correction of output (although this is the theoretical ideal), but for automatic exception reporting for management planning and control. Inventory decision rules are common examples of this type of control.

5. *Organization*—integration of the organization by utilizing its structure to design and implement the information system, notwithstanding the fact that modern integrated information systems frequently transcend conventional organizational structures. Conceptually, this linking of subsystems with and through the organization can be shown:

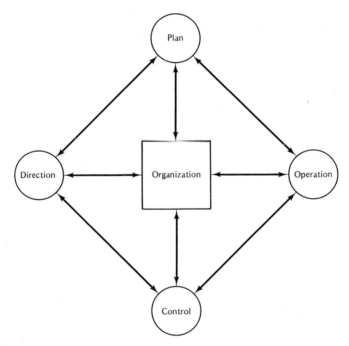

Due to the complexity of modern organizations, the various levels of management within them, and the decentralization of operations, it is frequently the case that staff people or departments that develop plans are not the ones that subsequently make them operational or control them. It is therefore necessary that everyone speak the same language. In other words, management information systems must be developed under a plan that recognizes this complexity and provides for integration through the media of information systems. A corollary objective is the integration of computer languages, data classification, and degree of detail for both the planning and performance data.

Integration of Resources

For purposes of systems design, *integration* can be defined as the design of subsystems in such a way that data are processed in a continuous stream until the use of such data has been completed in the total system. Now, since *operational* (as opposed to information) subsystems can be described in terms of their information needs, it follows that the integration of the resources contained in the operational systems can be improved by proper design of the information system. Indeed, it has been made abundantly clear that information is the nervous system, the bloodstream, the physiology giving direction to the operations that make the transformation process possible. Therefore, in advancing our objective of integration through information, we are at the same time allocating scarce resources in a more economical way.

A useful concept to keep in mind is that of the modular elements of information having commonality across different uses or structures. If the lowest-level information elements (as defined by the designer) are called *modules,* then integrative operational systems can be constructed from a collection of modules. Indeed, this notion is the basic approach to the design of integrated systems. It is illustrated in Figure 9-1, which depicts unique as well as common modules. In this illustration the common modules are sales orders, project control, purchasing, and accounts receivable. For some purposes two or more of these modules may be combined to provide a modular operational information system.

Horizontal integration of resources may be achieved by systems that interrelate and interlock the lateral functions of the organization (i.e., product development, marketing, operations, finance, personnel, etc.). It keeps the managers of these functions apprised of information concerning interfaces and their impact on other functions. This integration is not and cannot be achieved by the "islands of mechanization" or "automate now, integrate later" approaches to systems design, because development under that approach often proceeds without regard to the interlocking nature of subsystems.

Consider, for example, the rather common situation where the outputs from an otherwise sophisticated production planning and control or project control system are not utilized or received by personnel, despite the fact that these systems are designed to forecast the types and amounts of skills required for a project or production plan. Or consider the personnel system that maintains an up-to-date skills bank but whose output does not go to the training system.

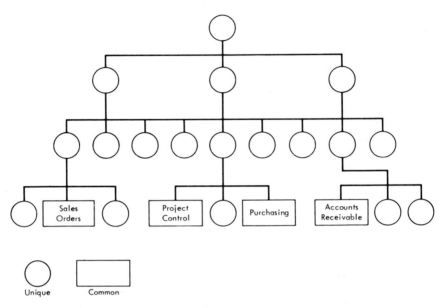

Figure 9-1   Integration of Organization Through Information

Integrated design takes account of subsystem interfaces. The manner in which subsystems design can be utilized to integrate functions horizontally and levels vertically is shown in Figure 9-2.

Vertical integration is achieved mainly through the characteristic of hierarchical systems whereby higher-order systems are dependent on lower-order subsystems for input. Lower-order systems are, in turn, dependent on more elementary or still lower-order subsystems for input.

It becomes evident that information systems are a vital tool for integration and economical operation of these vertical systems. The longer or deeper down in successively lower levels that planning and programming for all elements can be integrated, the higher the probability that the systems "mix" will be in optimal balance. Equally evident is the improved nature of planning and control information when all the pertinent interdependent elements and subsystems are correlated vertically.

Integration of Management Levels

If, as we have demonstrated, the integration of functions, programs, and resources is desirable in systems planning, then it follows naturally that the integration of the levels of management is also to be sought. A rather arbitrary but nevertheless traditional view of the levels of management and the tasks can be shown:

Management Level	Task	Decision Making	Type Information Used
Top	Management	Setting objectives and selecting courses of action from among alternatives	Decision information
Staff	Operational planning and scheduling	Identification of alternatives, analysis and evaluation of alternatives	Operating and some historical information
Functional	Line supervision at lower and middle organizational levels	Control of operations	Historical and some operating information

Despite the definition of top management's job in terms of decision making, research indicates that computer information systems have had little or no effect on the manner in which this task is performed. Even at middle-management levels, the effect of computer-based systems has been very slight to moderate. The general lack of use at these levels for decision making leaves only the lower levels of management and supervision. These latter groups depend largely on historical information and clerical applications. Such a situation cannot continue to exist if, like resources, management levels are to be integrated both horizontally and vertically.

The answer to better integration of management levels appears to lie in improved systems planning and design. Despite some lack of appreciation and a frequently defensive attitude on the part of a large segment of management, better systems design effort should be aimed at developing a greater understanding of the factors influencing management decisions. Also helpful would be better education of all levels of management concerning the capability of computer-based information systems to assist in areas of decision analysis.

A large part of the systems design effort can be devoted to upgrading historical information to the operational or decision-making category; or at the very least, design future systems with decision making and management in mind. The objective is *integrated* systems. The integration of management levels will be advanced by designing information systems around a data base that provides for a minimum of input, a multiple or joint use of the same data at all levels, and a maximum access for anyone with a need to interrogate any part or all of it. There should be no duplication, excess, or inadequacy of informational content flowing between organizational elements, horizontal or vertical.

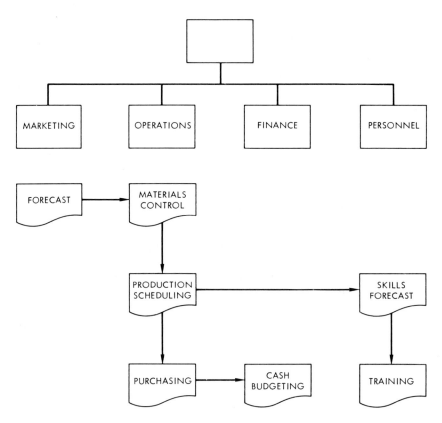

Figure 9-2   Horizontal and Vertical Integration of Functions and Resources

CLASSIFICATION OF SYSTEMS

An orderly classification of information systems is a fundamental prerequisite to good systems planning. Classification is the very beginning of the organization of facts and information. Without it there can be no systems design.

We have referred frequently to the prevailing tendency to build systems around some existing classification such as the charts of accounts or simply to automate existing reports. Such one-for-one changeover in systems design results in nothing more than attempted automation of existing files. As one designer stated it, this approach is "the perpetuation of inefficiencies at an accelerated rate." It is rather clear that if integration is our primary goal of systems design, we must begin with some kind of scheme of systems classifications. A classification is designed to organize the facts and information concerning the activities of an organization by the grouping of items of similar characteristics, traits, and relationships. The major purpose of such classification is the retrieval of the information by persons desiring it for a particular use. These persons and these uses may vary, but one major objective of the classification of information systems is a balance between the costs of classification on one hand and the costs of retrieval on the other. Systems that are too detailed and complicated are not only expensive to design but expensive to utilize in terms of the cost of data processing. This is known as the "see-saw" rule of classification: *as costs of classification go up, the costs of using the classification go down.* The reverse is also true: *as the costs of classification go down, the costs of using the classification go up.*

Throughout the design of MIS and the related classification schemes, master plans, and data banks, three perspectives should be kept in mind:

MIS as data converter—where the objective is to provide data conversion operations at the operating level for transaction data. The output is normally for housekeeping activities such as payroll and accounting subsystems.

MIS as a provider of scheduled reports—wherein a determination is made of what information is needed by whom, how often it is needed, and the necessary *scheduled* reports designed to meet the need.

MIS as a provider of demand reports—the objective of which is to collect a pool of data (data bank) from which managers can draw information *upon demand* as they encounter problems requiring decisions.

Approaches to Classification

The point should be abundantly clear by this time that regardless of how the manager views integrated data-processing and management information systems, the single overriding need is to work from a *grand scheme, a master plan.* A fundamental, indeed necessary, element of such a plan is some type of classification of systems, a conceptualization if you like. We are not referring to the detailed classification or coding of data (although the same principles apply), but to a basic *structure* or overall framework that will give us the *systems* perspective of the information network in an organization. This perspective, or structure, should yield a model of the organization consisting of the systems and their relationships.

Information systems have been classified:

1. *Management operating systems* are used to produce working papers, such as purchase invoices, job orders, or paychecks.

2. *Management reporting systems* are used to aid management in the making of decisions.

Others prefer to use the classifications of *major* and *minor* systems:

Major Information Systems

Accounting
Material Flows
Periodic Planning Information
Special Reports
The Grapevine
Scanning

Minor Information Systems

Competitive Information
Research and Development
Sales Forecasting
Special Systems

These two classifications are interesting and useful for some purposes but of little use in the development of an overall plan for systems development to structure our systems during the design phase.

For the purposes of systems development and design and in order to meet our planning objectives, a combination of the following approaches to classification is available. Information needed to manage an organization can be classified:

1. *Task*—the job, the function (selling, manufacturing, financing, etc.) representing the purpose for which the information is reported.

2. *Resource*—the objects or events reported upon (personnel, equipment, money, etc.) that are being used or acquired.

3. *Networks*—flows of information and resources representing a model of the organization: the focus of planning and control.

4. *Level*—three levels representing the hierarchy of planning and control in the organization: strategic planning, management control, and operational control.

5. *Environment*—the environment in which the firm operates, including information needed to set goals and objectives, information concerning other external environment (suppliers, government, etc.), and other external planning premises.

The job of the systems planner is to devise the master classification scheme that best fits his particular organization; he must keep in mind the need to design a *master plan* that will serve for integration of various additional applications over the near and long terms. In most cases a combination of the approaches cited will be sufficient, but *some grand scheme* is necessary if the planning objectives previously detailed are to be achieved.

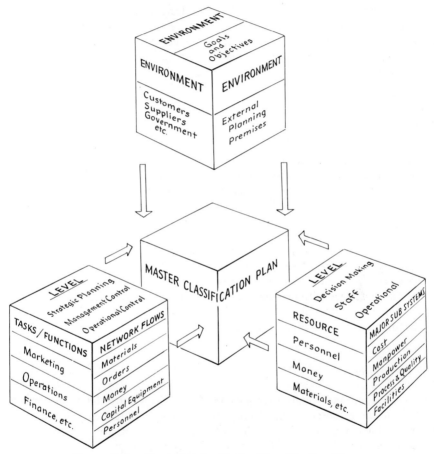

Figure 9-3　Elements of a Master Classification Plan

The task of selecting the proper classification framework can be described conceptually in Figure 9-3. From the "menu" offered, the designer must select the combination that suits the needs of management. The combination is multidimensional:

1. Two hierarchical classifications of systems (function and decision making),
2. The common tasks/functions among systems,
3. Resources to be managed in the transformation process,
4. Information and resource flows, and
5. The environment in which management sets goals and objectives.

In addition to these five dimensions, the designer is concerned with additional dimensions of a classification scheme: the common functions and resources among systems in the vertical hierarchy and informational elements that serve to construct integrated subsystems across horizontal boundaries.

Task or Function

The most logical and widespread type of categorization in information systems is organized around the job to be done, the task to be performed, and the use to which the information will be put. Classification in this fashion tends to develop for the same reason that most firms choose it— homogeneity of functions performed. This approach produces a natural subgrouping of work as well as the information required to plan and control this work. Moreover, this approach permits or encourages integration of subsystems, because different functional organizational entities frequently deal with the same resource or with different aspects of the same task. For example, sales orders from the marketing function have an important interface with production control and other subsystems.

Table 9-1 illustrates some of the major subsystems classified by task or function in a manufacturing organization.

Resource

A second and widely used means of classifying information systems is around the resource (people, projects, equipment, funds, etc.) to be managed. Each resource usually has characteristics that are peculiar to its description and hence to the information surrounding it. Resources tend to be organized around the functions of the organization: money around treasury department, personnel around personnel department, raw materials around production, and so on. Because of this association, there is naturally a great deal of overlap and integration between tasks (functions) and resources.

Table 9-1

Selected List of "Task-Oriented, Function-Related" Subsystems

Product Development	Operations	Finance	Manpower
Engineering	Classification	Accounts Receivable	Arbitration
Project Control	Cataloguing	Accounts Payable	Classifying
Bill of Material	Inventory Control	Billing	Interviewing
Research and Development	Labor Scheduling and Reporting	Cost Accounting	Placing
Styling	Manufacturing	Cash Receipts	Recruiting
	Cutting	Cash Budgets	Selection
	Welding	Financial Planning	Staffing
	Finishing	General Ledger	Testing
	etc.	Plant Accounting	Services
	Production Control	General Ledger	
	Process Control	Variance Analysis	
	Purchasing	Taxes	
	Quality Control	Timekeeping	
	Stores Control		
	Scheduling		
	Labor		
	Finished goods		
	etc.		
	Servicing		
	Maintenance		
	Repair		
	Materials Handling		
	Packaging		
	Receiving		
	Shipping		
	Warehousing		

For each major resource, an information system can be constructed with files containing information in subcategories; the personnel system contains a subsystem entitled Employee Benefits, which in turn has files on Insurance, Savings, Retirement, etc. Major elements of a resource classification system are illustrated opposite. Note also that several of the *task* subsystems are common to two or more *resource* systems. This makes the point once again that subsystems are seldom mutually exclusive; they are usually multidimensional, with dimensions of (a) hierarchy, (b) task, and (c) resource, each of which has two other dimensions of (d) vertical and (e) horizontal boundaries.

TASK/FUNCTIONAL INFORMATION SYSTEM

Resource	Purchasing	Inventory Control	Billing	Scheduling	Job Control	Personnel Adminst.
LOGISTICS						
Raw materials	x	x				
Finished goods		x	x			
Production facilities		x		x	x	
PHYSICAL ASSETS						
Property and equipment	x	x		x		
FINANCIAL						
Cash and credit	x		x			
MANPOWER						
Payroll					x	x
Benefits						x

Network Flows

Despite the fact that most existing information systems are organized around either resources or what might be called "task-oriented, function-related" categories, these approaches leave something to be desired. Conceptually, these classification approaches are static and do not adequately take account of the *dynamic* nature of the business firm. Yet we know that business is a dynamic organism composed of systems that process inputs into useful outputs of products or services. This processing or transformation of resources into outputs is made possible through an information system characterized by two notions: first, *movement* or *flow* through a complex interconnected system, and second, the *integrative* nature of the information that is used at multiple points throughout the organization. These characteristics are difficult to achieve in an information system organized by resource or task alone. What is needed is an additional dynamic dimension of *flow*. This concept can be applied to either information or physical resources, and these can be classified into *networks*. This notion of flow gives a greater conceptual grasp of the twin notions of upper management's development of plans and lower management's execution and control of these plans. To say it another way, we want to have operational planning and control systems. These may be achieved through an analysis of the flow process: its inputs, the transformation processes, its outputs, and the *decision points*.

The objects of the network flows are the inputs to the organization: facilities, materials, manpower, money, orders, and information. To illustrate how an information system can be built around such a flow network, let us take the *materials* flow. Conceptually (and practically), we can depict a system that plans and controls the acquisition of materials; their subsequent transportation to the factory; their allocation, storage, and production transformation within the factory; their transportation and distribution and final sale to a customer. We can see how an information system built around such an approach would *integrate* a number of activities that have traditionally been organized and managed by function (marketing, purchasing, etc.) or resource (plant, materials, etc.).

The *materials* network includes the flow and stocks of all materials, whether raw materials, work-in-process, or finished goods. An information system using this concept would include all decisions from the point where acquisition decisions are made through final delivery to a customer. Obviously, a number of other subsystems would need to be architecturally integrated with this flow because of interfaces. By taking the systematic network approach to design of this system, planning and control as well as time and cost considerations could be substantially improved over the traditional functionalism associated with management of materials. To illustrate, consider the traditional system where a sale triggers a change in the production schedule, which triggers a requisition for replenishment, which triggers a change in purchasing, and so on until the entire system is geared up to handle this input stimulus. Under a systems or network approach to materials flow, the initial trigger provided by the sale can stimulate responses all the way through the integrated system with much less delay and at less cost than the traditional organization, which is intent upon optimizing subsystem (department) objectives rather than the system (firm) as a whole.

The flows of *orders* are not physical objects but rather symbolic representations of what will become arrangements of other resources and the allocation of resources to meet the commitment of the order. Viewed in this light, orders become the vital catalyst that can provide the decision inputs for optimization of transformation resources.

It is important to design a system to track the *money* network, because money is the common language of managing and provides a tool for measuring results against plans. Moreover, money is a medium of exchange that reflects the firm's actions with its total environment, outside and inside. Outside, the money flow interfaces with banks, customers, stockholders, government (tax), labor, suppliers, and the community at large. Inside the firm, it is a yardstick to measure resource allocation and control. By focusing on the money flows within and without an organization, the integration of subsystems at both these levels should be improved, as well as the management of the individual functions, resources, or outside entities.

Other network flows consist of the *personnel network,* the *facilities network,* and the *information network*. The first two of these work in much the same fashion as those discussed previously, in that they improve decision making, cut down on the time involved in decision making, and integrate the subsystems of an organization for greater economies and efficiencies. The *information network* is in a category by itself because it represents the other flows and provides the linkage that causes the other networks to operate on each other in the manner of a *total system.*

These categories or *networks* comprise an arbitrary classification around which the systems designer may begin to construct a master classification plan. Regardless of the extent to which this scheme is utilized, it does provide us with an excellent sketch of the operation of the firm as a *dynamic system* whose total objectives can be achieved through the planning, allocation, and control of flows of inputs that are transformed into outputs.

Levels of Systems

In Chapter 3 we discussed the impact that the systems approach will have on the function of organizing and the structure of organizations. One major change will most likely be the elimination or reduction of the sharp lines of demarcation between existing departments as we know them: purchasing, accounting, sales, manufacturing, engineering. However, one essential feature of organizations will no doubt remain: the managerial hierarchy of planning and control. This hierarchy of management and organizational structure has been described in a number of ways, but almost invariably as having three levels. Some of the ways of structuring these levels have been by layer, task, location, function, and level:

		CLASSIFICATION		
Layer	*Task*	*Location*	*Management Function*	*Level*
FIRST	Strategic Planning	Management	Management	Top
SECOND	Management Control	Office	Planning and Control	Middle
THIRD	Operational Control	Factory and Field	Execution	Supervisor

Whatever the combination of classifications we choose to describe the organizational hierarchy, it is necessary that different levels and tasks be recognized and provided for in systems development and design. In Table 9-2, Blumenthal distinguishes among three levels: *strategic planning, management control,* and *operational control.* These levels are further extended to include an information systems perspective on this hierarchy of an organization: inputs, outputs, systems types, etc. These attributes and levels should be considered in adopting the master classification plan for information usage at different levels and for different purposes.

Table 9-2

	Level		
	Strategic Planning	Management Control	Operational Control
Organizational Identity	Corporation and Division Top Management	Corporation and Divisional Departments Profit Centers	Supervisors Foremen Clerks
Activities	Set Objectives Determine resources to be applied	Allocate assigned resources to tasks Make rules Measure performance Exert control	Use resources to carry out tasks in conformance with rules
Characteristics	Unpredictable Variable Staff-oriented External perspective	Personal style Organizational change Line-oriented Judgmental Internal perspective	Stable Logical Predictable Prescribed
Tempo	Irregular	Rhythmic (quarterly, monthly, weekly)	Real-time
Inputs	Staff studies External situation Reports of internal achievement	Summaries Exceptions	Internal events Transactions
Information Systems	Special onetime reports Simulations Inquiries (unrestricted)	Many regular reports Format variety Inquiries (restricted) "Data bank" —oriented	Formal Fixed procedures Complex Concrete
Outputs	Goals Policies Constraints	Abstract Decisions "Personal" leadership Procedures	Actions

SOURCE: Sherman C. Blumenthal, *Management Information Systems: A Framework for Planning and Development* (Englewood Cliffs, N.J.: Prentice-Hall, 1969), p. 29.

Environment

The classifications we have discussed thus far (task, resource, information flows, levels) have been for the most part concerned with the interaction of subsystems within the firm and information available inside the organization. However, some of the most vital sources of information are external to the firm and concern the environment in which it operates. Although the satisfaction of the manager's *total* information needs, including those external to the firm, is probably impossible, these needs must nevertheless be taken into account despite the two major difficulties of (a) little control over the environment, and (b) inability to design a system to capture this information.

Finally, it is desirable to recall that, except for the very top levels of management, the bulk of information needs of most managers can be met within the firm. Since most of them are involved with lower-level subsystems, their planning premises usually derive from higher-order systems, and their needs for execution and operational control come from within the firm as well. The point here is that for the vast majority of the managers within the organization, the needs for planning and control can be met from information systems designed to structure and communicate information from inside the firm.

DATA BANKS AND MASTER PLANS

In this chapter I have attempted to convey the notion that systems planning is an essential prerequisite to integrated management information systems. Without planning, the result is a piecemeal approach that results in "islands of mechanization."

Central to the concept and practice of systems planning are data banks and master plans. Each of these topics is complex and beyond the scope of this book. However, from a managerial point of view, certain ideas should be remembered.

The Data Bank

Central information files and data banks have become the subjects of widespread concern recently due to the news media's coverage of the intelligence files allegedly maintained by such government organizations as the FBI, the CIA, and the IRS. Indeed, the ordinary citizen may wonder whether Uncle Sam is watching him. Even the $1 bill has a sharp eye out for its owner. Get a $1 bill from your pocketbook, turn to the green side and look on the left at the reverse view of the Great Seal of the United States. At the tip of the pyramid is a big eye—gazing straight at you.

Until very recent years the development of data banks were pretty much a hit-or-miss proposition. The popular approach was to accumulate information in computer files and hope that it later turned out to be of some use. Of course, the aimless accumulation of marginally useful information is expensive and wasteful. Many experts view this practice as being one of the more serious economic problems associated with the computer age.

The problem then is twofold; determining what to store in the data bank and the organization of the information. To repeat, these are important but complex decisions. In this summary I can only offer a conceptual view of the process, which is shown in Figure 9-4.

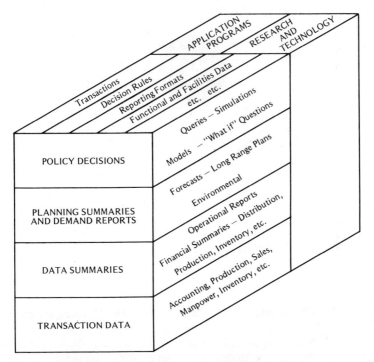

Figure 9-4   Organization of MIS Data Bank

The Master Plan

If the reader has kept pace with this book thus far he should be convinced that a master plan is an essential prerequisite for success in the design, implementation, and utilization of a management information system. The old cliche about planning in general applies here as well: "If you don't know where you're going, all roads lead there."

In designing the master plan, certain elementary cautions are in order:

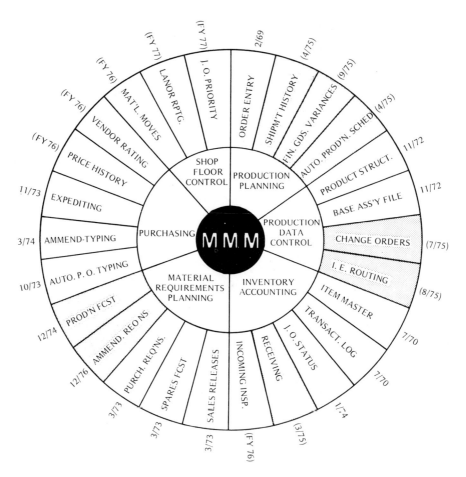

Figure 9-5 Master Plan for Mechanized Material Management

Don't rush to apply a narrow technical system, as a "Band-aid" or temporary solution, to a larger, longer-run problem. Inevitably, it will become necessary to redesign.

Distinguish between "lifestream" and administrative systems. Some systems (e.g., order processing, production planning, and control) are much more essential to operations and provide a much greater payoff potential than lesser support systems. Design the lifestream systems first, and let them be the central foundation of the total MIS.

Establish precedence relationships between and among subsystems or you will be engaged in redesign efforts to reestablish relationships.

Establish a priority setting organization. This should be some type of steering committee involving the EDP center and the users.

Choose, as the leadoff system, one that is common to all other systems in order to begin the establishment of commonality between diverse operations. This may be the employee system, the order processing system, or other common applications.

Figure 9-5 shows the master plan for mechanized material management in a leading firm in the instrumentation industry.

CHECKLIST FOR MIS PLANNING

	Yes	No
ORGANIZATION FOR PLANNING		
Do you have a formal structure for planning?	( )	( )
Are these planning objectives established:		
To offset uncertainty?	( )	( )
To improve economy of operations?	( )	( )
To focus on company and MIS objectives?	( )	( )
To control operations?	( )	( )
Are Information Subsystems Integrated and Related?	( )	( )
Are Additional Planning Objectives Established for Integrating Management Functions, Company Resources, and Management Levels?	( )	( )
CLASSIFICATION		
Is a classification scheme established?	( )	( )
Does it take account of transaction data, scheduled reports, and demand reports?	( )	( )
Does the scheme consist of one or more of these methods: task, resource, networks, level?	( )	( )
DATA BANK		
Is a plan underway and implemented for data bank file organization and structure?	( )	( )
Is it economical and does it avoid redundancy?	( )	( )
MASTER PLAN		
Is a MIS Master Plan in existence?	( )	( )
Is it kept updated?	( )	( )
Is it followed?	( )	( )
Does it lead ultimately to an integrated MIS?	( )	( )
Does it distinguish between lifestream and administrative systems?	( )	( )
Do you have a committee or other organizational entity for priority setting?	( )	( )

chapter 10

MIS design:
the manager's role

10

"One of the greatest handicaps to the fullest sensible use of the computer as an aid for senior management consists of the senior managers themselves. . . . If a manager has not found a computer useful to him in management, it means that he has not yet a competent team and that he does not yet understand how to obtain the benefits."

—Simon Ramo

Evidence continues to mount that the number one reason for poor utilization of the computer is the lack of managerial involvement in the design process and related areas of computer use. One executive of a computer manufacturer labels the resulting inefficient systems and low productivity a "20-year ripoff." A partner in the consulting firm of Mc-Kinsey & Company remarked that this lack of involvement results in the following typical life cycle of an EDP application:

Unwarranted enthusiasm,

uncritical acceptance,

growing concern,

unmitigated disaster,

search for the guilty,

punish the guilty,

punish the innocent, and

promote the uninvolved.

It is not difficult to make a case for managerial involvement. If for no other reason, it is economical; it has a payoff. This is shown in Table 10-1, which summarizes a McKinsey study report that concluded that more profit from computers was made by companies who got managers involved in a hands-on way.

There's an old saying in the EDP business: "When a systems man is up to his waist in alligators, it's hard for him to remember that his objective was to drain the swamp." Computer professionals frequently encounter alligators: new systems don't work as promised, users become disenchanted or irate, costs and schedules are overrun. It is therefore easy for the analysts and technicians to become wholly occupied with fending off the alligators, and to forget the real objective of MIS. This is why user participation in design is so important.

Table 10-1

Company Payoffs from Managerial Involvement With Computers

Area of Involvement	Less Successful Users	More Successful Users
	Percent of Involvement	*Percent of Involvement*
Identifying computer opportunities	22	72
Specifying payoffs	17	74
Defining requirements	33	83
Accountable for results	17	50

BASIC STEPS IN MIS DESIGN: MANAGERIAL PARTICIPATION

In this chapter we will answer the question: what are the design steps involved in management participations? Let me emphasize that these are the *minimum* involvement. The user should also be familiar with the essentials of detailed design contained in Chapter 11.

Our examination will be from the point of view of the manager-user and not the computer specialist. The assumption is made that a computer installation is already available and that preliminary investigation has been completed to the extent of authorizing a systems study to further refine or design the information system. With this in mind it will be convenient to examine the managerial contribution to systems design as a process with seven steps:

1. Set system objectives
2. Establish system constraints
3. Determine information needs
4. Determine information sources
5. Detail the system concept
6. Test and implement the system
7. Evaluate the system

These steps in design are not separate and distinct. Indeed, most of them are along a continuum, shade into each other, overlap, and are recycled. In other words, the process as shown in Figure 10-1 is iterative. Designers are constantly required to return to an examination and modification of prior steps in light of what is learned in subsequent ones.

There are several approaches to the design of a system. All of these have in common the development of the *input–processor–output* con-

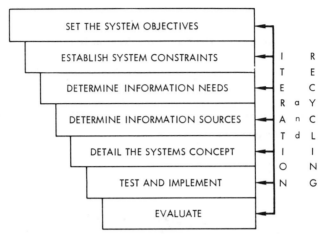

Figure 10-1   Steps in the Design of a Management Information System

structs at the subsystem level. The model for such a *data-processing system* (product demand) is shown in Figure 10-2. Although the analyst and the computer technician are concerned with the details of operations of the *processor,* the manager is involved only to the extent that he understands the general nature of this system element and how it affects the *inputs* and *outputs* to *his* information system. Therefore the methodology discussed in this chapter is not specifically concerned with the processing of data but with the inputs and outputs to achieve a system objective. The processor will remain essentially "black" for purposes of designing systems concepts.

Illustrative Subsystems

Throughout this chapter each design step will be illustrated as it applies to selected subsystems. These subsystems are: inventory, accounts payable, purchasing, production control, and project control.

SET SYSTEM OBJECTIVES*

This first step in systems design is perhaps the most difficult and is a step that must be stated and clearly understood before design can continue.

---

*This step is frequently described in terms of the *problem* to be solved, i.e., identify, isolate, state, or analyze the problem. For an approach to problem definition, see Chapter 11.

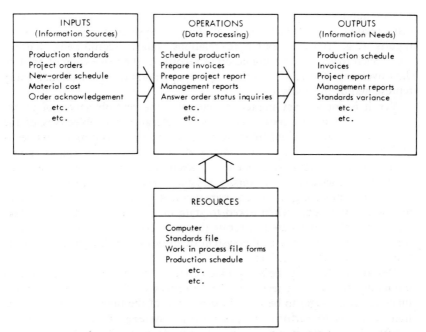

Figure 10-2   Input-Processor-Output Model of a Management Information System (Production Control Subsystem)

Yet, despite our clear understanding of the nature and need for objectives in other areas of the company, it is frequently quite difficult to have them stated in the systems design context.

Unlike the *technician* who frequently turns to topics such as file structure and retrieval techniques, and who views the objectives of subsystem only in terms of its input to a larger system, the *manager* must define system objectives in terms of legitimacy of information demands and not in terms of satisfaction of demands that are not related to an objective. Often the value of systems is measured in terms of transactions rather than of the benefit to the user. I have frequently heard systems analysts and computer salesmen state the objectives of systems design in terms of processing efficiency rather than of management effectiveness of the information processed. Several staff and functional supervisors have advised me that their objective was "to complete the required report on time for management use," without regard to the legitimacy of the report or its subsequent use for planning and control. I have witnessed the design of information systems in several government agencies where the objective was the automation of hundreds of reports without regard to management of the many tasks related, or to functional or resource subsystems represented by the reports (e.g., training, employee relations, safety, recruitment, staffing, etc.). Such focus on the automation of records or the processing of existing data overlooks the real objectives of the operational organizational entity represented by the subsystem.

Yet, it is not an easy matter to determine the real objectives of an information system any more than it is to determine the objectives of the operational system served by it. A common fallacy in stating objectives is emphasis on the obvious or statement of objectives in vague terms: "reduce costs," "improve efficiency," "keep accurate records," "meet the production schedule." A university president may reply, "Provide quality education," and the government bureaucrat may say, "Provide more jobs for the unemployed," when asked to state their objectives. Yet in neither case is the objective stated in terms that are specific enough to provide a measure of performance of the system or to design an information system to help achieve the objective.

Despite its difficulty, being specific is necessary. Systems objectives must ultimately be stated in terms of the objectives of the department, group, function, or manager to be served, or in terms of the functions the information system is to perform. In other words, systems objectives should be expressed in terms of what managers can do after their information requirements have been met. Such expression may use descriptive statements, flow charts, or any other means that will convey to management the objectives that the systems designer must meet in order to develop the system. If possible, the objectives should be stated in quantitative rather than qualitative terms, so that alternative system designs as well as system performance can be measured for effectiveness. In other words, a statement of objectives should include exactly what it is that the system is supposed to accomplish and how it will be subsequently evaluated.

Figure 10-3 contains a statement of objectives for the material control system of one of the nation's major manufacturers. Notice how specific objectives are defined.

In summary, the first step in systems design attempts to answer the questions: What is the purpose of the system? Why is it needed? What is it expected to do? Who are the system's users, and what are their objectives? These questions relate to the *what* of systems design; the remainder of the steps relate to *how* the systems design will do the *what*.

Finally, the establishment of systems objectives cannot be divorced from a consideration of organizational objectives, near-term and long-range. Over the near term, systems objectives can usually be framed in terms of management planning and control and decision making (lowering costs, strengthening operating controls, improving data flow, meeting customer

Figure 10-3   Objectives of Material Control System—Major Manufacturer

Subsystem	Objective
Routings	Establishment of a system to capture routing information and time values that can be used by manufacturing for cost of completes, labor status by contract, effect of changes by rerouting, etc.
Status	Establish a system that can be used by manufacturing to determine workload in shop, effect of accepting additional work, overload in various cost centers, status of self-manufactured work in process, etc.
Tools	Establish a system to capture all tool information that can be used by manufacturing to determine tool status *prior* to release of work to shop and maintain a tool inventory by contract for auditing purposes.
Cost Control	Establishment of an overall system that can be used by manufacturing to very quickly determine labor costs, material costs, tool costs, overruns, etc., by contract.
Exception Reports	*Of primary importance,* any establishment of mechanized systems will be predicated on the basis that when information is required by manufacturing, the system will have the ability to give us selective feedback on an immediate basis.
Scheduling	Establishment of a general-use scheduling system that can be used by manufacturing to determine effect of engineering changes, lack of material, tool shortages, etc.
Make or Buy	Establish a system that can be used by manufacturing to make intelligent decisions on those items to subcontract based on cost, load, schedule, etc.
Request for Proposal	Establishment of system that will be used by manufacturing to determine break-in points, effect of breaking in changes, and configuration of units when shipped.
Elapsed Time Reporting	Analyze, improve, and prepare an orderly procedure that can be used by manufacturing to report elapsed time, if required by contractual obligation.
Inventory	Optimize inventory costs through the design of decision rules containing optimum reorder points, safety stock levels, and reorder quantities, each capable of continuous and automatic reassessment.
Accounts Payable	Pay 100% of invoices before due date.
Purchasing	Provide performance information on buyer's price negotiations with suppliers in order that purchase variance can be controlled within set limits.
Production Control	Identify cost and quantity variances within one day in order to institute closer control over these variables.
Project Control	Identify performance against plan so that events, costs, and specifications of the project can be met.

and external requirements). These short-range systems objectives must, however, take into account the environment in which a business will be operating five to ten years hence. *Today's* systems design must take account of *tomorrow's* environment. Some factors that may shape long-range objectives would include:

1. New product information
2. Forecasts of changing markets and customers
3. Information concerning the marketing effort: sales force, distribution channels, service requirements
4. Projections of manpower needs
5. The external environment
6. Suppliers, manufacturing methods, plant expansion, etc.
7. Financial needs and sources

Objectives can be demonstrated by taking each of our illustrative subsystems and giving an objective for each.

DETERMINE INFORMATION NEEDS

A clear statement of information needs is fundamental and necessary to good systems design. Too many companies spend lavish sums on hardware and software to perpetuate existing systems or build sophisticated data banks without first determining the real information needs of management —information that can increase the perception of managers in critical areas such as problems, alternatives, opportunities, and plans.

Unless managers can provide the specifications for what they want from an information system, the design effort will produce something less than optimum results. If, on the other hand, the manager-user can define his objectives and spell out those items of information that are needed to reach the objective, he is then at least halfway home in systems design. Failure to be specific on these two steps probably accounts for the downfall of more design efforts than any other factor.

Too often systems design begins without a clear-cut statement of objectives and information needs. If this happens and the manager fails to provide them, the systems analyst or technician will provide *his* objectives and *his* information needs.

Information requirements should be stated as clearly and precisely as possible. Yet it is not easy for a manager to spell out the specific information requirements of his job, and therein lies a basic frustration in the improvement of systems. In an attempt to get a clear statement of information needs, the analyst frequently meets with an interviewing situation somewhat like the one represented in this typical exchange:

Analyst: Could you tell me what the objectives of this cost accounting system are as you see them?

Financial Manager: Sure . . . to get the reports out faster . . . to do something about keeping the costs in line . . . to keep management informed. . . .

Analyst: Yes, I understand . . . let me put it another way. What are your responsibilities as you see them?

Financial Manager: Whatta you mean? . . . I'm in charge of the treasury department.

Analyst: Yes, I know, but we need to get a better statement of your department's objectives, how the cost accounting system can further these objectives, and what information is needed to do this.

Financial Manager: Well, we need the information we've been getting but we need it faster and with a lot more accurate input from those fellows in operations.

This hypothetical conversation reflects the difficulty of getting managers to be specific about information needs. One approach, sometimes used by consultants, is to get top management to require in writing from subordinate managers a statement containing: (a) a list of four to five major responsibilities for which the manager believes himself to be responsible, and (b) the four to five specific items of information that are required to perform the responsibilities. These requirements could be framed in terms of duties performed or decisions made; the idea is to get the manager to think of information needs. If this can be done, the information system is well on the way to being designed.

Another approach is avoidance of the direct question: What information do you need? Instead, the designer requests that the user describe what occurs in the decision-making process; then the designer concerns himself with the identification of the questions that are to be resolved in the activity for which the system is being designed. This approach is also a good one for the manager-user, because he is intimately familiar with his operation and presumably with the difficult decision operations in it.

Managers need information for a variety of reasons, most of them concerned with the management process. The type of need that he will have at various times and for various purposes is largely dependent upon two factors: the personal managerial attributes of the individual manager, and the organizational environment in which decisions are made. Brief examinations of these follow.

Personal Attributes

Knowledge of information systems. If the manager is aware of what computer-based systems can do, his information requests will probably be more sophisticated and more specific. His knowledge of capabilities and costs places him in a much better position to aid in the design of a good system.

Managerial style. A manager's technical background, his leadership style, and his decision-making ability all affect the kinds and amount of information he requires. Some prefer a great amount of detail and others like to decide with a minimum of detail and in personal consultation with subordinates.

Manager's perception of information needs. "You tell me what I need to know" and "Get me all the facts" represent two opposite perceptions of information needs. This dichotomy is due partly to the fact that many managers are ignorant of what information they need. Another dimension of the problem is the widely differing views of managers regarding their obligation to disseminate information to subordinates and to groups outside the firm. The manager who cannot or will not delegate authority is likely to keep information closely held.

Organizational Environment

Nature of the company. Problems in communication and in controlling operations seem to be a function of the company's size and the complexity of its organization. The larger, more complex firms require more formal information systems, and the information needs of these systems become more critical to operations.

Level of management. We outlined in Chapter 9 the three levels of management (i.e., strategic planning, management control, operational control) and the varying needs for information at each. Each level needs different types of information, generally in different form. Top levels need the one-time report, the summary, the single inquiry. The management control level needs the exception report, the summary, and a variety of regular reports for periodic evaluation. The operational control level requires the formal report with fixed procedures, the day-to-day report of transactions in order to maintain operational control of actions as they occur. Managers at *all* levels have changing information needs, depending on the nature and importance of the particular decision.

Structure of the organization. The more highly structured the organization, the easier it is to determine information needs. Where authority and responsibility are clearly spelled out, relationships understood, and decision-making areas defined, the information needs of managers can be determined more easily.

Returning to our illustrative subsystems, some information needs might be stated:

Subsystem	Information Needs
Inventory	Need to know daily those items that have fallen below minimum inventory level, in order that expediting action can be taken.
Accounts Payable	In order to conserve cash, invoices should be paid no sooner than two days prior to due date. Therefore, incoming invoices must be coded according to "days to due date."
Purchasing	The performance of each individual buyer indicated by comparing actual purchase with hypothetical purchases at base or standard prices.
Production Control	Exception report to identify by shop order and lot number the variances in cost and quantity that are over or under standard by 5%.
Project Control	Need to know weekly the progress against plan for those events in critical path. Also need to know where float exists in other events so that resources may be shifted.

Summary—System Objectives and Information Needs

The importance of these first two design steps—set system objectives and determine information needs—cannot be overemphasized. It is estimated that if these steps can be accomplished successfully, the user has completed fifty percent of his design participation. And yet, these two important steps do not involve the user with the computer hardware or other computer manifestations that so frequently make him apprehensive.

Without a clear understanding of information needs, no MIS can be designed. The overwhelming majority of systems analysts list "getting the user to specify his information needs" as their number one problem. About the only solution is a clear directive from top management that users establish job responsibilities accompanied by their information needs.

ESTABLISH SYSTEM CONSTRAINTS

The iterative nature of the systems design process is easily understood when we consider the next step in the process, establishing constraints.

Sometimes called *problem boundaries* or *restrictions,* constraints enable the designer to stipulate the conditions under which objectives may be attained, to consider the limitations that restrict the design, and to add dimension to the objective. To state it another way, constraints, which are provided by the manager-user or the designer himself, limit freedom of action in designing a system to achieve the objective. It is clear then that a constant review of objectives is necessary when considering system constraints. Indeed, the two steps of the design process may be considered as one: setting objectives and establishing constraints.

Although constraints may be viewed as a negative limitation on systems design, there is a positive benefit as well. We should not let our desire to design sophisticated systems run away with reality or to make promises that cannot be kept. Although identification of the problem or setting the objective may be evident, the solution is not always easy. Moreover, the designer who thinks his system can run the organization is as mistaken as the manager who believes he can run his organization without a system. Establishing constraints will help insure that the design is realistic.

Constraints may be classified as internal or external to the organization. This concept is shown in Figure 10-4, which forms the basis of the following discussion.

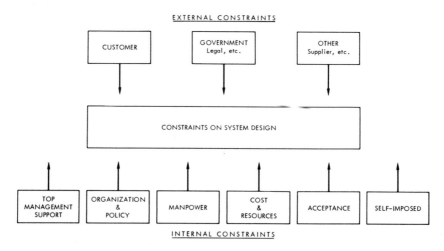

Figure 10-4   Constraints on Management Information Systems Design

Internal Constraints

If top-management support is not obtained for the systems concept and for the notion that computer-based information systems are a vital tool for management planning and control, the type of design effort discussed in these chapters cannot be implemented. A good environment for information systems must be set, and one essential ingredient is the approval and support of top management, a constraint that definitely influences the kind of system the manager-user may design.

Organizational and policy considerations frequently set limits on objectives and modify an intended approach to the design of a system. The structure of the organization as well as the managers occupying various positions influence information flow and use of system outputs. In a decentralized multiplant organization with a wide product line, the design of common systems in cost accounting or production control is obviously less acceptable than in a more centralized organization with fewer products. An additional organizational difficulty is related to the turnover of managers. More than one head of computer operations has told me that his major difficulty is the abandonment of redesign of systems due to the turnover of manager-users. Likewise, company *policies* frequently define or limit the approach to systems design. Among these policies are those concerned with product and service, research and development, production, marketing, finance, and personnel. For example, a "promote from within" personnel policy would have an impact on the type of systems designed to build a skills inventory. Other important considerations surrounding design are those concerning audit.

Manpower needs and personnel availability are a major limiting factor on both the design and utilization of information systems. Computer and systems skills are among the most critical in the nation, and rare indeed is the manager who admits to having sufficient personnel to design, implement, and operate the systems he desires. Additional considerations concern the nature of the work force and the skill mix of users. Elaborate and sophisticated systems are of little value if they cannot be put to use.

Cost is a major *resource* limitation. The cost to achieve the objective should be compared with the benefits to be derived. You do not want to spend $20,000 to save $10,000. Although a cost-benefit analysis is frequently difficult, some approach at priority setting must be undertaken. Considerations similar to those surrounding cost apply also to the use of resources. Computer capacity and other facilities relating to operation of data-processing systems should be utilized in an optimum way.

Perhaps the most significant constraint of all is the one concerning people. "People problems" are probably most often mentioned where failure to achieve expected results is concerned. Here we have the difficulties associated with the natural human reaction to change, the antagonism and the lack of interest and support frequently met in systems design and operation. These reactions are to be expected, however. Automation, computer systems, and systems design often call for the realignment of people and facilities, organizational changes, and individual job changes. These should be anticipated in designing systems to achieve the objective.

Self-imposed restrictions are those placed on the design by the manager or the designer. In designing the system to achieve the objective, he may have to scale down several requirements in order to make the system fit with other outputs, equipment, or constraints. Usually, he will also restrict the amount of time and effort devoted to investigation. For example, he may want to design a pilot or test system around one product, plant, or portion of an operation before making it generally applicable elsewhere. Functional requirements also define constraints placed on the system by its users. The data requirements, the data volumes, and the rate of processing are constraints imposed by the immediate users. More remote users impose constraints by the need to integrate with related systems.

External Constraints

Foremost among the considerations surrounding the external environment are those concerning the *customer*. Order entry, billing, and other systems that interface with systems of the customer must be designed with his needs in mind. If certain outputs from the system are not acceptable to the customer, a definite limitation must be faced up to. He may require that bills be submitted in a form that provides input to his system of accounts payable. For example, standard progress reporting and billing procedures are among the requirements imposed for processing data under many military procurement programs.

A variety of additional external constraints should be considered in addition to the customer. The *government* (federal, state, local) imposes certain restrictions on the processing of data. Among these are the need to maintain the security of certain classes of information (e.g., personnel) in order to comply with law and regulation in the conduct of business (e.g., taxes, reporting) and to meet certain procedures regarding record keeping and reporting to stockholders (e.g., outside audit). *Unions* can and do affect the operation of systems involving members in matters such as compensation, grievances, and working conditions. *Suppliers* are also an important group to be considered when designing information systems, because these systems frequently interface with that group.

In summary, it is important to recognize the constraints that have an impact on systems design. Having recognized them and made appropriate allowance in the design function, the manager will then be in a position to complete the remaining steps toward the design of an operating system that will achieve the objective he has previously determined.

The nature of constraints is illustrated here by taking our selected number of functional subsystems and stating a hypothetical constraint for each.

Subsystem	Statement of Constraint
Inventory	Regardless of reorder points and reorder quantities, the supplier will not accept orders for less than carload lots for raw materials 7 and 12.
Accounts Payable	The individual who prepares the check for payment of invoices must be separate from the individual who approves payment.
Purchasing	It is not necessary to negotiate purchases in amounts under $500.
Production Control	System output for shop control will be identified by department only and not the individual worker or foreman.
Project Control	We are required to report weekly to the Department of Defense any slippages in time or cost exceeding 10% of any event in the project control critical path.

DETERMINE INFORMATION SOURCES

The step of determining information needs is hardly completed before it is necessary to consider the information sources. Indeed, these two steps are overlapping and, as we stated before, iterative.

Although some systems require considerable external information, for the most part the natural place to turn for information is inside the firm: books, records, files, statistical and accounting documents, etc. Thus, most analysis refers to the step of determining information requirements as analyzing the present system.

The extent to which the *existing* system should be studied in a redesign effort of a *new* system has long been the subject of debate. One school of thought maintains that detailed analysis of the existing system should be a preliminary step to determining information requirements and that as much information as possible should be gathered and analyzed concerning the in-place system. This approach is justified on four grounds:

1. A minor modification in the existing system may satisfy the information requirements without a major redesign effort.
2. A look at the existing system is required in order to determine the specific areas that need improvement.
3. Since most systems utilize some common sources of input, a study of existing systems is necessary to determine these common inputs.
4. A study of existing systems is necessary to determine the data volume and costs associated with new designs.

The second theory of systems design, sometimes called the "fresh approach" or the "logical approach," holds that detailed analysis of the existing system is not necessary because the new system will be substantially changed and should not be predicated on the restraints of the existing one. Moreover, too close an identification with existing systems may compromise objectivity in the construction of logical methods to satisfy the information needs required to meet the systems objectives.

Whether the manager or the designer chooses one or a combination of these approaches is probably a matter of the state-of-the-art of information systems in the company under study, the objectives and existing information sources of the subsystem being designed, and the preferences of the manager himself. Sooner or later during design, some examination of existing company files as well as of external sources will become necessary if only to determine the source in order to satisfy a portion of the new information needs. It will also be necessary in order to integrate the subsystem under study with the total for the organization.

Analysis and Integration

During this step in systems design, the determination of information sources, the form of the new system begins to take shape. We must not only uncover information sources for the particular subsystem under consideration but also take into account how they fit into the overall integrative structure of the entire firm. We should therefore examine sources of information as well as techniques of analysis.

Sources of information may be categorized:

1. *Internal and external records.* Internal records most often take the form of written materials and could include examples of inputs or outputs, file records, memoranda and letters, reports containing information about the existing system, and documentation of existing or planned systems. External data may come from a variety of sources, such as trade publications, government statistics, and the like.

2. *Interviewing* managers and operating personnel is a valuable method of identifying possible sources of information and for analyzing the existing system. This form of data gathering can be the most fruitful method of securing information, provided it is conducted properly. Unlike the written record, the gathering of facts from an interview involves human communication problems; these can be largely overcome by proper planning and by gaining the confidence of persons interviewed.

3. *Sampling and estimating* methods may become necessary when the

accumulation of data is so large that only a portion of it can be examined. The major advantages of utilizing sampling techniques lie in the saving of time and cost, particularly on nonrecurring events for which data are not available. One frequently used form of sampling is *work sampling,* which can be used to analyze the actions of people, machines, or events in terms of time. *Estimating* is an acceptable method of analysis and is a time saver. However, estimates should be checked to control totals or be verified by interview where possible.

A number of *techniques of analysis* and synthesis have been published and are in widespread use. For our purposes in discovering information sources, two of these are of particular interest—input/output analysis and multidimensional flows. These two techniques permit us to summarize the available information sources, so that we can avoid duplication by integrating the various sources of information input.

Some type of *input/output* analysis will reveal sources of information and help to avoid duplication. Figure 10-5 demonstrates this kind of analysis with the input-output chart, which is a visual portrayal of information inputs to a system and the information outputs that results. By listing inputs along the left side and outputs across the top, the relationship can be established by the dot at the point of intersection. For example, to produce an output of invoices, the formulation designated by the dots for company order number, tax data, net price, and shipping papers is required as input.

Figure 10-5 also demonstrates how data can be reduced and subsystems integrated through proper design. The top half, or "before analysis" portion, reveals that several items of output appear also as input, indicating rehandling and reprocessing of the same information to produce an output. The bottom half of Figure 10-5 illustrates how consolidation and integration can reduce the number of information sources (i.e., input items). Figure 10-6 demonstrates the multiple uses of information sources and how information requirements may be identified and combined in a systems design that can serve more than one user. Files of input can be utilized by various organizational elements and various information subsystems.

Multidimensional flow is an additional technique of organizing information sources or depicting the existing design of a subsystem. A flow chart can be constructed to trace the routing or flow of information from origin to destination and arrange this flow in a chronological sequence showing the progression of information through the organization. Although not specifi-

BEFORE ANALYSIS   OUTPUT DATA

INPUT & SUPPORTING DATA	Invoices	Shipping papers	Shipping labels	Quantity shipped	Back orders	Replenishment orders	Net price	Shipping terms	Shipping register	Stock ledgers	Stock bulletin	Stock report	Billing & cost dist.	Price realization	Tax reports	Royalty reports	Face sheets	Unfilled orders ($)	Orders entered ($)	Statistical analysis
Customer orders																				
Order number		•	•			•														
Quantity ordered				•	•				•									•	•	•
Item ident.		•		•					•									•	•	•
List price						•												•	•	•
Company ord. no.	•	•	•		•			•	•											
Customer reg. record																				
Pricing policy (Dis.)	•					•	•											•	•	•
Traffic routing		•						•												
Tax data	•																			
Quantity shipped		•																		•
Net price	•																			•
Invent. cost at stand.													•	•	•					•
Stock replen. proc.				•	•				•											•
Receipts				•	•				•											•
Invoices													•	•	•	•	•		•	•
Shipping papers	•		•					•	•											
Stock ledgers			•	•						•	•	•								•
Price & cost refer.													•	•						
Peg board forms													•	•	•	•				
Royalty ident. codes																•				

AFTER ANALYSIS   OUTPUT DATA

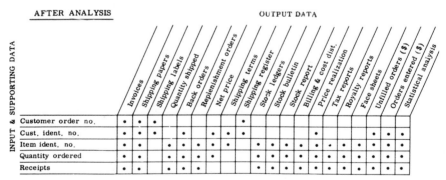

INPUT & SUPPORTING DATA	Invoices	Shipping papers	Shipping labels	Quantity shipped	Back orders	Replenishment orders	Net price	Shipping terms	Shipping register	Stock ledgers	Stock bulletin	Stock report	Billing & cost dist.	Price realization	Tax reports	Royalty reports	Face sheets	Unfilled orders ($)	Orders entered ($)	Statistical analysis
Customer order no.	•	•	•				•													
Cust. ident. no.	•	•	•		•		•	•	•						•			•	•	•
Item ident. no.	•	•		•	•	•	•		•	•	•	•	•	•	•	•	•	•	•	•
Quantity ordered				•	•	•	•		•	•	•	•	•	•	•	•	•	•	•	•
Receipts	•	•		•	•	•			•	•	•	•	•	•	•	•	•	•	•	•

Figure 10-5   Input/Output Chart (Customer Order Processing). SOURCE Victor Lazzaro, ed., *Systems and Procedures*, 2nd ed. (Englewood Cliffs, N.J.: Prentice-Hall, Inc., 1968), p. 435.

ACTIVITY	Customer File	Product File	Open Order File	Master Assembly and Parts File	Labor Planning File	Plant Master Schedule	Vendor File	Open Purchase Order File	Accounts Receivable, Credit, and Collection	Accounts Payable	Employee Master Record	Product Development Resource File	General Ledger and Subledger Account File
Pre-Award	X	X		X		X						X	
Order Processing	X	X	X										
Design and Document Product			X	X			X					X	
Buy Materials, Supplies, and Services				X		X	X	X		X			X
Make Product	X		X	X	X	X		X			X		X
Distribute Product and Service It After Installation	X	X											
Plan and Control the Above Activities											X	X	
Report Job Status	X	X	X	X	X	X	X	X	X	X	X	X	X
Report Job Cost	X				X				X	X			X
Report Personnel Statistics											X		X

Figure 10-6   Multiple Uses of Information. SOURCE Donald F. Heany, *Development of Information Systems* (New York: The Ronald Press, 1968).

cally required for identification of information sources, the factors of frequency, volume, time, cost, and physical distance can also be shown on such a chart.

Summary—Information Sources

Now that information *sources* have been identified with information needs, the next design step is to prepare a list that matches needs and sources. Such a list is evaluated and re-evaluated until a final valid list of information requirements is generated to match previously determined information needs. This matching can take the form of a matrix diagram, a valuable device for the integration of subsystems as well as for use in the remainder of the systems design process. Figure 10-7 illustrates how such

	Accounting	Production	Purchasing	etc.	
Ordering Costs	X				
Carrying Costs	X				
Requirements		X			
Consumption Time		X			
Usage Rate		X			
Lead Time			X		
etc.					

Figure 10-7   Information Needs/Information Sources Matrix

a matching process might be useful for the economic order quantity sub-system of the inventory management system.

Information sources can be further illustrated by giving examples for our selected subsystems:

Subsystem		*Information Sources*
Inventory	*Need*	Items falling below minimum inventory level
	Source	Stock-level determination subsystem comparing current balance against minimum inventory level
Accounts Payable	*Need*	Code invoices "days to due date"
	Source	Coded upon entry into accounts payable sub-system
Purchasing	*Need*	Performance of individual buyers
	Source	Purchasing system comparing outgoing purchase prices against predetermined standard
Production Control	*Need*	Cost variances over or under 5%
	Source	Integration of costing with manufacturing applications: shop control, stores requisitioning, labor distribution, etc.
Project Control	*Need*	Progress against plan for events in critical path
	Source	Project control subsystem

DETAIL THE SYSTEM CONCEPT

At this point, sufficient information has been accumulated to begin a more detailed description of the system concept. This description includes essentially a flow chart or other documentation of the flow of information through the system, the inputs and outputs, and a narrative description of the operations.

Here we are describing the manager's participation in systems design and not the detailed specifications and documentation included in subsequent expansion by the designer. The manager's involvement in the design process is analogous to the homeowner's participation in the architect's planning. As with such plans, the basic design and many of the details are shaped by the wishes and needs of the person buying the house. So it is with a computer-based information system. The manager should be involved to the extent that the system provides information for his needs; the designer is concerned with the nature of the materials and equipment as well as with the technical processing considerations. Later details will be worked out by the designer. These details will include explicit instructions that will dictate what *data* are to be captured and *when,* the *files* that are to be used, the details of how *processing* is to be done, what *outputs* will be generated by the system, and how the outputs and files are to be *distributed.*

General System Flow

The general system flow chart of the type shown in Figures 10-8 and 10-9 is a common method of indicating the general specifications of a computer-based information system. Shown in such a chart is the description of the data-processing logic in general terms. The system flow also reflects the design efforts that have gone on before this step: setting objectives, establishing constraints, determining information needs and information sources.

The system flow, as illustrated, is quite general in nature and indicates only the main components of the system. At this stage in the design the chart does not indicate what processing occurs at particular steps in the flow or what specific data, equipment, or people are involved. However, the chart is of utmost importance because it provides the foundation upon which a great deal of detailed specifications will follow.

Notice some important characteristics about Figures 10-8 and 10-9.

1. System *objectives* are achieved and reflected in the flow diagram (e.g., optimize inventory costs through the design of decision rules containing optimum reorder points, safety stock levels, and reorder quantities).
2. Information needs and information sources are designed into the system.
3. Decision rules and decision points are shown.
4. Inputs and outputs are designated.
5. Most important—*subsystems are integrated.*

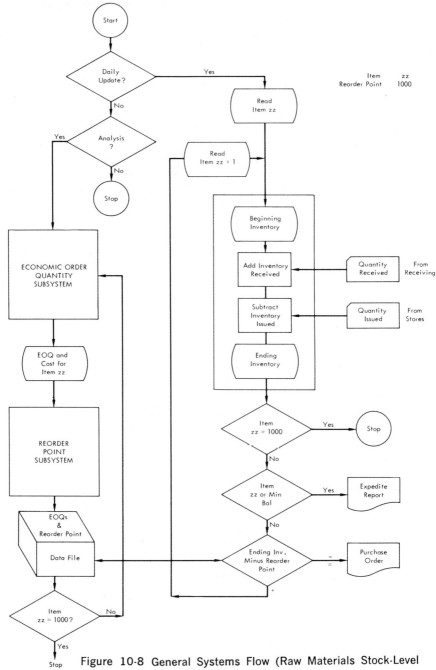

Figure 10-8 General Systems Flow (Raw Materials Stock-Level Subsystem of Inventory Control System)

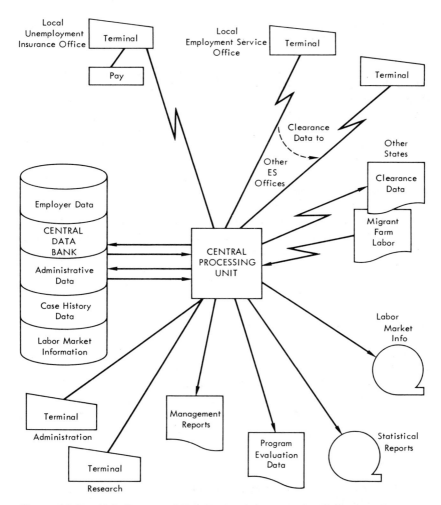

Figure 10-9   U.S. Bureau of Employment Security Management Information
System Conceptual Design

System Inputs

From the user's point of view, the inputs have been structured mainly
when information sources were determined. However, there remains the
task of design of input format. Since inputs frequently have to be accepted
in the form in which they are received from outside the firm (e.g., sales
orders, shipping documents, receiving papers, personnel information),
input design becomes a matter of converting these to machine-usable

form. When inputs are from other subsystems within the firm, the problem becomes one of integrating these systems through common data elements and other means.

More detailed input data specification includes the sources of data, i.e., where they come from, what form they are in, and who is responsible for their production. Notice that in Figure 10-9 some inputs are machine-readable and some must be converted. Because *forms* are so often used in collecting inputs and for other aids in operating a system, they are indispensable in modern business. Forms design is a major consideration for the systems designer.

Although the manager is not concerned in detail with these input specifications, he should be aware that the designer must specify the source of each input, its frequency, volume, and timing, plus its disposition after processing is completed. Since input must be checked for validity and volume, the editing procedures for accomplishing this are also required. Another important consideration is the specification of how inputs are to be converted into machine-readable form. These and other details of input design are usually contained on forms designed for that purpose.

System Outputs

From the technical standpoint, output-data definition includes the specification of destination; i.e., where they go, in what form they are, and who is responsible for receiving them. Included in these specifications are the distribution of output (who gets what, how many copies, and by what means), the frequency with which output will be called for and its timing, and the form the output will take (tape, hard copy, data terminal, etc.). Questions that the designer will ask in the process of developing output specifications include:

1. What form are the output reports to take? Can it be off-line?
2. Should the information be detailed or summarized?
3. What can I do with the output data that will be reused?
4. What kind of output form will be required? How many copies?
5. Are reports generated on demand? By exception? On schedule?

Despite the need to answer these details of output specification, the manager is concerned primarily with getting his information needs as previously determined in some type of output format. In other words, the consideration is how to *present the information to the eye or the ear of the manager*. The answer to this question lies in the content and form design of the output document. This form design is a direct function of information needs and should be designed to provide those needs in a timely fashion. Care should be taken not to ask for *too much* information *too frequently.* "Management by exception" and "information by summary" should be the guiding principles.

Three illustrative subsystems that we have been using for design in this chapter are inventory management, production control, and purchasing. Figure 10-10 shows examples of outputs that might be designed to provide managerial information needs determined earlier in the design process.

Remember—the system output is the most important element in an information system. It is the reason why we design an MIS, and the system exists for the sole purpose of providing the output. Information for decision making and for planning and controlling operations is provided by the output, and it is therefore of primary concern to the manager.

Other Documentation

Other frequently used means of describing or documenting the system concept are the activity sheet and the system narrative. Figure 10-11 is a system description for our illustrative inventory management system and is designed to provide information on volumes, time relationships, and specific functions or requirements.

The system narrative is another means that can be used to document and describe a system. The justification for such an approach is based on the caution of the system designer: "If you haven't written it out, you haven't thought it out." The following excerpt from our inventory management system indicates the kind and level of system description that should be available at the end of detailing the system concept.

Inventory Management of Raw Materials

This system is concerned with inventory control of raw materials for manufacturing. There are four plants, each with its own computer and each utilizing the same inventory control system. Raw materials move from receiving to storekeeping and thence to manufacturing, as required by the production planning and control system. There are three major groups of operations within the system: *stock level subsystem,* based on transactions; *reorder point subsystem,* including purchase order preparation; and *economic order quantity subsystem.*

I. *Stock Level*
   1. As material arrives at receiving, the receiving report is marked to show quantity and quality acceptance. The receiving report is then matched against the receiving order file (prepunched card), and actual quantity received, data received, and quality acceptance are key-punched. The receiving order card is then transmitted to the computer center for updating the inventory file.

DAILY RAW MATERIALS EXPEDITE REPORT

Item Number	Description	Unit	EOQ	ROP	Bal	On Order	Del.	Received	Action
zz	Gasket Material	yd	900	400	327	900	6/6		Expedite with vendor
f73	Spring	doz	60	10	12	60	7/3	42	Check receipt

SHOP VARIANCE REPORT

No.	Lot	Description	Unit	Run	Start	Due Compl.	Shop		Variance $\pm$ 5%
3B2	R44	Alum. Tube	each	2	6/13	6/19	Weld		Cost variance + 7.2%
zzx4	R44	Alum. Tube	each	3	6/13	6/26	Bend		Time over 7 days

BUYER NEGOTIATIONS VARIANCE REPORT

Material	Unit	Part No.	Vendor	Standard Cost	Actual Cost	Variance	
Steel Pl.	Lb.	274345X	Bay Metals	.32	.35	.03	9.4% +
Dr. Shaft	ea.	B33-165	Zimmer	9.55	8.72	.83	8.7% **

Figure 10-10   Selected Outputs for Three Subsystems: Inventory Management, Production Control, Purchasing

ACTIVITY: Inventory Control

	Key	Name	Volume
Stock Level Subsystem		Inputs	
Freq: As received	1600	Receipts	100/day
Inputs: 1600, 1610, 1620	1610	Issues	1000/day
	1620	Misc. Transact.	100/day
Reorder Point Subsystem		Outputs	
Freq: Daily			
Inputs: 3610, 3640	2600	Stock Status	400/day
	2610	Purchase Orders	25/day
Reporting	2620	Expedite Report	1000 lines/day
	2630	Exceptions	200 items/day
Daily	2640	Stock Status	5000 lines/week
Inputs: 3610			
		Files	
	3600	EOQ & ROP File	5000 records
	3610	Master Stock	5000 records
	3620	Receiving File	5000 records
	3630	Vendor File	100 records

Note: Purchase orders for commodity class 7Q4 must be in carload lots.

Figure 10-11   System Description—Activity Sheet for Inventory Control Subsystem (Materials Control)

2. As the storekeeper issues items from stores, a prepunched
card is . . . etc. . . . . etc. . . . .

Aside from this documentation, which is a part of the design concept,
there is additional formal documentation prepared during the detailed
design steps. Although the manager-user is generally not involved in the
details of the preparation of these documents, he should be aware of their
existence and general nature. Detailed design documents include:

System Summary. An identification of the computer configuration and
the programs and software components of the system.

General System Flow Chart. A graphic version of the system summary
(see Figure 10-9), which represents the interfaces with other systems.

Run Summaries. Additional detail to the system summary, the run summary describes one segment of the total set of processing operations.
Input-Data Definition. Defines the medium for input (punched cards,
tape, etc.) and the format of each input record.

Master-File-Data Definition. General description of each file, its relation to other files, and how records making up the file will be processed.

Output-Data Definition. Generally the same as input-data definition. Report descriptions are included.

Data-Processing Logic. Conveys to a programmer the functional specifications of what a program is to do with input in order to produce the required output.

In addition to the foregoing system documentation, a *user's manual* is usually prepared. The purpose of such a manual is to describe to operating people how the system works so that it may be used as a reference document at operating levels.

TEST AND IMPLEMENT THE SYSTEM

The last two steps in systems design from a managerial point of view are involved with testing the soundness of the design process to this point and developing a plan for implementation.

Testing the System

After conceptual design of the subsystem has been completed, including the nature of its integration with other subsystems, the design can be tested to see whether it yields appropriate outputs to meet the previously defined objectives and information needs. If not, the system may require redefinition or redesign efforts at the conceptual level and a review of the process leading up to the test.

Testing of some sort is almost invariably done prior to the implementation of a system in order to provide a systematic review of all specifications. The importance of the test and the degree to which it is extended depend upon the importance of the system and what effect it has on the operations of the firm. Systems that propose major modifications in manufacturing control and distribution would naturally receive more extensive test efforts than those concerned with internal data flow of minor systems within the firm.

System testing prior to implementation also makes good economic sense. It is generally conceded that less than 20% of the effort devoted to an operational system is used for writing instructions for the computer; 80% or more is for self-analysis, planning, and design. Clearly, the larger investment in design should be tested prior to further implementation efforts.

The initial effort in testing should be devoted to determining whether the input (information sources) can be converted into output (information needs). If input data cannot be converted into output, the system logic is unworkable and redesign effort is indicated. Systems designers have taken a page from the engineer's book and categorized system tests as (a) desk check, (b) component test, and (c) system test.

The *desk check* is similar to the bench test of the engineer. The information system is represented by the flow chart, and the designer searchingly examines it for omissions and errors. "Have I provided for every contingency? Are there any loose ends?" The path of every input must be followed through the processing to determine if the output is correct. Decision rules must be examined carefully and tested for correctness and validity. The desk check gives the manager-designer the opportunity to trace and check the data-processing logic as well as the overall design to determine whether it meets the objectives as stated.

The *component test* views the system as a group of individual or clusters of "black boxes," which may operate independently or serially. A malfunction in the entire system may be isolated by testing the components separately because each is complicated in its own right. Since a change in one may have little effect or a marked effect on the other, the only way to determine this to to test each separately.

The component approach to system testing can be illustrated by viewing the three subsystems in Figure 10-9: stock level, economic order, and reorder point. Although taken together, these subsystems operate serially; each can be tested separately. Indeed, the decision rules for EOQ and reorder point can be tested mathematically by manipulating them with synthetic or historical data.

Finally, in order to test the way in which the entire logic of the system performs, a *systems test* may be used. Several iterations of the test are normally required before the system becomes operable. One popular method is the *parallel test*, which involves running past and current data through the new system without eliminating the old system it is to replace. After the new system is debugged and has proved workable, the old system is abandoned. This method has been used in the past when the consequences of failure of the new system were great or where there was serious doubt concerning the workability of the new system. Payroll, inventory, and accounts receivable are typical systems that usually run in parallel until the new system is proven. A *pilot test* is another type of systems test that uses a part of the new system for test on the assumption that the part is representative of the whole. A good example of a pilot test is a payroll system that uses one plant, one shift, or one department to test whether the system should be adopted company-wide.

Modeling

Modeling is rapidly becoming an important tool of system testing, and its use is almost certain to grow in the future. As information systems become more complex and the consequences of poor design become greater, the costs involved in using this basic operating device of systems analysis will be justified.

Computer simulation of the system is a special case of modeling, growing in use and importance as a tool of system analysis and design. Simulation is similar to the trial-and-error approach to decision making except that simulation permits exploration of alternatives in the system "on paper" without the costly mistakes frequently associated with trial-and-error operation in which decisions are actually implemented. Simulation involves the experimental use of models to study the behavior of a system over time. Thus it permits the manager to "play" his decision and to predict the outcomes of various alternatives.

Implementing the System

Implementation is a rather indefinite term covering the herculean job of converting the system specifications into an operating system that achieves the objectives and information needs determined early in the design phase. Implementation is the longest and most costly step in systems development. However, prior planning and involvement in the design process will pay off manyfold in the implementation phase. The tendency of managers is to reach the implementation phase and say, "Fine, let the technicians carry it the rest of the way." This attitude would negate to some extent the design efforts so painstakingly undergone in earlier stages. If the manager is going to use the system, then he should plan and oversee its implementation. Specifically, he should become involved in:

1. The data-processing plan.
2. The establishment of application priorities.
3. The selection of equipment.
4. The organization of his department to utilize information systems.
5. The establishment of authority/responsibility assignments to develop, implement, and utilize computers and systems.
6. The staffing of study and project teams.
7. The provision of a good environment for information systems.

Developing a plan for implementation is essential. The extent and detail of the plan depend upon the system to be implemented. Although the designer has the best experience and overview of the situation to develop such a plan, the manager should become involved in its development and subsequent control. For the more complicated plans, *documentation* is important. This may take a variety of forms but should always include a time schedule and responsibility assignment. Figure 10-12 illustrates the "milestone" chart, a typical method of documenting an implementation plan.

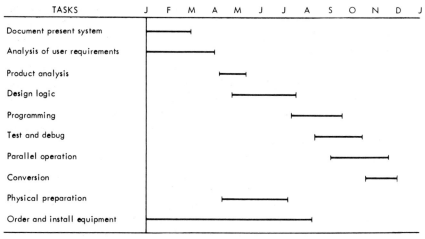

TASKS	J	F	M	A	M	J	J	A	S	O	N	D	J
Document present system													
Analysis of user requirements													
Product analysis													
Design logic													
Programming													
Test and debug													
Parallel operation													
Conversion													
Physical preparation													
Order and install equipment													

Figure 10-12   Milestone Chart of System Implementation

Training is a major consideration in implementation. Care should be taken that the training does not become an orientation to the technology of information systems and computers. The avoidance of such an approach makes a strong argument for managerial involvement in the training process. Proper organization of training sessions also provides an opportunity to *orient users,* another vital step in implementation. Without the cooperation of users, the system is bound to fail. In this regard, *input conversion* is a major problem: it cannot be achieved unless the operating people— the system users—are involved and understand the process of conversion.

A final word about implementation concerns the systems component that outweighs all others in importance—the people involved. The natural tendency in systems development is to treat the computer as just another machine and to consider the conversion to computer-based information systems nothing more than faster processing of data. This is a painless way to squander money and talent on systems effort. Once again, we meet the argument head-on that if information systems are to be used to *manage* the organization, then *managers* must be involved in their design and implementation. This includes gaining acceptance and setting a climate for "managerial," not "clerical," information systems.

EVALUATE THE SYSTEM

There is no doubt that the companies that have been the most successful in systems utilization have achieved their success by managing their computer systems in much the same way that they control other complex parts of their business, by planning and controlling the operation. Control requires some sort of measurement, some standard of performance, some *criteria of effectiveness.*

Very little attention has been paid to criteria, or measures of performance, in information systems operations. This neglect should not be permitted. A major problem is to determine or to evaluate the results we get from the accelerating expenditures on systems. Generally, the cost of running the systems effort can be estimated, but putting a value on what these efforts are worth is difficult.

Evaluation of effectiveness has generally been clouded by the fact that the people primarily responsible for the computer have been making the evaluation. Hence, no true measure has been available because the overwhelming tendency has been to evaluate performance by cost-savings measured by clerical displacement or data-processing efficiency. Not only is EDP proficiency a rather poor measure of effectiveness but it is far outweighed by the value of management improvements in an effective control network.

The true value of an information system should be measured in terms of whether or not it does efficiently what it set out to do. Does it achieve the systems objective *effectively* and *efficiently?*

Effectiveness

The relationship between *effectiveness,* efficiency, and systems objectives has been expressed by the U.S. Navy:

> *Effectiveness* refers to success in achieving objectives, as contrasted with *efficiency,* which is minimization of resources used in achieving objectives. Efficiency can be measured substantially without reference to the specific objective of the effort. Effectiveness, on the other hand, cannot be considered other than in relation to the objectives established.

The heart of the task of measuring effectiveness is no different from the process of controlling other operations—the selection of standards of performance or measures of effectiveness. Essentially, the purpose of these measures is to disclose whether the objectives selected for the system are being achieved. In selecting these measures, we should take care to insure that they are valid—that is, they should measure the real objectives of the system. For example, if the objective is to reduce shortages, a measure might be the percentage reduction in shortages as a result of system installation. It follows that where possible, measures should be capable of being expressed in quantitative terms such as rates, dollars, volume, items, people, and programs. These quantitative measures can frequently be applied to changes in operating ratios. Good indicators are such items as:

1. Personnel reductions.
2. Better maintenance of delivery promises to customers.
3. Reduction in shortages of inventory.
4. Improved customer-inquiry response time.
5. Reduction in number of product changes.
6. Improved operating ratios in accounts payable and accounts receivable.
7. Effect of cost reduction and elimination of waste.
8. Improved flexibility in operations.

Any operating index directly affected by system installation should be watched as a possible measure of effectiveness. Since managers almost invariably participate in setting the operating policies that affect these measures, it becomes clear that they can be calibrated with systems effectiveness measures without the bias so often found in the staff of computer installations.

Efficiency

The *efficiency* of the systems effort is also a criterion of performance and should be watched. Efficiency refers to the relationship between costs and value returned. The natural tendency in measuring efficiency is to start at the recording end of the business and compare current processing costs with those prior to the computer. Though *processing* efficiency is important, it is certainly secondary to considerations of costs versus value received in management applications and improved performance.

The efficiency of the system as reflected by relating cost and value can be accomplished through three types of analysis:

1. *Profit and loss*. Cost-value relationship can be predicted by projecting estimates of future revenue and expense figures on a "present" basis

Costs in thousands (000)

		1st Year	2nd Year	3rd Year	Total	
1	PRESENT SYSTEM – Operating Costs	400	450	500	1350	
2	PRESENT SYSTEM – Inventory Level	3000	3400	3700	10100	
3	PROPOSED SYSTEM – Operating Costs	500	550	550	1600	
4	PROPOSED SYSTEM – Inventory Level	2000	2100	2400	6500	
5	Operating Costs – Difference	-100	-100	-50	-250	
6	Inventory Level – Difference	1000	1300	1300	3600	
7	Inventory Reduction (estimated)	300	340	340	980	
8	Net Operational Cost Reduction	200	240	280	720	
9	Equipment and Implementation	800				
10	RETURN ON INVESTMENT – 30% (Divide Average Yearly Savings by System Costs)					
11						

Figure 10-13   Return on Investment Analysis of System Implementation

and then on a "proposed with system" basis. Or, if an after-the-fact assessment is desired, the values can be derived historically.

2. *Return-on-investment.* Cost-value relationship is computed on the proposed or existing system by compiling estimates of return-on-investment. This analysis demonstrates the value of the systems investment in terms of earnings by measuring the difference between income with and without the system. Figure 10-13 shows the result of this kind of analysis.

3. *Cash flow.* An increasing measure of any investment is its influence on cash flow. This analysis should show how the total investment in systems improvement (e.g., inventory reduction, operating cost reduction) would, over the near and long term, improve the cash flow position of the company.

SUMMARY

From the point of view of the manager-user, systems design consists of seven steps. Each of these has been examined in terms of its meaning for management participation in the design process.

Setting systems objectives refers to the questions: What is the purpose of the system? and, Why is it needed? The objectives must be framed in terms of what they contribute to the organization's objectives and how the processes of planning, organizing, and controlling are furthered. The second step is concerned with the establishment of systems constraints. These refer to those external and internal resource and environment limitations that affect the optimum design of the system.

Once systems objectives and constraints are established, the manager-designer can proceed to the third and fourth steps of determining information needs and sources. These should be matched in order to evaluate whether information is available and whether information needs as defined will accomplish the objectives as previously determined.

The fifth step involves the detailing of the system concept. This is a description that normally includes a flow chart or other means of documentation of the flow of information through the system. It is during this step that the actual inputs and outputs are specified and designed for meeting information needs. In the more sophisticated managerial systems, we might include modeling and simulation as part of the design for providing appropriate decision information.

The last two steps in design are concerned with the testing and the soundness of the design process and in developing a plan for systems implementation. Testing involves the determination of whether the system yields appropriate outputs to meet the previously defined objectives and information needs. Implementation is the process of converting the systems specifications into an operating system. Finally, the evaluation step involves measuring systems performance against a criteria of effectiveness to determine whether objectives are being achieved.

CHECKLIST FOR
MANAGERIAL INVOLVEMENT

	Yes	No
PARTICIPATION BY MANAGERS		
Has top management set a participative climate?	( )	( )
Do users participate in the design process?	( )	( )
Do managers get hands-on involvement?	( )	( )
SETTING SYSTEM OBJECTIVES		
Do users set the MIS objective?	( )	( )
Are objectives specific?	( )	( )
Quantifiable?	( )	( )
Verifiable?	( )	( )
Related to performance and results?	( )	( )
INFORMATION NEEDS		
Do users establish their own needs?	( )	( )
Are information needs specific?	( )	( )
Does top management insist on matching responsibilities with information needs?	( )	( )
SYSTEM CONSTRAINTS		
Internal constraints identified?	( )	( )
External constraints identified?	( )	( )
Constraints considered in design process?	( )	( )
INFORMATION SOURCES		
Does user determine in cooperation with analyst?	( )	( )
Are additional and new sources investigated?	( )	( )
Are input/output charts or other tools used?	( )	( )
Are information sources matched with information needs?	( )	( )
SYSTEMS CONCEPT		
General systems flow	( )	( )
Narrative	( )	( )
Flow chart	( )	( )
Objectives met	( )	( )
Needs and sources of information	( )	( )
Inputs/outputs indicated	( )	( )
Subsystems integrated	( )	( )
System outputs	( )	( )
Designed by user	( )	( )
Meet information needs	( )	( )

	Yes	No
Provide for summaries and exception reporting	( )	( )
Specifications	( )	( )
Form, frequency, copies, detail	( )	( )

SYSTEM DOCUMENTATION

System adequately documented?	( )	( )

SYSTEM TEST

Has system been adequately tested?	( )	( )

SYSTEM IMPLEMENTATION

Are tasks defined?	( )	( )
Are tasks scheduled?	( )	( )
Responsibility assigned?	( )	( )
Planning and control chart?	( )	( )

SYSTEM EVALUATION

Is a criteria of performance established?	( )	( )
Does it measure attainment of objective?	( )	( )
Procedure established for measurement?	( )	( )

chapter 11

MIS analysis and design: the team of analyst and user

11

"If you, the manager-user, can define clearly enough what kind of information you want to capture, what you want done with it, and how you want the answers printed out, any competent systems analyst and programmer can get the information for you."

—Alfred M. King, vice-president of finance,
American Appraisal Associates, Inc.

In the preceding chapter we examined the major steps in MIS design from the manager-user point of view. This description was limited to the design minimum involvement that *he* (the manager) should undertake in the design of *his* MIS. In this chapter we will go into somewhat greater detail regarding systems design and describe how the technician (usually the systems analyst) goes about the process of designing and implementing the system.

There are two major reasons why the user should have some detailed familiarity with the design process. First, a speaking knowledge of these activities will vastly improve his chances of success, because such knowledge will enable him to communicate better with the analyst and guide the design effort to a greater payoff. Second, his improved knowledge will lend added expertise to the EDP effort so that the end product will better meet his needs and with less expenditure of time and money. In summary, participation is both effective and economical.

The "cutting edge of the art" in systems design is not sharp. A number of approaches to the problem may be taken. Over time, I have found that the steps described in this chapter are understandable and usable by the manager and provide an excellent background for the analyst or technician who aspires to the design of *management,* not *data,* systems.

The approach that is taken in this chapter will be from these basic *iterative* steps:

Define the Problem (System Objective)
The Feasibility Study
Data Gathering
Data Analysis
Determine Alternative Designs   **FEEDBACK**
System Controls
Documentation
Implementation of the System

DEFINE THE PROBLEM (SYSTEM OBJECTIVE)

For centuries managers have been told that they cannot solve a problem until it is defined. This caution is justified because you certainly cannot solve a problem if you don't know its dimensions. Moreover, if you don't do a good job during the *problem definition* phase, you will find that the real problem goes unsolved while you are spinning your wheels on a *symptom*. For example; low inventory turnover (usually identified as the problem) may only be a symptom of underlying trouble in pricing, product obsolescence, sales techniques, shipping or any one of several underlying *causes* of the *symptom*.

> When you complain to a medical doctor: "I have a problem with my stomach" or "my problem is a sore throat," the doctor does not diagnose your problem as a stomach ache or a sore throat. No! These are symptoms. The *real* problem is infection, diet, nerves, smoking, or some other underlying cause that is traced to the symptom.

In some respects a business organization can be defined as a set of problems to be solved. Indeed, this is the approach of many theorists and practitioners. This view is reflected in Figure 11-1 and suggests that the primary role for the manager is to *solve problems with information.* At any rate, if a system is to be designed from the solution of a problem, it is clearly necessary to first formulate and state the nature of the problem. This process of problem definition is one that both managers and analysts so frequently overlook. The result is a great deal of wasted time expended on a solution to the wrong problem.

Formulation of the problem requires a statement of the elements: (a) the present state, (b) the desired state, (c) the constraints involved in solving the problem, and (d) the criteria by which the solution will be judged. These elements comprise the factors that are relevant to describing the various states and the relationships among the factors.

Consider the illustrative problem description of Figure 11-2. This is a rather elementary but typical problem situation that exists in the accounts receivable department of many companies, and there should be no difficulty in stating the problem. Do you agree? Despite the straightforward nature of the problem situation, fewer than 5% of the managers and analysts in my experience are able to correctly state the problem. Perhaps you would care to try a problem statement before turning to Figure 11-3, which contains the elements that lead to a clear statement.

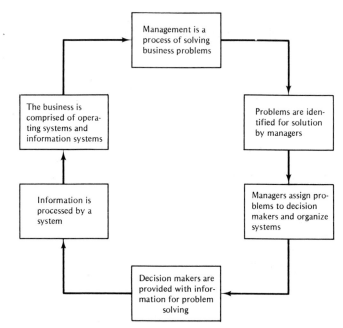

Figure 11-1   The Business Organization as a Problem Solving Process

These are typical problem statements that result from the description of Figure 11-2:

"Improve the collection process."

"Design a better receivables system."

"Send out invoices faster."

"Insist on faster payment or cut off credit."

"Speed up collection."

"Revise the aged trial balance."

"The problem is bank loans."

Each of the above statements are either off-the-top-of-the-head attempts to jump to a quick solution or they misdirect attention to the *symptom* rather than *the statement of the problem for systems design.*

Figure 11-3 is a problem formulation for the problem description contained in Figure 11-2. It shows a step-by-step problem formulation discipline that is easy to understand and leads to a logical problem statement by the MIS user or the analyst. This will save everyone involved a lot of time, effort, and expense. As one successful analyst observed, "The user,

By early 1976 the National Manufacturing Company had continued to grow in sales and product line expansion, but top management was becoming increasingly concerned with information systems, program plans, and related procedures. This was particularly acute in the controller's department where responsibility for coordination lay.

A real problem existed in Accounts Receivable where the amount of receivables was increasing at twice the rate of sales. The level had reached the critical stage in March when the bank indicated that the company's line of credit might not be renewed unless receivables were brought into line. Loss of the line of credit would seriously hamper growth plans and hurt the company's "best supplier" reputation.

John Flynn, the controller, established an objective "to reduce billing time by three days in order to reduce the level of receivables." In his research surrounding this objective he discovered the following industry statistics:

	Industry Average	National Manufacturing
Sales in $millions	174	188
Average collection days	43	67
Average A/R outstanding ($mil)	18.9	37.6

In discussing the accounts receivable problem with John Flynn, the chief executive stated: "John, we've got six months to get our receivables down to the industry average, because that is the deadline for our line of credit renewal. And by the way, I would very much like to see us beat the industry average by 5% in the next 12 months. And incidentally, John, I think you have sufficient computer hardware and personnel for this system so don't ask for more resources."

On the way back to his office John Flynn reviewed his present system in his mind:

1. Sends out invoices weekly.
2. Follows up on past due accounts after sixty days.
3. Begins personal telephone contacts for collection after ninety days.

What is the statement of John Flynn's problem?

Figure 11-2   An Accounts Receivable Problem

PROBLEM ANALYSIS

Describe the Present Situation (Including identification and location of deviation)

The average level of receivables is $37.6 million.
The average collection days is 67.

Describe the Desired Situation

Reduce average level to industry average (10.8% of sales = $20.3 million).
Reduce average collection days to industry average (43 days).

Constraints (Time, cost, manpower, equipment, organizational, etc.)

Time: level must be reduced in six months.
Time: level must be reduced 5% below industry in 12 months.
Resources: no additional personnel or equipment.

Criteria for Evaluation of Problem Solution

Average collection time of 43 days and receivables level of $20.3 million to be achieved in six months.
These levels to be improved by 5% in twelve months.

Statement of the Problem

The accounts receivable level must be reduced to $20.3 million and the average collection days to 43 in six months, and these figures must be reduced by 5% in the following six months. There can be no increase in personnel or equipment to achieve these objectives.

Figure 11-3   Problem Formulation Technique

together with the systems designer, has to peel the problem down like an onion. Otherwise he will design a system that provides the right solution to the wrong problem."

THE FEASIBILITY STUDY

A feasibility study is not to be confused with an analysis of whether or not you need a computer. It is an analysis of whether it is technically practical and economically viable to change your methods of handling information processing. The primary objective is to arrive at a conclusion of whether or not a new project, program, or system should be undertaken.

A secondary objective is to explore alternative ways in which system goals can be achieved, and in this process it is only natural that valuable information is collected for subsequent use if the decision to go ahead with the design or the modification is affirmative.

The feasibility study usually consists of two major steps: *the study plan* and *the study implementation.* The scope of the study will depend upon the extent of new design or modification.

The *study plan* normally includes a statement of these items:

1. *Study objectives.* A statement of objectives usually leads to the question: "Can we solve the problem stated in the problem definition by system design or modification?" If the answer is no, your study is over.

2. *Study scope.* A definition of how far-reaching the study will be in terms of applications, departments, procedures, equipment, and related considerations.

3. *Restrictions.* Constraints such as time, manpower, budget, equipment, and cost that limit the study. Normally these constraints are similar to those internal/external constraints discussed in Chapter 10.

4. *Manpower requirements.* The composition of the study team, its membership and skills required, and the degree of participation from user departments or staff departments.

5. *Study phase segmentation.* This includes:
   (a) Design activities (including data gathering, data analysis, documentation, and design).
   (b) Target completion dates for each design activity.
   (c) Cost estimates for each phase.

6. *Project control.* Provision for progress reporting on the study.

The *feasibility study* itself is normally undertaken by using these principal steps:

1. *Identify large users of the information.* This is for the purpose of adequately considering all major users of the proposed system.

2. *Identify information needs.* This is perhaps the most important step in the feasibility study because it provides the basic foundation upon which the system will ultimately be designed. It includes not only a definition of the operating and management needs of the organization (or department concerned) but a projection of these needs for the future. For major system design or modification, these needs should be projected about five to seven years into the future because it will take that length of time to recover your investment.

3. *Define alternative system designs or processing methods.* Design general system concepts that meet the information needs defined in step 2. Examine these to determine which are technically practical.

4. *Conduct cost/benefit analysis.* (See Chapter 8.) Weigh the cost of each alternative against the benefits to be derived, and select the lowest cost alternative that can do the job.

5. *Examine the intangibles.* This is to make sure that none of the very important nonquantifiable benefits and limitations have been overlooked.

One conclusion of the foregoing analysis might be to cancel or delay further system design because it is not feasible.

> Dick Brandon, a noted computer consultant, says that a feasibility study can't be delegated downward; it's a management study, requiring management participation and management direction. At least half of the team performing it should be company managers, with less than half information systems technicians. [*Important:* keep equipment salesmen out of range.]

DATA GATHERING

In preparation for design of the new system, it is necessary to gather and document considerable information about the existing system and about the information needs, boundaries, and interfaces between related systems. Ideally the systems analyst should be a collector at heart.

In the data gathering phase we are concerned with what data to gather, the sources of this data, and some techniques for gathering it.

What Data Shall I Gather?

In answer to this question, the analyst should collect samples of all documents and records used in the system, and document all of its activities. These should include:

1. *Inputs to the system.* The first type of inputs are usually those comprising the source documents that describe the initial business transactions. The second are the actual records and forms used to put data directly into the system.

2. *Outputs from the system.* The primary output of interest are those reports or other forms provided to managers and other users. A secondary type of output are those that provide reports to other systems.

3. *Processing operations* are the individual clerical (data-processing) operations performed on the raw data and are gathered and documented in order to establish the precise means by which the data transformation takes place.

4. *Decision points* regarding the type of processor activity to be performed in the system and the criteria for the decision. For most clerical type decision points, a decision table is very useful for this documentation.

5. *Information files* that are used in the system. It is desirable to document the filing sequence to provide index identification. Note should also be made of how long the information is retained, as well as the source of information.

6. *Controls.* The techniques that are used to maintain the integrity of the existing system.

Sources of Data

In addition to the information and knowledge he has by reason of his experience in the organization, the analyst must seek out additional sources of data to complete his background study in preparation for design. The following sources are the most frequently used for this purpose.

1. *Policy and procedures manuals* set forth the guidelines and actual procedures for decision making and data processing operations throughout the firm. It is essential that the analyst be familiar with the present procedures of the system under study and the policies that may have an impact on design.

2. *Job descriptions* contain the functions and duties that are performed by a particular job or position. This information is useful in determining whether the proposed system will meet the information needs of the persons occupying the job and whether the incumbent is able to carry out the functions required by the proposed system.

3. *Organizational charts* depict authority relationships and communications channels. These are helpful in determining the source and flow of information between departments. They are also useful in determining who is responsible for enforcing procedures and information system details.

4. *Sample forms and reports* are essential—they are the basic inputs and outputs of the system. They are also helpful in answering questions relating to the originator of the report, deadlines, frequency, volume, originating department, system interfaces, and the general usefulness of the document.

5. *Previous studies* are particularly helpful if properly documented. Examination of studies on related systems can frequently shorten research time by providing information that relates to the system under study.

6. *Attitudes and opinions* regarding the proposed system can frequently provide valuable comments on how it might be improved or how potential problems can be avoided.

Techniques of Data Gathering

Several techniques are available to the analyst for gathering the data necessary for systems design. The most prevalent of these is the interview. Other methods are discussed below.

1. *Interviewing* is the most widely used and the most important technique for gathering information. Most information surrounding a system under study has never been written down, and the analyst must depend upon the personal interview to obtain it. It is a very useful means for developing both general background information and the details needed in the investigation.

Interviewing requires a high degree of diplomatic skill and sales ability. Unfortunately most analysts do not possess these attributes. The result is a less-than-optimum output from the interview.

The points listed below will aid the successful conduct of an interview during the system investigation:

(a) Schedule the interview in advance. Make an appointment, usually with the manager of the organizational unit involved, and provide him with advance information about the nature of the meeting.

(b) Develop background for the interview. As a minimum this would include the general boundaries and information goals of the system as well as information of a personal nature concerning the user.

(c) Structure the interview; outline it, rehearse it.

(d) Record the interview. Make notes, or record it on tape for future reference.

(e) Be a salesman and a diplomat. Don't subvert the interview with your own behavior. Stay away from technical jargon and personal opinions. Consider the human aspects of system design and implementation.

2. *Observation* is the second most frequently used technique. It involves actually observing the operation of a particular set of procedures. The objective is to determine whether the procedure is being followed and whether it could be improved by a modification in the system.

3. *The questionnaire* is an economical technique for getting a large amount of information, and it is particularly useful when remote locations

are involved. The general rules for good questionnaire development (e.g., avoid narrative answers, provide deadlines, identify respondent, avoid lengthy questionnaires) apply also to those developed to gather design information; follow the rules.

4. *Suggestions* from employees are frequently helpful and may be either oral or written. After all, the persons directly involved in system operation are in the best position to suggest improvements.

5. *Formal meetings* are very useful for purposes of coordinating efforts and for gaining approval of the project as it unfolds.

6. *Publications* from industry sources, associations, and of a general professional or managerial nature are frequently a good source for suggestions on improved design. A good research of the literature may uncover a company or individual who has experienced your problem and designed a system to overcome it. There is no reason to re-invent the wheel.

DATA ANALYSIS

After the data gathering phase is complete, the data gathered will range from the irrelevant to the highly important. The analyst must then decide how to organize his information for analysis.

The first question to answer is: "Do I retain the data?" The following questions will help him to make a determination:

Does it help define the problem?

Does it represent a restriction or constraint?

Does it specify a criteria of performance?

Does it identify a resource that will be useful in later stages of systems design?

If the answer is no to any of the above questions the data should be categorized under "miscellaneous" and filed. But don't throw it away. The chances are good that you will be searching for it at a later stage in the analysis and design process.

After the data have been segregated into two categories, "miscellaneous" and "to be retained," the next step is to *arrange* the *retained* category for ease of retrieval and analysis. Two alternative arrangements are suggested.

1. *The general, operational, and programming method.* Useful for larger projects, this arrangement separates the data into three categories:

(a) *General* information that defines goals, objectives, constraints, performance criteria, and the general system description.

(b) *Operational* data that includes the narrative descriptions, narrative procedures, flow charts, and other documentation relating to the processing.

(c) *Programming* data that includes file specifications, logic diagrams, record layouts, and information relating to computer programs.

2. *The input/output/processor method.* This method is frequently used for the smaller project or one dealing with a known specific application. The arrangement categories suggested are:

(a) *Inputs*—The transactions, files, and other input data.

(b) *Outputs*—The reports, statements, documents, registers, updated files, and queries or decisions.

(c) *Processes*—Data entry and verification (how inputs are generated), the actual processing steps and procedures, and exception procedures for nonstandard transactions.

(d) *Input/Output Relationships*—Descriptions of inputs that are required to provide specific outputs; usually a list that is cross-referenced to exhibits that may be contained elsewhere.

(e) *Controls*—Control description, frequency, and auditing procedures.

Analysis of the Retained Data

At this point the analyst is ready to begin the analysis of his data for the purpose of developing alternative designs. It is here that his capacity for creativeness is taxed to the utmost, because analysis is essentially a creative process. It is concerned for the most part with an analysis of the existing system with the objective of improving on the system to be.

No step-by-step or structured approach to analysis is available; one is not desirable in view of the large number of options that are open. The process involves asking pertinent questions (of himself and others) regarding each part of the existing system and the proposed system. For example:

System Activities

What activities are performed in each step of the system?

Why are these performed in this way?

When and where are they performed, and who performs them?

System Operation

Can the operation be simplified, combined with another, or eliminated?

Can the sequence of operations be changed?

What are the differences between formal and actual procedures?

Are input documents standardized? Can exceptions be reduced?

How frequently are files updated? What changes in file organization are necessary?

Are computer programs safeguarded and documented?

System Decision Making

Can the decision-making process be simplified or eliminated?

Can it be formalized as a set of rules?

Can it be delegated to operating employees?

Are existing or planned output reports necessary? Can copies be eliminated or exception reports designed?

Although the process of analysis is creative and unstructured there are certain commonly accepted tools to assist in the process. The most common of these are shown in Figures 11-4 through 11-8 and are briefly described below:

> Figure 11-4. *Forms Analysis Chart of Recurring Data.* Useful for definition of data elements when developing a common data base. This form also indicates overlap and duplication of forms by showing those that use the same data elements.
>
> Figure 11-5. *File Description Sheet.* This describes the different files that comprise the system.
>
> Figure 11-6. *Document Usage Analysis Questionnaire.* Useful for determining frequency, number of copies, location, and content of existing or proposed documents.
>
> Figure 11-7. *Work Distribution Chart.* Procedural disposition or "who does what" with each system step.
>
> Figure 11-8. *Forms Distribution Chart.* Flow of documents between departments. Shows interfaces and distribution of copies of each document.

In addition to the *qualitative* analysis described above, there are a variety of *quantitative* techniques for the analysis and presentation of data. These range from the analytic techniques of statistical averages, ranges, and trends, to the presentation techniques of frequency distributions, graphs, scatter diagrams, and histograms to name a few. These analytical techniques are very valuable for data analysis leading to design of the system.

DETERMINE ALTERNATIVE DESIGN CONCEPTS

Upon completion of the data analysis step, a number of alternative design concepts should begin to emerge. These might involve different

FORMS ANALYSIS CHART OF RECURRING DATA	Title of Form				
Date:					
Activity:					
Name or Analyst					TOTAL
ITEMIZED DATA	Form No.	Form No.	Form No.	Form No.	
1.					
2.					
3.					
4.					
5.					
6.					
7.					
8.					
9.					

Figure 11-4   Forms Analysis Chart

FILE DESCRIPTION SHEET

Name and Description of File _____

_____

File Organization:_____Sequential_____Random_____Other_____

Record Format: _____Fixed_____Variable

File Sequence (Control Field or Fields)_____

Security Classification_____

Current Records in File_____

Projected Records in File_____

Retention Period_____Frequency of Update_____

Storage of File_____

Other Remarks_____

_____

_____

_____

Date_____Analyst_____

Program/System_____

Figure 11-5   File Description Sheet

"mixes" of equipment, processing steps, data bank organization, input/ output combinations, and other factors. Each "mix," or each alternative will have advantages and disadvantages. Only rarely will one concept dominate all others by every yardstick of measurement. More often, some formal evaluative approach is necessary to select the best alternative. Such

DOCUMENT USAGE ANALYSIS QUESTIONNAIRE

Document Name _____

Origin: Own Dept _____   Outside Dept _____

Preparation Frequency: _____   No. of Copies _____

Disposition of Copies: _____

_____

_____

_____

Filing of Document:

Where is document filed?   _____

What order?   _____

How long retained?   _____

How frequently used?   _____

What is ultimate disposition?   _____

How is document used during normal working day (frequency, purpose, edit, review, who uses it, etc.)

_____

_____

_____

_____

Describe interaction with file and other departments

_____

_____

Sample copy of document attached with indication of special codes and data elements

Name _____   Date _____

Department _____

Figure 11-6   Document Usage Analysis Questionnaire

ACTIVITY	Total Hours	Al Sklar Supervisor	Total Hours	G. Peterson Editor	Total Hours	T. Robbins Invoice Edit
AUDITING INVOICES	24	Handles problems with sales department. Handles problems with vendors. Writes to vendors			32	Edits and approves routine invoices. Reviews special invoice cases with supervisor. Contacts vendors
ORDER PROCESSING	32	Reviews customer orders requiring special attention	4 3	Edits customer orders for price, stock number, etc. Supervises open order file		
CUSTOMER ADJUSTMENTS CLAIMS RETURNS CREDITS	24	Reviews all credits, claims, and returns and clears with traffic and sales department	6 4	Clear adjustments with supervisor. Processes adjustment as directed by supervisor		

Figure 11-7 Work Distribution Chart

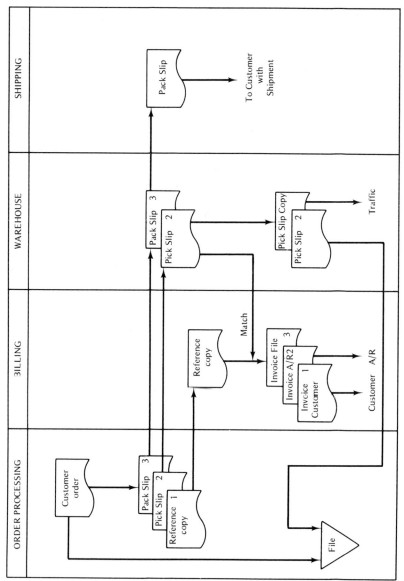

Figure 11-8   Forms Distribution Chart

National Components Inc. manufactures high technology proto-
type models of major equipment both for itself and outside customers. When the engineering department wishes to order materials,
it sends a materials request form to purchasing where one
of several vendors is selected from among those that meet the
engineering specifications. The resulting purchase order must be
signed by engineering management and, depending upon the
amount, by the finance department, or even the general manager.

The vendor encloses a packing slip with delivery of the items,
and the company's receiving department sends a receiving report
to both engineering and accounting. The vendor also sends a separate invoice to the accounting department to bill the company.
The company checks the invoice, the packing slip, the receiving
report, and the purchase order. If they all agree, the bill is paid;
otherwise an investigation is initiated. Problems arise when partial
shipments are made.

The new engineering manager is appalled at such a cumbersome
system, claiming that it is a bottleneck and prevents planning and
control of material expenditures. He wants a fast system that
doesn't delay the design effort and one that permits budgetary control.

Figure 11-9   A Purchasing Problem in the Engineering Department

an approach will naturally take into account a number of criteria. Some of
these are suggested by the following questions:

Does the alternative design meet system objectives?

Does the alternative design provide the information needs?

Is the alternative design the optimum from a cost/benefit standpoint?

Can the system be implemented within allowable time?

Does the alternative design meet imposed constraints?

The Factor Analysis Technique

Factor analysis is an excellent method for weighing design alternatives
and for bringing some *quantification* to what is otherwise a *qualitative*
decision. The method is not limited to MIS design alternatives but has
wide application in a variety of qualitative decision situations.

Consider the problem situation described in Figure 11-9. You may

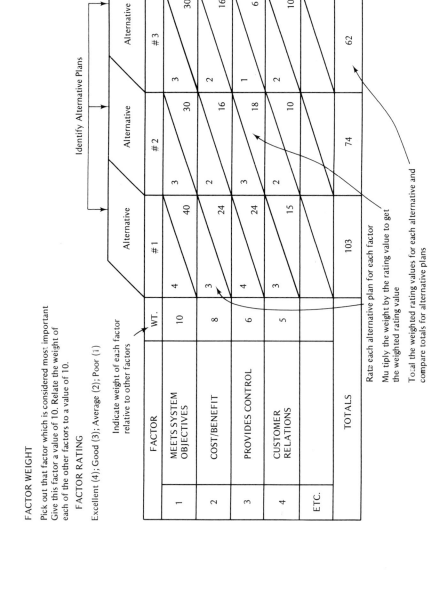

Figure 11-10 Factor Analysis

FACTOR WEIGHT

Pick out that factor which is considered most important.
Give this factor a value of 10. Relate the weight of
each of the other factors to a value of 10.

FACTOR RATING

Excellent (4); Good (3); Average (2); Poor (1)

Indicate weight of each factor relative to other factors

Identify Alternative Plans

	FACTOR	WT.	Alternative #1		Alternative #2		Alternative #3	
1	MEETS SYSTEM OBJECTIVES	10	4	40	3	30	3	30
2	COST/BENEFIT	8	3	24	2	16	2	16
3	PROVIDES CONTROL	6	4	24	3	18	1	6
4	CUSTOMER RELATIONS	5	3	15	2	10	2	10
ETC.								
	TOTALS			103		74		62

Rate each alternative plan for each factor

Multiply the weight by the rating value to get
the weighted rating value

Total the weighted rating values for each alternative and
compare totals for alternative plans

286

arrive at a number of alternative designs to solve the problem, but assume for the moment that these are limited to three:

Alternative 1. Establish "open purchase" accounts with selected vendors, and allow engineering to order direct.

Alternative 2. Engineering selects vendor (if amount is under $500) and sends requisition to purchasing.

Alternative 3. Vendor ships direct to engineering where purchase order is certified for payment by accounts payable.

A factor analysis approach to the selection of the best alternative of the three mentioned would break down each criteria of measurement (factor) surrounding each alternative, and analyze each one. The procedure involves the following steps:

1. List all factors that are considered important—the criteria of measurement against which you wish to weigh the effectiveness and overall value of each alternative. These factors may include such yardsticks as cost, return-on-investment, probability of success, customer service, payback time, whether objectives and information needs are met, and so on. For the case problem of Figure 11-9, the factors in Figure 11-10 show the *factor analysis* technique.

2. Weigh the relative importance of each factor against other factors. This involves establishing *weight* values for each factor. A good way to do this is to pick the factor (e.g., meets system objectives) that you consider most important and give it a value of ten (10). Then relate the weight of other factors to ten (10). For the case problem of Figure 11-9, the weights are shown in Figure 11-10.

3. Rate the alternatives against one factor at a time. Rate across the form, considering each of the alternatives for one factor at a time. This allows a constant interpretation of each factor for the various alternatives. See Figure 11-10.

4. Extend the weighted and rated values and compare the total value of each alternative. The one with the highest weighted value should be the best alternative.

See Figure 11-10, which indicates that Alternative 1 is the best design selection.

SYSTEM CONTROLS

Jacob Guzik (Al Capone's bookkeeper) once said, "I can steal more with a pencil than ten men with guns."

If Mr. Guzik were alive today, he would probably be surprised to find such new opportunities as computer equipment, which is 100 million times as fast as his old key-driven equipment. Along with this increased speed has come increased chances for theft and a variety of computer foul-ups, either intentional or accidental.

Recent statistics indicate that the average bank embezzlement loss via manual systems has been about $100,000 per incident. The average computer embezzlement loss (not including equity funding) is about $1,000,000. Horror stories abound. In 1974 the Stanford Research Institute published a report describing 140 of these stories. Two typical incidents indicate the need for *control:*

> To impress his employer with the need for additional security, a programmer designed an undetectable program to automatically write payroll checks for several of his relatives, including a two-year-old girl. He ran the system for three months, keeping the checks in their unopened envelopes, then he dropped the entire collection of 30 checks on the security director's desk. He is now in charge of EDP security.

> An Atlanta computer center, located in a fireproof floodproof building two floors above the street level, was left knee-deep in water by a faulty fire sprinkler.

To many managers, security means an elderly, gray-haired guard sleeping out his semi-retirement at a factory door, silver tape around the windows and a fire extinguisher hanging in the hall. Security talk is just like that description . . . dull! Dullness notwithstanding, somebody must be concerned with security and computer controls.

Although security is not the primary responsibility of most managers and the topic is somewhat outside the scope of this book, a minimum familiarity with the subject is desirable. This familiarity is provided by a summary of common controls and how these relate to EDP systems and security.

EDP Controls

Manual Controls

Authorization. There must be evidence of approval and authorization of all source data before it is processed. Usually authorization is furnished by the user department.

Control Totals. Dollar amounts, quantities, transaction counts, or other batch processing control totals should be provided by the originating department.

Document Registers. A document, maintained in EDP center, in which is recorded all data that is received and delivered. Controls in the register may include initials, routing slips, time stamps, etc.

Cancellation. In order to avoid duplication of input data or processing input data more than once, documents should be cancelled after processing. Methods include stamping after punching, different colors for different days, and filing with a lead card after processing.

Rejected and Corrected Data. When the computer rejects data or processes it subject to correction, adequate measures should be taken to ensure that the data is corrected.

Output Checks. Output must be reasonable and provision should be made to check it for reasonableness, completeness, and control totals. Sometimes this is called "eyeballing the output."

Mechanical (Machine) Controls

Conversion to Machine-Readable Form. Many opportunities for clerical error occur in the process of converting original information into machine-readable form. Methods for reducing this error include:

Key verifying	Form standardization
Self-checking digit	Programmed check
Mark sensing	Optical scanning
Other source data automation	Batch control totals

Application Processing Programs. These are self-checking hardware programs built into the computer. They include:

Record counts	Batch total checks
Sequence checking	Code validity
Record completeness	Reasonableness tests
Program constants	

System Software. Programming routines that sense problems that occur during input or processing. Other routines prohibit the accessing of files or accepting of data unless proper identification is made.

Hardware Controls. Controls built into the circuitry of the computer that provide recovery and control capabilities.

Operational Controls for the EDP Center

Run Manuals. Detailed instructions for operators for each run. In addition, instructions should cover handling of input/output data and the disposition of tapes, card decks, and disk packs.

System Log. Records that permit identification of time on the computer for each run and sufficient detail to permit identification of each program run.

Library Security. Provisions to ensure the safety of programs and files. These include adequate physical facilities as well as proper labeling and

EDP Center Security. Organizational and physical removal of the center and restricted access to facilities.

controlled access to files.

System Backup. Adequate provision for recovery of lost or damaged files (such as duplicate files) and utilization of standby equipment in case of loss or breakdown.

Recreation of Files. In the case of tape files, the "grandfather, father, son" principle will ensure the availability of a current file. For direct access files, the saving of transactions originating between file dumps will accomplish the same result.

Personnel Controls

Reference Check. Make sure that EDP personnel have adequate references.

Bonding. For sensitive employees, the bonding company investigation is quite efficient.

Mandatory Vacations. This breaks up permanent contact with a particular application or system.

Instant Departure of terminated employees prevents sabotage.

Separation of Duties. Make sure that certain tasks (operator, library, programmer, etc.) are not performed by individuals with related duties.

DOCUMENTATION

If there is one word that should be engraved on the forehead of every analyst, the word is *document!* This process is one of the most important steps in systems analysis and design, and it is one that is frequently overlooked or inadequately performed.

The reasons for documentation are self-evident. Should the original designer leave the organization or if a major modification to the system is necessary, the previous documentation is invaluable for reference purposes, and it will save time and additional design effort. Even the original designer may find that documentation is essential as design proceeds or as redesign becomes necessary. A properly documented system also provides a source of educational material for users and operators; it serves as an operational and reference source for trouble-shooting the system, and it helps to provide adequate security and control measures.

The Documentation Package

A complete documentation job would include most, if not all, of the items listed below. However, in smaller systems or in redesign of systems that are already partially documented, the analyst may wish to use this list for check-off purposes or for filling in vacant spaces in the existing documentation package.

User Project Request. This is the document of understanding with the user department regarding the scope of the system; it provides the basis upon which further design effort proceeds. It may be submitted in a format prescribed by the EDP department, but in most cases it includes all or part of these items:

Statement of the problem
Description of service requested
User justification for the design effort
Necessary approvals by the user department
Estimates of and constraints on implementation costs
Approvals of EDP department

Cost/benefit Analysis. Estimates of costs as well as benefits. The benefits can be both tangible (manpower and cost savings) and intangible (timely reporting, better controls, improved customer relations).

Document of Understanding. As opposed to the project request, the document of understanding spells out such matters as a definition of responsibilities, schedules, and costs.

User Design Specifications. These are the major design elements that will be incorporated into the system; they include:

System concept
System flow charts
Source documents
Inputs
Processing
Outputs
Forms, schedules, and reports
System interfaces

System Controls. Manual, operating, hardware, and other controls.

Procedures. These are developed for use by clerical and operating personnel and include:

> *Flow diagrams*—general (input/output relationships) and detailed (procedure steps by application)
>
> *Procedures narratives*—standard procedures, exception procedures, controls at each step, source and disposition of documents and files; and responsibility for task performance
>
> *Disaster recovery procedures*—procedures in case of power failure, equipment breakdown, etc.

Computer Programming. Documentation related to programs, including:

> *Program description*—functions it performs, frequency of use, inputs required, outputs produced, configuration
>
> *Logic diagrams*
>
> *Coding sheets*
>
> *Operating instructions*

Implementation Summary. This is the historical record of implementation after it has been completed. Useful for future reference.

IMPLEMENTATION OF THE SYSTEM

Once the analyst has completed the data gathering and analysis phases and has obtained approval for one of his alternative designs, the problem becomes one of planning, scheduling, and controlling the many tasks and work packages involved in system implementation.

The management of MIS design and implementation lends itself very well to the methods of project management. Normally, these utilize the techniques of PERT/CPM (Program Evaluation and Review Technique/Critical Path Method).

The major stages in MIS project planning, implementation, and control usually take the following four forms:

1. *The work breakdown structure.* This begins with the total end result desired and terminates with the individual detailed tasks. It is a natural *decomposition* of the project end result. Major categories of work involved in implementation are first defined, and then the detailed tasks under each category are listed. Although the following list of major categories is not exhaustive, it does indicate the nature of the category definition. The de-

tailed tasks under *Program coding and testing* are listed to illustrate the work breakdown structure for that particular category. Tasks for large projects can run into the thousands.

1. Detail the system flow
2. Evaluate and select personnel
3. Program coding and testing
   (a) Define program processing specifications
   (b) Prepare program logic diagram
   (c) Code program
   (d) Keypunch program, and perform desk check
   (e) Prepare test data for program test
   (f) Operator instructions
        etc.
4. Install and test the system
5. Acquire the hardware
6. Design the forms
7. Generate the files
8. Application cutover
9. Systems maintenance
   etc.

2. *Establish a network for scheduling tasks.* A network (PERT) diagram provides a scheduling device as well as an excellent visualization of the plan of action. It depicts the sequence of tasks as well as the relationships among them. Figure 11-11 demonstrates an elementary diagram for illustrating task relationships.

3. *The budget.* The cost for completing each milestone (major task category) on the network should be established as a part of the plan. This will provide subsequent control over costs if the rate of expenditure is budgeted and subsequently controlled.

4. *Project control.* As the project unfolds and the events in the network are accomplished, it is essential that control be maintained if the plan is to be achieved within time and cost constraints. For this purpose a Gannt chart is very useful. A typical control package of milestone (Gannt) charts to accompany the project network is shown in Figure 11-12.

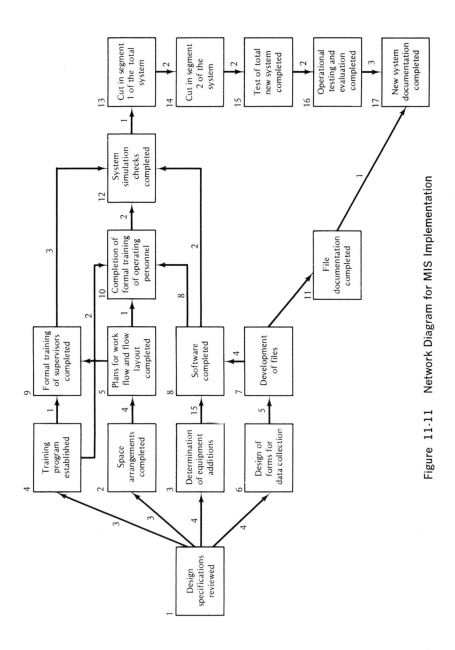

Figure 11-11   Network Diagram for MIS Implementation

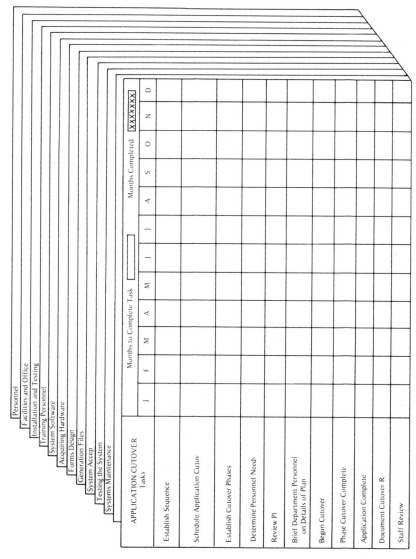

Figure 11-12 Milestone Charts for Systems Implementation

Personnel
Facilities and Office
Installation and Testing
Training Personnel
System Software
Acquiring Hardware
Forms Design
Generation Files
System Accep
Testing the System
Systems Maintenance

APPLICATION CUTOVER	Months to Complete Task								Months Completed				XXXXXXX	
Tasks	J	F	M	A	M	J	J	A	S	O	N	D
Establish Sequence												
Schedule Application Cutov												
Establish Cutover Phases												
Determine Personnel Need-												
Review PI												
Brief Department Personnel on Details of Plan												
Begin Cutover												
Phase Cutover Complete												
Application Complete												
Document Cutover R												
Staff Review												

CHECKLIST FOR MIS
ANALYSIS AND DESIGN READINESS

	Yes	No
PROBLEM DEFINITION		
Do you have a formal structured problem formulation approach?	( )	( )
THE FEASIBILITY STUDY		
Do you conduct a feasibility study prior to embarking on systems design?	( )	( )
Do you develop a feasibility study plan?	( )	( )
Does your study contain an identification of information needs, alternative design concepts, and a cost/benefit analysis?	( )	( )
DATA GATHERING		
Do you identify major categories of information to gather?	( )	( )
Do you utilize all available sources?	( )	( )
Are interviews structured in advance, outlined, and recorded?	( )	( )
Are all techniques of data gathering utilized?	( )	( )
DATA ANALYSIS		
Do you have a preplanned system for the organization and retention of data?	( )	( )
Do you utilize the common techniques of data analysis shown in Figures 11-4 through 11-8?	( )	( )
Are you using quantitative techniques of data analysis?	( )	( )
DETERMINE ALTERNATIVE DESIGN CONCEPTS		
Do you have a form approach to the selection of alternative designs?	( )	( )
Does the approach quantify the values and weigh the alternatives?	( )	( )
SYSTEM CONTROLS		
Have you established and do you practice the commonly accepted control procedures:		
Manual controls?	( )	( )
Hardware controls?	( )	( )
Operating controls?	( )	( )
Personnel controls?	( )	( )

	Yes	No

DOCUMENTATION

Do you have an established system of documentation? ( ) ( )

Does your system contain the commonly used categories of the documentation package? ( ) ( )

SYSTEM IMPLEMENTATION

Do your implementation procedures contain the basic elements of a project planning and control method:

Work breakdown structure? ( ) ( )

Scheduling network? ( ) ( )

A budget that costs each milestone? ( ) ( )

A project control devise such as Gannt charts? ( ) ( )

index